Epistemologies of Land

GLOBAL EPISTEMICS

In partnership with the Centre for Global Knowledge Studies (*gloknos*)
Series Editor: **Inanna Hamati-Ataya** (University of Cambridge)

Global Epistemics is a transdisciplinary book series established in partnership with the Centre for Global Knowledge Studies (gloknos) based at the University of Cambridge, that aims to foster, promote, and disseminate empirically grounded and theoretically ambitious research on knowledge as a cultural and natural phenomenon. The series welcomes innovative contributions that serve its mission, regardless of their methodologies, conceptual frameworks, levels of analysis, temporal scope, or specific objects of investigation.

Learn more about the series at tinyurl.com/GlobalEpistemics | https://tinyurl.com/RLgloknos

Titles in the Series:

Imaginaries of Connectivity: The Creation of Novel Spaces of Governance

Edited by Luis Lobo-Guerrero, Suvi Alt and Maarten Meijer

Mapping, Connectivity, and the Making of European Empires

Edited by Luis Lobo-Guerrero, Laura Lo Presti and Filipe dos Reis

Invisible Labour in Modern Science

Edited by Jenny Bangham, Xan Chacko, and Judith Kaplan

Scientific Freedom: The Heart of the Right to Science

By Sebastian Porsdam Mann, Maximilian Martin Schmid, Peter Vilmos Treit, and Helle Porsdam

Epistemologies of Land

Edited by Felix Anderl

Epistemologies of Land

Edited by Felix Anderl

ROWMAN & LITTLEFIELD
Lanham • Boulder • New York • London

Published by Rowman & Littlefield
An imprint of The Rowman & Littlefield Publishing Group, Inc.
4501 Forbes Boulevard, Suite 200, Lanham, Maryland 20706
www.rowman.com

86-90 Paul Street, London EC2A 4NE

British Library Cataloguing in Publication Information Available

Library of Congress Cataloging-in-Publication Data

DataNames: Anderl, Felix, editor.
Title: Epistemologies of land / edited by Felix Anderl.
Description: Lanham : Rowman & Littlefield, [2024] | Series: Global epistemics | Includes bibliographical references and index.
Identifiers: LCCN 2023042202 (print) | LCCN 2023042203 (ebook) | ISBN 9781538176443 (cloth) | ISBN 9781538176467 (ebook)
Subjects: LCSH: Land use--Philosophy.
Classification: LCC HD111 .E657 2024 (print) | LCC HD111 (ebook) | DDC 333.73/13--dc23/eng/20231102
LC record available at https://lccn.loc.gov/2023042202
LC ebook record available at https://lccn.loc.gov/2023042203

Contents

Series Editor's Note

I am very grateful to Felix Anderl for conceiving this innovative and timely project for the Global Epistemics series and for his dedication in guiding and coordinating a most successful cross-disciplinary collaboration over the past three years. *Epistemologies of Land* is a bold collective intervention that illuminates the various meanings of land as an object of thought and theory, experience and practice, policy and existential struggle. In doing so, it invites us to reflect on the implications of the multivalence of land as the foremost condition and common source of our life on this planet.

The contributions to this volume show us how, across multiple domains of human social existence, defining the nature and value of land constitutes a primordial performative act that establishes the structure and legitimacy of our social order, understood as an order created by and around our relation to land and all the relations land makes possible or necessary. The concept of land epistemology provides a powerful single prism to make sense of this process, which each contribution expertly unravels to lay bare its origins, complexity, and profound implications for the present and future well-being of human society.

In thus (re)claiming epistemology as a common human practice anchored in the most existential processes of our lives, *Epistemologies of Land* reinstitutes the rightful ownership of claims to knowledge that scholarly discourse has thus far exclusively claimed for itself. I hope the volume inspires practitioners to reflect on the responsibilities such ownership entails and encourages academics to ponder what they might or could owe to the knowledges of others.

Inanna Hamati-Ataya
Cambridge, 13 July 2023

Acknowledgments

Even though this is a book about land, its creation was strangely decoupled from it. Largely a product of pandemic times, the original writers' workshop we had planned in Cambridge, as well as almost all follow-up conversations, needed to happen in digital spaces, thus ironically contradicting one of the arguments in the introduction: that the social sciences need to come to terms with land as the material space of its production. The volume getting published despite this drawback is only due to the fact that a very energetic and hugely inspiring group of scholars was committed to the project of land epistemology from beginning to end. I am very grateful to all contributors for their inspiration and wisdom but also for their mutual encouragement and patience.

The greatest appreciation is due to Inanna Hamati-Ataya. Not only has she created an incredibly inspiring place of mutual exchange and intellectual production in the Centre for Global Knowledge Studies (gloknos), but also her decision to hire me in her project the Global as Artefact at the Centre for Research in the Arts, Social Sciences, and Humanities (CRASSH) at the University of Cambridge was truly life changing. Furthermore, she encouraged us to keep going, despite the impossibility of meeting in person, by creating a webcast series under the wings of gloknos in preparation of this volume and bringing a bunch of interesting people together on a regular basis. For the support of this webcast series, I also thank Samantha Peel.

For their contributions to the preparatory workshops, I sincerely thank Bikrum Gill, Matthew Holmes, Eduardo Machicado, and Laksmi Savitri. Many thanks to Elda Berdeja for her diligent work in support of the final manuscript and Natalie Mandziuk, Yu Ozaki, and Crystal Branson of Rowman & Littlefield for the smooth, supportive process and the professional advice.

I also thank the participants of the roundtable Land and Territory at the Pan-European Conference of the European International Studies Association in Athens, 2022, and the participants of the Internationalised Politics Colloquium at the Institute for International and Intercultural Studies at

Bremen University, particularly Klaus Schichte, Anna Wolkenhauer, Alex Veit, Roy Karadag, Sarah Penteado and Kressen Thyen.

This book was funded by the European Research Council (ERC) under the Horizon 2020 Research and Innovation Programme (ERC Consolidator project the Global as Artefact, grant no. 724451). I herewith acknowledge this financial support. The funding allowed me to allocate research time to the book, as well as to the organization of the online workshops via gloknos, and importantly treated us to the Open Access fee. I am truly grateful for this support. Views and opinions are, of course, those of the authors only and do not necessarily reflect those of the European Union or the ERC Executive Agency.

Introduction

Felix Anderl

What is the meaning of *land*? This question is far from trivial, for depending on the context, land can mean the ground on which we walk or the soil that we prepare for planting; it refers to the countryside more broadly, and in some languages, it is even used as a synonym for country. *To land*, furthermore, means to go off the water from a boat or to come down from the air and rest on the ground. But even if scholars agreed on what they mean when they say land by settling on one of these connotations, they would still not know what land means. This is because land means something different to different species and to different groups of people at different times and in different places. This is arguably one of the reasons for the frequency of conflicts over land, in which not only its distribution but also its meaning and purpose are heavily contested (Borras and Franco 2013; Hall 2013; Wolford 2010). Parties to land conflicts are therefore trying to make the broader public understand what land means *to them*. In a declaration of landless people who assembled in Honduras, the following statement was agreed upon: "Land provides the base for all human life. Land, appropriately called Mother Earth by the natives of the Americas, feeds us: men, women, boys and girls; and we are deeply bound to her. . . . We therefore reject the ideology that only considers land as merchandise" (La Vía Campesina 2000). This declaration is instructive because it contrasts two different understandings of land. In the latter one, land is treated as a commodity that can be traded and invested in, just like any other private good. In the former understanding, land is the basis for human survival and stands in a reciprocal relationship of care with the people it feeds; it is celebrated as Mother Earth. This implies that land in such an understanding is not only an object but also a subject.

These two understandings of land—as commodity and as a caring subject—do not only convey political differences; they also suggest two different forms of scientific inquiry: One lends itself to statistical, economic analysis; the other to investigations of the cultural or spiritual aspects of land and its relationships to humans and other species (Tuhiwai-Smith 1999, 12). In turn, the way scientists have historically treated land has heavily shaped what is considered its nature, meaning, and value. Across the globe, over the course of the last century, a broad coalition of transnational corporations, governments, and scientists have been mainstreaming an extractivist and rationalistic understanding of land, often in the name of development (Ferguson 2012; Li 2014a, 2014b). In this extractivist understanding, land is a lifeless resource that can be calculated and exploited rather than known through intimate relationships (Alcoff 2022, Kimmerer 2013).[1] In an extractivist understanding of land, there is thus no accountability toward land: knowledge is reduced to perfecting the ways in which land can be governed and exploited. This meaning of land has become so dominant that alternative approaches to land seem backward, esoteric, and unfit for purpose in a world in which land is a core asset in the globalized economy of food production, resource extraction, and the real estate industry (Akram-Lodhi 2022, 278; Clapp and Isakson 2018).

THE PLURAL MEANINGS OF LAND

Empirically, however, this extractivist paradigm is far from the only thinkable approach to land. People all over the world, whether rural or urban (consciously or unconsciously), live off the land. For agricultural producers particularly, land is livelihood. But the meanings of land diverge across time and space, even between those with a similar occupation, as well as in places of similar geographical conditions, where many different meanings are attached to land simultaneously. For instance, in a report on the meanings of land in Myanmar, a variety of such meanings are portrayed (Franco et al. 2015). Beyond livelihood, land to the interviewed farmers is also tradition and remembrance: "Land is very meaningful for us not only for our livelihood but also as an inheritance to work on and relay across the generations" (Farmer in Shan State cited in Franco et al. 2015, 12).

This is not restricted to countries in the periphery. Consider Nettie Wiebe, member of the Canadian National Farmers Union, who told Annette Desmarais about a similar connection to land: "If you actually look at what 'peasant' means, it means 'people of the land.' Are we Canadian farmers 'people of the land'? Well, yes, of course. And it's important to take that language back" (Desmarais 2008, 139). For rural families, land often means family continuation across generations but also togetherness and community (Franco et al. 2015). Individual and collective identities are heavily entangled with the land on which they flourish (Berberich, Campbell, and Hudson

2012). This bond to land often inspires collective identities, as in connections to *a homeland*. And individual identities—particularly those of farmers and peasants—are linked with the land on which agricultural technologies come to bear. In that regard, land provides security both emotionally and economically, and has immediate connections to health and well-being.

This volume brings to the fore the plurality of meanings of land in order to understand their histories, relationships, and effects. It fosters a more comprehensive theorization of land by bringing its different understandings into conversation, particularly by exploring how we can understand the social world better if we look at land through different eyes. An epistemology of land designates an inquiry into knowledge production about land, with land, and by land. This project has concrete political, social, and ecological implications. Current relationships to land are often unsustainable. Based on the assumption that this is connected to a specific understanding of land (limited to a resource), this volume contributes to the discussion about alternatives to the current, unsustainable relations to land by offering more nuanced, more holistic ways of knowing land. This, in turn, can be the epistemological basis that alternative practices can be grounded in. Such a discussion is already underway and advanced among rural social movements (e.g., Nyéléni Europe and Central Asia 2020), particularly Indigenous communities (Hill 2017; Simpson 2021, chap. 9) but has so far not been sufficiently developed for a reflection on academic knowledge production.

Farmers, peasants, and many other people living and working in rural areas emphasize that it is not enough to have knowledge *of* the land: Land stores knowledge passed from one generation to the next. This knowledge is passed *through* the land, land being the link between people's past, present, and future. Building on this historical and temporal focus, epistemology in this volume is understood as a process and scientific practice that sheds light on why we have come to understand land in the ways we do; why certain understandings of land have become dominant in specific historical contexts; what consequences this dominant understanding of land has on people, animals, and the environment; and how these understandings become contested. The outcome of this book, thus, cannot be one such understanding. Rather, we ask what the conditions of possibility for specific sets of land knowledge are and which aspects of alternative land knowledges can possibly be recovered.

Not only the meanings of land are plural, but so are the ways in which we can learn about these meanings. In different disciplines, scholars have studied how land has been known in different sociopolitical contexts. The contributors to this volume bring them together to reflect on how they have been searching for meanings of land. They adopt very different approaches and geographical foci but are united by their interest in the role of knowledge in fields like politics, history, economy, and law of land. What connects these different approaches is that they not only strive to know what is meant by land or what land means to different actors but also that they aspire to know *through* (the material substance of) land. Collectively, they make significant advances toward a theory of knowledge of land.

TOWARD AN EPISTEMOLOGY OF LAND

How can we understand the role that land plays in different fields of study? For this volume, scholars from various disciplines reflect on the role of land in their research and the epistemological perspective on land that they utilize. These reflections bring to the fore that this relationship goes both ways. It is not only about taking a specific epistemological perspective and then grasping the role of land. Instead, all contributions show that land in itself shapes the way we can understand the social. Epistemologies of land therefore acquire a double meaning: Land can be understood and made meaningful in quite diverse ways: that is, it matters *how* we look at land as an object of research. But land also potentially drives us to change our views once we really take it into account. It stores near and distant memories, assembles a variety of artifacts, so clearly guides our means of production, and influences the ways of connecting to our own species and others. In sum, it isn't just a space in which social relations happen, but also it conditions and coproduces those relations.

Therefore, studying land through relations holds many possibilities. At first sight, this is nothing new, as the study of the social has always been the study of relations. Across disciplines, whether explicitly or implicitly, social orders, exchange, conflict, and cooperation are usually understood to be driven by humans relating to each other. Oddly, however, in most of the social sciences and humanities, these relations seem to be confined to a rather restricted segment of possible socioenvironmental scenarios. With few exceptions only, the social sciences are looking at a very limited facet of social life, both historically and geographically, by focusing on urban (and lately digital) relations, implicitly synonymizing them with society at large. Furthermore, cosmopolitan thought, transnational theories, and global studies have focused on relations that seem to transcend spaces, sometimes taking the form of flows or imaginaries that are detached from the land on (and in relation to) which they materialize.

In recent years, however, there has been a growing movement across disciplines to take place and space more seriously. The spatial turn has taken hold of the social sciences and humanities, putting a premium on theories that relate social action to the spaces in which they occur and to the characteristics of these environments. Space is constructed through social relations, which arise from the interests and actions of humans, particularly their means of production (Lefebvre [1974] 1991, 81). At the same time, the ontological turn has captured many debates, proposing in contrast that the "nature" of the worlds we inhabit determines to a great extent what kinds of relations can evolve in particular places, and what can be known about them (Blaney and Tickner 2017). This volume builds on the legacy of these turns because they both suggest a priority of socio-temporal space and its impact on social relations, hence pushing the social sciences to rethink how we conceive of humans in and in relation to their environment. In that sense, the project of knowing land stands in a diverse tradition in which the spatial and the ontological are analytical approaches for understanding how land is known in specific spatial contexts.

An epistemology of land therefore tries to understand the meanings of land at play in specific historical and spatial contexts, teasing out what land means to the people living on it and how this particular meaning has been constituted over time. Moreover, it engages with the question of how the meanings of land influence the ways in which people go about their lives, how they interact with each other and other species: that is, whether and how they relate through the land and the meanings that they attach to it. This kind of research is potentially possible regarding any kind of land, irrespective of whether it is pristine countryside, agricultural fields, or an urban center. Yet in the latter case, most inhabitants lack awareness of the land that they walk on, a fact that is both visible in and contested by the increasing willingness by such institutions as universities to acknowledge the land on which they were built. Oftentimes, this land acknowledgment recognizes Indigenous peoples, the traditional owners or stewards of the land, from whom it was violently taken by colonialists.[2] An epistemology of land in this case would ask which knowledges of the land are suppressed and forgotten due to colonization and how, in the process of acknowledging, a particular land knowledge is mobilized, staged, and communicated and with what effects. The contributions of this book focus on how such land knowledges change and with what consequences. Yet they do so mostly in agrarian regions because in agricultural practice, people tend to have a more explicit relationship to land and a stronger urgency to gain, keep, and communicate knowledge of the land. In turn, changed or lost knowledges of the land directly affect the land itself and vice versa, agrarian contexts thus being a crucial case of land epistemology.

ECONOMIZING KNOWLEDGES OF LAND

Engaging in epistemological questions can seem somewhat aloof. Why study the epistemology of land instead of, say, its ecology or economy? One of the most obvious changes in how humans have been relating to land throughout history is that an understanding of land as capital has developed from the sixteenth century onward and was fully globalized in the twentieth century. Nowadays, it is no problem for a trader in Frankfurt to buy land in Indonesia and sell it to another trader in New York the next day. Thus, emphasizing the diversity of meanings that land empirically has acquired across time and space—including material and spiritual meanings—stands in some contradiction to the fact that land has in recent decades been increasingly reduced to a commodity, a redefinition with terrible effects on many people and animals living on and from it (Engels and Dietz 2018, 7). Not only have rural lifestyles been disrupted and often made impossible due to the industrialization of agriculture, but also millions of people have been evicted and displaced by private companies, international financial institutions, and public-private partnerships that have grabbed their land in the course of rural development projects (Borras et al. 2011; de Wet 2005; Ziai et al. 2019). Growing up in most places of today's world, the understanding of land as a tradable good from which landlords and speculators can make a profit seems almost natural. It is this empirical normalization of one particular understanding that can be traced and critically evaluated with an approach that focuses on the history of knowledge of an object rather than (only) the object itself.[3] To recover and foreground alternative ways of knowing can contribute to a different practice. In her preface to *Caliban and the Witch*, Silvia Federici (2004, 9) suggests that hope for change can come from reconstructing these alternative understandings of land:

> In Nigeria I realized that the struggle against structural adjustment is part of a long struggle against land privatization and the "enclosure" not only of communal lands but also of social relations that stretches back to the origin of capitalism in 16th-century Europe and America. I also realized how limited is the victory that the capitalist work-discipline has won on this planet, and how many people still see their lives in ways radically antagonistic to the requirements of capitalist production. For the developers, the multinational agencies and foreign investors, this was and remains the problem with places like Nigeria. But for me it was a source of great strength, as it proved that, worldwide, formidable forces still contrast the imposition of a way of life conceived only in capitalist terms.

This quote is instructive in three ways: First, it correctly inscribes current conflicts over land into a long international history of land struggles. Second, it highlights the radicalization of the extractivist model that has developed during the rise of neoliberal economics in the second half of the twentieth century. Third, it showcases alternative practices of subtle resistance to or refusal of extractivist relations to land that can inspire new ways of knowing and living with land. But the catch is that since Federici's writing in 2004, this trend has even accelerated, leaving almost no place on Earth untouched by financial capital and its extractivist approach to land. In recent years, even such organizations as the Food and Agricultural Organization (FAO)—that previously could be seen as a counterweight to the interests of financial capital—tilted toward embracing large-scale investment into agriculture as the necessary cure for rural poverty (Canfeld, Duncan, and Claeys 2021; Duncan and Claeys 2018, 1418), leaving a trace of destruction in the countryside, with people evicted, climate change escalating, and alternative practices of relating to land becoming almost extinct (Akram-Lodhi 2022). This is why the project of rethinking how we know land is not just an academic curiosity but a project driven by a sense of political urgency.

Not only species and practices become extinct but also imaginations. Consider the following quote from an interview I conducted with a World Bank manager of extractive industries projects. Referring to a dialogue forum with civil society, she remembered that radical environmental advocates, especially those of Indigenous peoples' groups, spoke eloquently about their feelings, their habitat, or the land they lived on: "But it was very divorced from the conversations that we needed to have. It was almost like mystical at times" (Anderl 2022, 136). These advocates' relations to their land irritated the manager and her colleagues, who considered these interventions off-topic and therefore counterproductive to a constructive debate. They faced the challenge of not possessing an interpretative frame that would allow them to perceive the activists' discourse as rational knowledge. Consequently, they could only categorize it as mystical, resulting in a lack of common ground for mutual understanding. The manager could not accept as valid those knowledges derived from lived experiences. This situation raises the question of which knowledges are registered as such and whose experiences are disqualified as "single stories" that cannot be taken seriously (Anderl 2022, 71; see also Berman-Arévalo, this volume).

One problem of limiting one's epistemological perspective to a rationalist understanding of land as a commodity is thus that the rich and productive alternative knowledges cannot even be recognized as such but only as "backward" or "mystical," hence frequently making conversation impossible. This also means that exercises in participation, community outreach, and consultation before land acquisitions in the context of extractive industries or infrastructure projects cannot really perform what they are supposed to. Various types of land knowledges brought to the table are not recognized as such. But an epistemology does not only observe the shrinking plurality of knowledges; it also reconstructs why this happens and with what consequences. An important starting point here is that as the extractivist understanding of land becomes ever more pervasive, strategies of resistance also change. Instead of engaging in constructive debates, progressive and ecological social movements in the countryside become increasingly defensive and try to protect what is theirs. In an extractivist economic regime that is destructive for millions of people and the land on, with, and from which they live in cohabitation, being counterproductive to them often seems a reasonable first step in that it inserts alternative meanings into a debate—even though these may be dismissed as unprofessional (Anderl 2022, 71). This is also increasingly acknowledged in theories of resistance and mobilization, where the protection of what is left is becoming the primary focus of social movements, particularly those in the countryside (Sempertegui 2023; see also Tsing et al. 2017).

Finding, showcasing, and theorizing diverse knowledges of land not only serves as a potentially productive irritation but also is a basis for contestation. In this book, however, we go beyond showing "diversity." In a three-step process, we approximate the question of epistemology to go beyond its connotations as an academic metatheory. First, we investigate why one particular kind of knowledge, land as capital, has become dominant, asking how the knowledges of land have historically been reduced to conceptualizing land only in a commodified form, enabling an extractivist relationship to land that underlies the unsustainable practices of extraction that we currently observe the world over. Second, we look at contestations of these meanings of land, how they mobilize alternative knowledges, and how they open up possible new ways of relating to land. Third, we investigate the concrete implications of knowing and unknowing land in specific arenas, also showing the policy implications of changing meanings of and relationships to land.

COMMODIFYING (KNOWLEDGE OF) LAND

How, given the plethora of possible meanings of land, was the mainstream knowledge of land rendered extractivist? How is it possible that today it is taken for granted that the land we walk on is only an economic resource? In chapter 1, David Nally offers a close conceptual reading of the commodification of land. Building on Polanyi, he emphasizes the urgency and traction of an epistemological approach because the very process of commodification is fictitious, as land is not produced for the market, nor is it regulated by supply and demand. Nally critically discusses the material processes that underwrote the commodification of land. In Polanyi's account, land is commodified mainly through the force of ideas, whereas here, Nally foregrounds the instrumentalities that enclosed and assetized land, making it a resource object to be exploited for profit. In line with the perspective of this volume, he stresses that there used to be plural ways of relating to the land: before enclosure and privatization, most land was held in common. Referring to the example of the "quintessential English countryside"—the rectangular fields, dotted with walls and hedges we know from postcards—he highlights that these are historical artifacts, a landscape that cannibalized the open-field system characterized by topographic fragmentation and ecological variation. In fact, there were inner and outer commons, hinging on the idea that land was used but not owned: that is, one took only what was needed and no more because resources were shared with other commoners and, crucially, needs were aligned with ecological capacity (stewardship).

In this opening chapter, Nally does a great job illustrating how the current meaning of land is an impoverished form of a once pluralist system whose access was privatized while the majority forgot many of its functions and possibilities. Furthermore, he shows how an analysis of the physical material of land, its aesthetics, rules of access, and its ownership structure can teach us something about the meanings attached to land and their genealogy: that is, the power structures that they reflect. Drawing on Ingold, he argues that knowledge and meaning are not simply *attached to* land but also can be *gathered from* it (Ingold 2013, 155). The land itself holds knowledges; it can thus be seen *as* an epistemology that we must learn to mobilize. Building on this understanding, old political practices can be relearned anew, such as communing, agroecology, and mutualism.

Leo Steeds, in chapter 2, builds on this long-term perspective and investigates how the land that we know has been made and with what effects. With the methods of intellectual history, he traces the emergence of a discourse in which land is understood primarily or exclusively in terms of the revenues that it might yield to its owner: land as capital. Crucially, while there has been a discourse about land in economics in the seventeenth and eighteenth centuries, land was not considered a kind of capital. In fact, the two were strictly distinguished in the economic discourse of that period. Steeds shows that it was only later, in the late nineteenth and early twentieth centuries, that this theoretical orthodoxy was challenged and land came to appear to economists as merely one type of capital goods. While not the only influencing factor, the emergence of this understanding of land as capital within economic thought contributed to reducing the meanings of land over time.

Steeds makes an important twofold contribution to the epistemology of land: First, he shows how the understanding of land has shifted in economic theory, arguing that this shift rested on a prior and more fundamental epistemic rupture in understandings of land that in turn informed the birth of political economy. He describes how the understanding of land was transformed from being an irreducible materiality, as the essential basis of human subsistence, into one in which it was considered more narrowly in terms of the exchangeable value that it yields to its owner—that is, in terms of rent. Second, this transformation of how land was understood in consequence marked the birth of economic knowledge in a recognizably modern form. That is, again, Steeds shows how we can learn *about* land by tracing the meanings of land and how they were changed (i.e., reduced) over time, but looking at land also helps us understand bigger questions of society: in this case, political economy. We can understand them *through* land by considering how changes in political, legal, cultural, and administrative relations to land were necessary for land to appear as an object of economic analysis and in turn for economic thought to emerge as a body of knowledge.

The trend of commodifying land that Nally and Steeds trace is fully established and radicalized in the second half of the twentieth century, as Shailaja Fennell shows by reconstructing the epistemological dimensions of the "Green Revolution" (chapter 3). Fennell demonstrates what happens when food production is restricted to a form of economic output. Heavily influenced by conventional economics, with its singular attention on yields, food production has increasingly been reduced to a type of economic output by Green Revolution recipes. Value has thus been accorded solely to the final economic product (i.e., the commodity that is sold in national or transnational supply chains). The forms of agriculture that have been introduced in order to achieve this are bypassing the richer social dimensions of food within a farming community, as well as the processual aspects of food production that are its inherent features: the preparation of land, seed selection, harvesting, and sale of agricultural produce.

This reductionist perspective on agricultural practice has changed the relation of agrarian communities to the land that they work on, reducing it to a machinelike means of production. What is more, even the original products—such as millets in the case of many African communities—were degraded by international interventions due to discourses around efficiency and development, leaving millions of people with a worse deal and an environment in which suddenly their staple foods were looked down upon and exchanged for some foreign grain. Fennell makes a strong case for an epistemology of land that takes the practices of people working it seriously as embodied knowledge. The narrow focus of the Green Revolution on increasing food-grain productivity in Asia and Africa has conceptualized agriculture as solely a matter of material production, neither taking into account the colonial and postcolonial history of the continued denial of land rights nor the traditional knowledges of producers and consumers about which crop will sustain local conditions and nourish the population, thus producing what she calls a "false economy."

By overlooking the importance of recognizing land tenurial rights and its implications for the ability to transform the lives of rural communities, this extractivist approach reduces land to the purpose of economic production. Yet it is not even delivering on that account because the extractivist economy that calculates context-independent land use plans on the drawing board is bound to fail. Instead, Fennell argues that expanding our land knowledge would mean to regard land not only as a resource but also in its social relationships and cultural values. The lived reality of communities and their understanding of how they work the land need to become the basis for mapping local supply chains, building on local notions of ecological knowledge that will ascertain what patterns and levels of agricultural productivity these communities are able to achieve and sustain. The project of land epistemologies may sound very abstract, but Fennell clearly elaborates its practical consequences and political demands that can be bolstered by our collective research on land knowledges.

CONTESTING LAND KNOWLEDGE THROUGH ALTERNATIVES

The reduction of land to a commodity has become the dominant way of knowing land at the beginning of the twenty-first century, but it still is not without critique and alternatives. But how can we uncover such alternative understandings of and relations to land in order to foreground them and make them productive? In the second section of this volume, we trace the contested character of land knowledges, particularly foregrounding the epistemological tools to uncover alternative meanings of land and their purchase on the societies that preserve and create them in their relation to land.

In chapter 4, Eloisa Berman-Arévalo uses stories to grasp the meanings of land. Her chapter is informed by a dilemma: What is the use of ethnographic and other methods for understanding a people whose relations to the land and environment has been so distorted by colonial interventions and their extractivist understanding of land? What else apart from the reification of relations of domination can we find through such ethnographic investigations? She starts by looking at maps, admitting that, as a geographer, she has an ambivalent relationship to them, necessarily using and being critical of them at the same time. In this regard, stories in which the forest and the land were ascribed a mythological and a social function act as an entry point to make visible social lives that had been rendered ungeographic by previous academic projects.

To map these stories and to render them visible is one promising approach of uncovering alternative knowledges of the land that preceded its colonization. Berman-Arévalo is able to encounter the "geographic domination" of Afro-campesino women by analytically foregrounding their everyday stories and storytelling as forms of knowledge. Her epistemological register thus interrogates ordinary life and the stories that, at first glance, appear as anecdote or gossip. As she argues, these stories narrate histories, geographies, and racialized and gendered agrarian political economies through the lens of ordinary life events, thus expressing detailed geographic knowledge that reclaims land and territory through gendered everyday practices of care and social reproduction.

Another option for analytically recovering alternative land knowledges and the contestation of the extractivist approach to land is to focus on the growing number of rural social movements, particularly the rising peasant movements since the 1980s, who have been resisting their dispossession and at the same time illuminating alternative relations to land for the international audience to see. Especially, by offering their traditional ways of knowing land, they have been showcasing the utility of such agrarian practices as agroecology, thereby underlining the functionality of their alternatives to the monocultures that resulted from the commodification of land. Their resistance furthermore highlights the violent practices that occur in the course of land grabbing, especially in countries of the global South, a problem that has received plenty of attention in academic discussions during the last years (Borras et al. 2011).

What has been less covered in the literature is the process of land grabbing and its contestation in European countries, and what it means for the people being expulsed there. Katarina Kušić portrays such processes in Southeastern Europe, arguing that through a focus on these episodes of dispossession and resistance, we can learn a lot about contested land knowledges, not only in terms of the motivations for resistance but also regarding the "perpetrators" and their rationales (chapter 5). As she impressively illustrates, there is a staggering diversity of actors and reasons for grabbing land, from investment funds trying to squeeze profit from the land to organic entrepreneurs trying to establish sustainable agrarian projects. During these processes, social, ecological, and political relations are being reshaped, creating paradoxes, and giving way to varied forms of contestation. Kušić aims to make these deals the "narrators of history" and critically reflects on the tools available for pursuing this project.

Again, this procedure shows that we can learn more not only about land when using an epistemological lens but also about society and politics when looking at them *through* land. This is why she offers productive ways of knowing land differently by asking what is at stake when land is grabbed. The chapter shows that it is not just resources, markets, and subsistence but ways of life—both social and more than human. Tapping into the literature on ontologies of land, she argues that these approaches are not just useful when theorizing Indigenous peoples' movements but also necessary for understanding land and its meaning in Southeastern Europe because the various forms of contestation that arise in the context of land grabbing there can only be understood properly when accepting the diverse political, ecological, and socioeconomic relations that turn land into a contested site.

Such strategies of contesting land commodification and extraction by showcasing alternatives are also at stake in chapter 6, where Sakshi analyzes the attempts by Indigenous communities in Australia to legally establish the reality of alternatives to the setter-colonial property regime in the practice of strategic litigation. Particularly, they mobilize the transformative role of land in establishing the novelty of Indigenous environmental justice as a segue from doctrinal environmental litigation to a more holistic justice-oriented jurisprudence in Australian courts. Sakshi contends that "environmental jurisprudence in a settler nation is an exercise in reading against the grain" but shows that contestation of the dominant ways of knowing can be successful even within institutions of settler states.

Drawing on such contestations by movements and communities in Australian courts, she shows that land is both a historical artifact that cannot be captured with such simple terms as *territory* and a resource for Indigenous peoples that they use in front of the court. Indigenous knowledges of the land can be an opportunity to change litigation. But this needs pedagogical interventions in which land is both the context and the process. Sakshi shows how these advocates have mobilized Indigenous philosophies in recent court cases, enriching the understanding of land and using it as a resource for the communities who make claims for compensation once their land has been taken away. But it is a difficult process in a system that only knows economic compensation and communities whose relation to land is so much more than that.

Contributing to the project of land epistemology, Sakshi's chapter highlights how knowledge can be expanded by looking at social relations through land, in this case in order to foster understanding of what *justice* means in material terms. As she argues, for Indigenous land claims and in environmental litigation, "land assumes many forms as it progresses through the filters of law and justice." Land is not limited to physical territory in these legal contestations but extends to water, natural resources, indigeneity, cultural representations, and knowledge forms within and outside of litigation. In terms of widening the meanings of *land*, Sakshi contributes three frames that she observed in these court cases: land as memory and pedagogy, land as justice, and land as sovereignty.

KNOWING AND UNKNOWING LAND

One of the core findings that this book delivers is how contingent and yet violent the histories of transforming land into a resource of the few have been and the similarities in those processes, despite their enormous geographic and temporal variation. Colonialism is the central concept to consider here. Settlers and imperial companies have been colonizing the land, and the ways in which land has been colonized over centuries continues to colonize our epistemologies. Understanding this has very practical consequences, as Anna Wolkenhauer shows in her research on social policies in rural Zambia (chapter 7). The so-called evidence-based rural social policies that she investigates are so intertwined with a particular understanding of land as a resource that despite all the new evidence that development planners accumulate, the outcomes remain destructive and lack emancipation for the rural poor, a goal that needs a different understanding of the land on, with, and from which they try to live, as Wolkenhauer argues. She shows how roles, identities, and responsibilities are being inscribed in rural people and places, how these ascriptions are maintained through agricultural policies, and what the material effects are for the communities affected by the resulting political decisions about state services, land reforms, and international aid.

One of Wolkenhauer's conclusions is methodological: to rethink and contest accepted futures of the rural cannot happen in the economistic knowledge that pervades political and academic discourses. Different forms of knowledge need to inspire political decision making, importantly those resulting from lived experience, while other forms of knowledge need to be unlearned, particularly those that have resulted from the extractivist understanding of land and are being channeled into prejudiced ideas about rural people who do not live up to these economistic standards. "Helping" them within the same epistemological register will not deliver on the goals of politicians and development agencies, however well meaning they may be.

In that regard, the delegate at the Global Soil Partnership quoted in chapter 8 is right, when highlighting the inherent political nature of land. Yet, as Maarten Meijer discusses, this political character cannot simply be overcome by retreating to the supposedly more scientific substance of soil. In this chapter, Meijer takes a critical perspective at the delineation of concepts and how they influence what can be known about them—and the attempts by policy makers at compartmentalizing certain aspects of land politics in order to govern them efficiently by that *un*knowing other dimension of the problems at hand. He showcases the merits of an epistemological perspective by elaborating that, differentiated from those of land, epistemologies of soil open up their own modes of politics. As he shows with reference to the increased interest of the European Union (EU) in regulating soil, these politics are best understood in terms of cosmopolitics, that is the ongoing (re)construction of worlds. From that vantage point, both soil and land, accordingly, are not to be taken for granted as stable objects but need to be interrogated as actively constructed, politically defined, and temporally dynamic entities that are (a) creating new spaces that can be governed and (b) affecting the people, animals, and plants living on and in them in the way that they become defined and distinguished.

Meijer outlines how the EU has been creating a particular "problem space" of soil governance in which soil (as differentiated from land) has become the matter of concern for Brussels, affecting the physical, financial, and legal interactions between farmers and their lands, as well as other dimensions, such as environmental, biophysical, and touristic interests. Yet, as the chapter also makes clear, the policy makers never quite succeed in governing and even delineating this problem space due to the inherent material instability of soil, especially the manifold and contradictory ways in which communities relate to it.

In all chapters, the epistemological perspective on land contributes a productive and fascinating approach that illustrates how changing knowledges of land correlate with its usage and ownership, and their reconstruction therefore offers purchase on broader questions of societal change and political economy that would otherwise be out of sight (see also Wojnarowski 2023). I started this introduction by stating that the way scientists have historically treated land has heavily shaped what in consequence is being considered its nature, meaning, and value. With these last two chapters, Wolkenhauer and Meijer also close the volume by circling back to knowledge production in modern institutions and thus also to universities.

In the outlook, which I asked Inanna Hamati-Ataya to write, she radicalizes the perspective of what can be known and unknown regarding land, its knowledge, and the knowledge of its knowledge. Underlining the fundamental significance of agriculture for our knowledge of land, she not only doubles down on this book's strategy of focusing on agrarian contexts for understanding the meanings of land, but she also argues that the sets of knowledge that current societies operate by are fundamentally anchored in the "agrarian mode of life"; that is, the transition to agriculture has created a distinctive historical modality of being, the "Agrocene" that has since then been constituting land as a distinctive artifact of human knowledge and labor that has become a condition of human life. That is why, she argues, we have trouble even imagining epistemologies other than the ones connected to the Agrocene (previous to agriculture), for all the tools to make sense of the lived world are themselves the product of our agrarian paradigm of life. In that sense, both caring and extractivist epistemologies of land can be understood as types (cultures) of the agrarian paradigm that is distinctive of the Agrocene.

Zooming out to such a degree does not only confirm to necessarily conceive of epistemologies in the plural, but it also allows Hamati-Ataya to imagine a transformation away from this particular social structure. Epistemology in such a deep anthropological fashion "inscribes the formation of the structures of our consciousness in the most fundamental life processes that produce and reproduce us as natural and social beings." As such, this also allows us to speculate about a postagrarian modality of being in which the production of food may one day be decoupled from land. This will, of course, neither be an uncontested process, nor will it free the study of epistemology (of land) from being squarely inscribed in the domain of the contested, hierarchical social order. As Hamati-Ataya observes about the chapters in this book, "it is difficult—and perhaps even unwise—to untangle social claims to land from epistemic claims about land and to treat them—analytically and practically—as different categories of statements about the world or even as different types of engagement with the world." "Sometimes the truth is buried in the land" (Nagle 2021). As the following chapters show, sometimes you have to dig a little deeper, but where it gets rocky, the treasures are still contested.

NOTES

1.There is a big debate about the meanings of *extractivism* and *neoextractivism* (Acosta 2013; Svampa 2019). I am concerned with the general understanding of land as a resource from which valuables can be extracted in contrast to understanding it as a living matter with which humans stand in codependence. The specific political underpinnings of this extractivist understanding vary, but the general trend is observable during the twentieth and twenty-first centuries.

2.See, for example, Northwestern University (n.d.).

3.Even though the academic production of said object is always in danger of coproducing it at the same time, particularly in cases so encompassing as neoliberalism (Bacevic 2019).

REFERENCES

Acosta, Alberto. 2013. "Extractivism and Neoextractivism: Two Sides of the Same Curse." In *Beyond Development: Alternative Visions from Latin America*, edited by Miriam Lang and Dunia Mokrani, 61–86. Amsterdam: Transnational Institute, Rosa Luxemburg Foundation.

Akram-Lodhi, Haroon. 2022. "Food Regimes and Agrarian Questions." In *Essential Guide to Critical Development Studies*, edited by Henry Veltmeyer and Paul Bowles, 275–83. New York: Routledge.

Alcoff, Linda M. 2022. "Extractivist Epistemologies." *Tapuya: Latin American Science, Technology and Society* 5 (1), DOI: 10.1080/25729861.2022.2127231

Anderl, Felix. 2022. *Broken Solidarities: How Open Global Governance Divides and Rules*. Bristol, UK: Bristol University Press.

Bacevic, Jana. 2019. "Knowing Neoliberalism." *Social Epistemology* 33 (4): 380–92.

Berberich, Christine, Neil Campbell, and Robert Hudson. 2012. "Introduction: Framing and Reframing Land and Identity." In *Land and Identity: Theory, Memory, and Practice*, edited by Christine Berberich, Neil Campbell, and Robert Hudson, 17–41. Leiden, Netherlands: Brill.

Blaney, David L., and Anne B. Tickner. 2017. "Worlding, Ontological Politics and the Possibility of a Decolonial IR." *Millennium* 45 (3): 293–311.

Borras, Saturnino M., and Jennifer Franco. 2013. "Global Land Grabbing and Political Reactions 'from Below.'" *Third World Quarterly* 34 (9): 1723–47.

Borras, Saturnino M., Jr., Ruth Hall, Ian Scoones, Ben White, and Wendy Wolford. 2011. "Towards a Better Understanding of Global Land Grabbing: An Editorial Introduction." *Journal of Peasant Studies* 38 (2): 209–16.

Canfeld, Matthew C., Jessica Duncan, and Priscilla Claeys. 2021. "Reconfiguring Food Systems Governance: The UNFSS and the Battle over Authority and Legitimacy." *Development* 64: 181–91. https://doi.org/10.1057/s41301-021-00312-1.

Clapp, Jennifer, and S. Ryan Isakson. 2018. *Speculative Harvests: Financialization, Food and Agriculture*. Rugby: Practical Action.

de Wet, Chris. 2005. *Development-Induced Displacement: Problems, Policies, and People*. Oxford, UK: Berghahn.

Desmarais, Anette A. 2008. "The Power of Peasants: Reflections on the Meanings of La Vía Campesina." *Journal of Rural Studies* 24: 138–49.

Duncan, Jessica, and Priscilla Claeys. 2018. "Politicizing Food Security Governance through Participation: Opportunities and Opposition." *Food Security* 10: 1411–24.

Engels, Bettina, and Kristina Dietz. 2018. "Contested Extractivism, Society and the State: An Introduction." In *Contested Extractivism: Struggles over Mining and Land*, edited by Bettina Engels and Kristina Dietz, 1–20. London: Palgrave.

Federici, Silvia. 2004. *Caliban and the Witch: Women, the Body and Primitive Accumulation*. New York: Autonomedia.

Ferguson, James. 2012. "How to Do Things with Land: A Distributive Perspective on Rural Livelihoods in Southern Africa." *Agrarian Change* 13 (1): 166–74.

Franco, Jennifer, Hannah Twomey, Khu Khu Ju, Pietje Vervest, and Tom Kramer. 2015. *The Meaning of Land in Myanmar: A Primer.* Amsterdam: Transnational Institute. https://www.tni.org/files/publication-downloads/tni_primer-burma-digitaal.pdf.

Hall, Derek. 2013. *Land*. Cambridge, UK: Polity Press.

Hill, Susan M. 2017. *The Clay We Are Made Of: Haudenosaunee Land Tenure on the Grand River.* Winnipeg: University of Manitoba Press.

Ingold, Tim. 2013. "The Temporality of the Landscape." *World Archaeology* 25 (2): 152–74.

Kimmerer, Robin Wall. 2013. *Braiding Sweetgrass: Indigenous Wisdom, Scientific Knowledge, and the Teaching of Plants*. Minneapolis: Milkweed.

La Vía Campesina. 2000. "Declaration of the International Meeting of the Landless." San Pedro Sula, Honduras, July 28.

Lefebvre, Henri. (1974) 1991. *The Production of Space*. Translated by Donald Nicholson-Smith. Hoboken, NJ: Blackwell.
Li, Tania M. 2014a. *Land's End: Capitalist Relations on an Indigenous Frontier*. Durham, NC: Duke University Press.
———. 2014b. "What Is Land? Assembling a Resource for Global Investment." *Transactions of the Institute of British Geographers* 39: 589–602.
Nagle, Rebecca. 2021. "1. Solomon's Sword." *This Land* (podcast). August 23, 2021. MP3 audio, 47:14. www.crooked.com/podcast-series/this-land.
Northwestern University. n.d. "Land Acknowledgment." Accessed July 6, 2023. https://www.northwestern.edu/native-american-and-indigenous-peoples/about/Land%20Acknowledgement.html#:~:text=What%20is%20a%20Land%20Acknowledgment,Peoples%20and%20their%20traditional%20territories.
Nyéléni Europe and Central Asia. 2020. *Your Land, My Land, Our Land: Grassroots Strategies to Preserve Farmland and Access to Land for Peasant Farming and Agroecology*. Brussels: Nyéléni Europe and Central Asia. https://www.eurovia.org/wp-content/uploads/2020/05/EN-Your_Land_My_Land_Our_Land1.pdf.
Sempertegui, Andrea. 2023. "Weaving the Spiderweb: Mujeres Amazónicas and the Design of Anti-Extractive Politics in Ecuador." *Studies in Social Justice* 17 (2): 204–21.
Simpson, Leanne B. 2021. *As We Have Always Done: Indigenous Freedom through Radical Resistance*. Minneapolis: University of Minnesota Press.
Svampa, Maristella. 2019. *Neo-extractivism in Latin America: Socio-environmental Conflicts, the Territorial Turn, and New Political Narratives*. Cambridge, UK: Cambridge Elements.
Tsing, Anna, Heather Swanson, Elaine Gan, and Nils Bubant. 2017. *Arts of Living on a Damaged Planet: Ghosts and Monsters of the Anthropocene*. Minneapolis: University of Minnesota Press.
Tuhiwai-Smith, Linda. 1999. *Decolonizing Methodologies: Research and Indigenous Peoples*. London: Zed Books.
Wojnarowski, Frederick. 2023. "Settling Land, Unsettling People: Living with and Contesting Land, Social Change and Grand Schemes in Rural Central Jordan." *History and Anthropology*: 1–26. https://doi.org/10.1080/02757206.2023.2220342.
Wolford, Wendy. 2010. *This Land Is Ours Now: Social Mobilization and the Meanings of Land in Brazil.* Durham, NC: Duke University Press.
Ziai, Aram, Daniel Bendix, Eva Gerharz, and Dustin Schäfer. 2019. "Vertreibung durch Entwicklungsprojekte." *Peripherie—Zeitschrift für Politik und Ökonomie in der Dritten Welt* 39: 154–55.

PART I

Commodifying (Knowledge of) Land

Chapter 1

The Land Organism

On the Multispecies Commons and Its Enclosure

David Nally

> *What we call land is an element of nature inextricably interwoven with man's institutions. To isolate it and form a market for it was perhaps the weirdest of all the undertakings of our ancestors.*
>
> —Karl Polanyi ([1941] 2000)

Karl Polanyi famously argued that one cannot understand land as separate from the landscape and the ecology in which it is embedded, yet this is precisely what our ancestors attempted to do when they constituted a land market and invented the concept of private ownership in land. The abstraction and isolation of land as property—its invention as a "fictitious commodity," to adopt Polanyi's ([1941] 2000) terminology—conjured into being new links with the soil (and with it, the emergence of the landed estate), new ideas about utility and wealth (particularly ideas about profit maximization and improvement), and new modes of political subjectivity (the birth of the self-interested individual and landlord). While land may not have been the first form of property, there is no doubting its signal importance, especially as a site for articulating the defense of exclusive ownership. Moreover, the form of property that coalesced around land eventually percolated out and downward in society, such that today, rival powers vie to annex distant planets [a move that potentially inaugurates a new phase of astrocapitalism (Abrahamian and Ebel 2018)] and corporations strive to patent and privately own genes and, in some cases, whole life-forms. It is easy to forget just how revolutionary the development of private ownership was and just how central the property form is to our understanding of the modern world.

Before enclosure and privatization, most land was held in common (Nichols 2020). Consider, for example, the quintessential English countryside—the uniform landscape of rectangular fields, dotted with walls and hedges and inhabited by single farmsteads (Hoskins [1954] 2013). This field pattern is a historical artifact, of course, a landscape built on a cannibalized open-field system characterized by topographic fragmentation and ecological variation (Evans 1973). Under the earlier medieval open-field structure, a peasant might enjoy use rights to several noncontiguous strips, an outcome that ensured that good and bad ground was distributed evenly among villagers, and the land was not prematurely exhausted from raising one crop intensively over an extended area. Typically, a peasant had ground equivalent to one days' work, meaning the use of land was carefully calibrated to individual needs, communal work rhythms, and the ebb and flow of seasons. Livestock animals grazed on common grasslands or on the open field after harvest, and the absence of fences, walls, and hedges—which of course defines the *open* field—meant that this practice was easily accommodated. Beyond the confines of the village lay still other lands—mountain, heath, moor, marsh, forest, and wetland—where peasants rough-pastured their animals; foraged for herbs, medicinal plants, and bedding litter for animals; snared and hunted game; cut peat for fuel and gathered wood for tools and furniture; caught fish, shrimp, and shellfish; and scavenged seaweed for fertilizer. Like the communal lands of the manorial village, this "outer commons" (Greer 2017, 249) provided a cornucopia of goods and services that was intrinsic to rural life. Both inner and outer commons hinged on the idea that land was used but not owned (usufruct); one took only what was needed and no more (the "humble harvest"); resources were shared with other commoners (mutualism); and, crucially, needs were aligned with ecological capacity (stewardship; Kimmerer [2013] 2020; Scott 1976; Thompson 2010). In short, peasants used land in ways that sustained their daily lives and made social reproduction possible (Federici 2014). In turn, the land imprinted on the peasantry, shaping their outlook, customs, mores, and values.

In this sense, the landform was inseparable from the formation of the peasantry. Or to put this more directly, the medieval peasantry were land people whose very life was not merely dependent on the commons but also fundamentally inseparable from it. They were commoners—a term that did not carry the pejorative connotations it does today (Linebaugh 2015, 110)—whose personal and communal well-being was umbilically tied to the practical maintenance of their land environment. For this very reason, historian of the commons Peter Linebaugh insists on seeing the commons as a *practice* as much as a place—and thus he speaks of "commoning," reminding us of the immense range of customary activities that the commons both supported and made possible: *pannage*, meaning the right to pasture pigs in woods and forest (sylvo-pastorialism); *piscary*, connoting the right to access waterways and aquatic foods; *estovers*, describing rights to take timber for fuel, tool making, and home repair; *agistment*, connoting grazing rights; and *chiminage*, describing the rights of passage through woodlands (Linebaugh 2008, 73, 125).

The commoners who accessed grasslands, woods, and waterways of the medieval world also worked to shape and maintain them. Fire was used to create clearings, for instance, so that different plants could thrive and livestock could graze in newly made glades. The land was also a site of considerable cognitive and symbolic investment (Abram [1996] 2017; Jeffs 2022). For the medieval Italian peasant, writes Paolo Squatriti (2013, 4), woodlands were "simultaneously physical, botanical facts, and cultural artifacts." Moreover, their longevity, seasonality, and liminal status—uniting "aerial, terrestrial, and subterranean" domains—gave woodlands an exalted, sacred status (Squatriti 2013, 5), a worldview that likely acted as a brake against overuse and exploitation (Merchant [1980] 1990).

In a similar vein, coastal peoples managed kelp beds and other littoral resources in ways that exemplified care and respect. For the Channel Islander, seaweed, known locally as *vraic*, could be harvested from the beaches where it was deposited at high tide, or it could be cut loose from the rocks with sickles (*vraic scie*). The latter practice was heavily regulated, however, to ensure the health of the coastal ecosystems was maintained over time. In this way, production was thoughtfully aligned with social and ecological reproduction (Hocart 2016). In the vertical commons of the Andes, peasants domesticated potatoes (*Solanum tuberosum*) in ways that demonstrated a careful partnership between the people and their land environment. Dramatic variations in soil, gradient, humidity, and precipitation produced intense selection pressures that favored versatile cultivars with a broad-based adaptive capacity (Ochoa 2001; Wust 2001; Zimmerer et al. 2017).

However, and just as importantly, a culture of reciprocity and mutualism, with high rates of seed-tuber exchange, created an additional stimulus for crossings and gene flow, as did the practice of growing domesticated varieties in fields fringed by the potato's wild, tuber-bearing relatives (*Solanum L. sect. Petota Dumort*; Nally and Kearns 2020; Pollan 2001; Spooner and Hetterscheid 2006). This partnership between peasant, potato, field, and climate nurtured tubers that were not only hardy and adaptable but also diverse in texture, taste, and usability. Thus, the result—the harvest—was the outcome of generations of learning, dwelling, and experimentation, a process that Tim Ingold (1993, 153) characterizes as the "education of attention." Significantly, for Ingold, knowledge and meaning are not simply *attached to* land; on the contrary, they are more commonly *gathered from* it (Ingold 1993, 155). In other words, the land itself holds epistemological treasures. Land imparts and teaches, creating a store of practical knowledge. We might therefore consider land *as* epistemology rather than thinking more narrowly about (human) epistemologies *of* land.

****

This attunement to the land and the companion species that coinhabit it is one of the fundamental ways that hunter-gatherers, pastoralists, and peasant communities interact with and know their worlds. Their knowledge is tacit, born of experience, the sort of practical and contextual knowledge that James Scott (1998) terms *metis*. In *The Other Side of Eden* (2001), Hugh Brody similarly describes how hunting communities in the Arctic traverse the land noting topographical features, sharing stories, watching, listening, sensing. Storytelling, poetry, and singing become ways of fostering "intimate connections" between land, animals, plants, and people (Brody 2001, 205). Significantly, Brody notes that the "egalitarianism" often observed within Indigenous communities is profoundly *functional*—what Kimmerer ([2013] 2020, 126) elsewhere identifies as "practical reverence." Thus, failure to take care of the land is hazardous because it undermines the very basis of community survival (Brody 2001, 146). There is a broad recognition here that "we are at stake to each other," as Donna Haraway (2016, 55) memorably puts it, and that ultimately "all flourishing is mutual" (Kimmerer [2013] 2020, 15). To take more than one gives back—what we might label extractivism—is to undermine the prosperity of the land, to refuse its hospitality, to treat its gifts as so many fungible assets available for exploitation.

Taking a step back, it is apparent that the principles of commoning are perforce principles that guide relations to land, as well as relations with the nonhuman residents who share the land with us. Thus, the commons are always *multispecies* sites, places conjured out of partnerships and reciprocal arrangements that operate among and between species (Baynes-Rock 2013). "Nothing exists by itself," writes Arturo Escobar (2020, 19), "we interexist with everything." Interexisting *is* commoning, in the fullest sense of that term. Natural scientist and member of the Potawatomi community Robin Wall Kimmerer sees this ontology of connection as the very foundation of an Indigenous land ethic. For Kimmerer, the commons is a great "covenant of reciprocity" that begins with the metabolic connection of "life flowing into life": "plant breath for animal breath, winter and summer, predator and prey, grass and fire, night and day, living and dying. Water knows this, clouds know this. Soil and rocks know they are dancing in a continuous giveaway of making, unmaking, and making again the earth" (Kimmerer [2013] 2020, 194,

344, 383). Here again the commons is an awakening to the sense that "we are at stake to each other" (Haraway 2016, 55). Arguably, it is only through such multispecies commoning that we animate the world. Philosopher Emmanuele Coccia powerfully reminds us, "We, the living, have never stopped exchanging bodies, and what each of us is, what we call our 'species,' is only a set of techniques that each living being has borrowed from others" (2021, 4; cf. Coccia 2020).

The land partnerships and linked metabolisms that we call commoning involve connections that scientists are only beginning to unlock and understand. Take the corn-bean-squash complex, otherwise known as the Three Sisters. Widely grown by Indigenous communities across North and Central America, this vegetative troika demonstrates an acute grasp of companion planting, including the phenomenon of overyielding: that is, when two crops cultivated together yield more than when planted apart. Sown together, the beans twist around the corn stalk, providing the bean with stability and ready access to sunlight. At the base of the corn and beans, the squash provides a thick carapace of leaves that smother late-growing weeds and protect the soil from excessive heat and rain. Remarkably this reciprocity extends below ground, where soil-dwelling *Rhizobium* bacteria forge an alliance with the roots of the bean plant to produce nitrogen fertilizer, which is then shared with the corn and squash (see especially Kimmerer [2013] 2020, 133–34; Merchant 1989, 76–78). Behind the corn-bean-squash complex lies an intricate web of *synchronized interdependencies*. "Alone, a bean is just a vine, squash an oversized leaf," writes Kimmerer. "Only when standing together with corn does a whole emerge which transcends the individual. The gifts of each are more fully expressed when they are nurtured together than alone. In ripe ears and swelling fruit, they counsel us that all *gifts are multiplied in relationship*" (Kimmerer [2013] 2020, 140, emphasis added). Here, microbial partnerships below ground meet practices of caring relationality above ground (Puig de la Bellacasa 2017). What is typically called farming is nothing other than a coevolutionary compact to nurture such beneficent land relations.

The world over, land people have established partnerships of astonishing complexity with nonhumans. In Mozambique, young Yao men call and follow the diminutive bird, the greater honeyguide (*Indicatoridae*), to locate beehives. Alone, the men cannot locate the honeybee colonies among dense canopy or camouflaged in decaying tree trunks. Equally, while the greater honeyguide's intricate knowledge of the land means it can easily locate the honeybee colonies, the bird cannot easily access the larvae and wax cocooned in the hive. Only by working together, in alliance, can the Yao men and greater honeyguide collect the resources they need (Isack and Reyer 1989).

Such dramatic examples of partnership should not blind us to more everyday or prosaic forms of alliance making. Adding manure or night soil to land, clearing scrub, selecting and saving seed, fallowing fields, and rotating crops—these biotic interactions between people and land have fostered a commons with cascading benefits that go beyond the activities that are usually imagined under the sign of cultivation. When smallholders choose to save seed, for instance, they are directly shaping the genetic variance of a species. Equally, when foragers for wild strawberries (*Fragaria vesca*) remove only what they need and no more, their restraint becomes the condition for species survival and success. To fully appreciate the commons, then, one needs to grasp its multispecies entanglements and the tendency of life to survive and flourish through interdependencies that function at a range of scales. Too often the terms associated with the commons—*moral economy*, *mutualism*, *stewardship* (Scott 1976; Thompson [1963] 1991)—are understood in narrow anthropocentric terms (but see Kropotkin 1902), when in fact they might better describe modes of "interliving" and symbiotic dependence (Margulis 1998). The "land organism" (Leopold [1953] 1993, 146) is not only the *basis* for these relations; it is the *product* of them, too. Land is the ground upon which—and within which—different species bring each other into being.

****

The sociologist John Law has suggestively said, "Land doesn't belong to people. Perhaps it would be better to say that people belong to the land" (cited in Escobar 2020, 14). Many communities of people retain a deep and abiding attachment to land. For them, land is revered and sacred; it is identity and home as well as a source of food, medicine, beauty, and poetical inspiration. Yet for others, land is property, a resource that is privately owned and an instrument for accumulating profit. Thus, even as many land communities sought to preserve land as commons, new forces of extraction have worked to cleave land from its ecological and communal foundations, converting it into a commodity. How, then, is land as property fabricated (Bhandar 2018, 10)? What are the dominant regimes of extraction that enable not only the appropriation and control of land but also the appropriation of *land-based relations* that sustain ecologically vibrant communities?

The English enclosure movement was vital to the making of land as property (McDonagh 2013). Gaining momentum in the Tudor period and culminating with the "parliamentary enclosures" (Boyle 2007) of the eighteenth century—which saw a further 6.5 million acres of land privatized by legal fiat—the English enclosure movement saw the demise of open field and commons, as well as the curtailment, if not outright extinction, of the principles and customs that stood in the way of exclusive ownership (Linebaugh and Rediker 2007). In Ellen Meiksins Wood's (2017) view, it was the development of specific market imperatives—the pressures of competition, the compulsion to increase productivity and reinvest surplus—that hastened enclosures and the gradual discommoning of land (Linebaugh 2015; Nichols 2020). John Locke's *Second Treatise on Government* (Laslett 1960), with its emphasis on the improvement of waste, provided ideological ballast for landlords eager to put land to work in the service of capital (see chapter 2). For Locke, the value of land derived neither from nature nor from use but from the labor bestowed to make land more productive. In line with the new theory of mechanical nature derived from the Scientific Revolution (Laslett 1960; Merchant [1980] 1990), land was considered passive and inert, a resource base to be controlled and tamed for commercial benefit. The enclosure of wastes, the draining and improvement of fenlands, the pasturing of sheep for the woolen industry, the felling of woodlands for shipbuilding and fuel, the mining of mineral wealth below the Earth's crust: these extractive industries symbolized the breakdown of an ecological appreciation of land—what Aldo Leopold ([1949] 1968) called a "land ethic"—and its replacement by a new logic of unbridled economic growth. Now farmland would be measured by gains in yield, woodland by the quantity of the timber provided, pastureland by the volume of ungulates raised, and coastlands by the stocks of fish caught and sold. Land had a value, but that value was increasingly understood in narrow economic terms.

While the thinking of Locke and other Enlightenment scholars was a significant factor in these transformations, it is important to stress that these changes took root at the level of *material culture* (Merchant [1980] 1990, 61). In other words, the changing appreciation of nature was actualized, or grounded in, "changes in the land" itself (Cronon 1983). For instance, vast quantities of oak, ash, and elm were cut to provide the fencing and posts that were used to sequester animals, marking their new status as livestock. Stone walls and hawthorn hedgerows broke up the open-field system and established the boundaries for newly isolated farmsteads. Cattle runs and sheep walks replaced the arable commons (defenders of the commons deployed Thomas Moore's metaphor of sheep-eating men to decry this plague of ungulates). What was planted in fields also changed as agricultural production became more specialized and farmers turned to crops that fetched a higher price: hemp and flax for the textile industries, hops for brewing, woad for dyeing, fruit and vegetables to appeal to the diets of a rising middle class (Thirsk 1984).

The tenets of agricultural improvement also transformed animal lives as breeders sought to optimize the animal's body, converting dairy cows into milking prodigies, sheep into efficient fabricators of high-value wool, and hogs into superabundant producers of pork. "In the choice therefore of your sheepe," advised one seventeenth-century breeder, "choose the biggest boned, with the best wooll. These sheep . . . are alwaies the best butchers ware, and goe soonest away in the market" (cited in Davis and Beckett 1999, 1). Writing in 1610, Richard Carew tellingly drew links between the engrossing of land and improved breeds of ruminants:

> What time the shire, through want of good manurance, lay waste and open, the sheep had generally little bodies and coarse fleeces . . . But since the grounds began to receive enclosure and dressing for tillage, the nature of the soyle hath altered to a better graine, and yeeldeth nourishment in greater aboundance, and goodnesse to the beastes that pasture thereupon: so as by this meanes . . . Cornish sheepe come but little behind the easterne flockes for bignes of mould, finenesse of wooll, often breeding, speedie fatting, and price of sale. (cited in Davis and Beckett 1999, 9–10)

Seen this way, enclosure was a social force that shaped the evolutionary trajectory of animal lives (via selective breeding) as much as it altered the social practices of animal husbandry. More and more, nature was treated as technics, a living substance that could be worked on and altered to become more amenable to commodification (Boyd 2001; Schrepfer and Scranton 2004).

****

It was, of course, in the colonies where these sorts of interventions were most fully expressed. For instance, the Tudor reconquest of Ireland proceeded through the policy of plantation, whereby rebellious Gaelic and Hiberno-Norman lords and their supporters were forcefully deposed and their lands were resettled by English, Welsh, and Scottish colonists who undertook to settle the forfeited estates, develop towns, and practice commercial agriculture (Ohlmeyer 1998). The first plantations were established by Mary Tudor in the 1550s, and later, under Queen Elizabeth I, large parts of the province of Munster were confiscated and given over to plantation (Canny 1976). King James I continued Elizabeth's policy of plantation—confiscating large tracts of land in the northern province of Ulster—and further waves of dispossession and displacement followed Oliver Cromwell's military campaigns in the mid-seventeenth century. Between 250,000 and 300,000 colonists arrived in Ireland over the course of the seventeenth century, and their changes in the land were a direct effort to *deterritorialize* the old Gaelic order, replacing it with a new framework of property ownership and a new emphasis on commercialized trade (Smyth 2006). Sir William Petty's cadastral survey of Ireland—the first large-scale colonial survey and a precocious attempt to extend the "logic of quantification and measurement" to land (Bhandar 2018, 35)—aided the partitioning and parceling of land to the soldiers who served in Cromwell's New Model Army. Armed with new instruments for land control, such as the Gunter's chain (which replaced less exact poles and rods) and circumferentor (for measuring horizontal angles), Petty's surveyors mapped the civil boundaries for most of the island. Classifying land as profitable or unprofitable and producing accompanying books of data that recorded property titles on confiscated territory (Greer 2017, 282; Prendergast 1997; Smyth 2006), Petty's surveyors ably demonstrated the advantages of a new scientific culture dedicated to the instrumentalization of the land organism.

If maps, surveyor's chains, compasses, and theodolites were spectacular instruments of colonial property formation—"engineering colonization according to the laws of geometry" (Greer 2017, 273; Nichols 2020, 47)—then the actual possession of land was secured through more everyday or "micro" practices of inscription (Greenblatt 1991; Li 2014). For example, the authorities overseeing the plantation of Ulster stipulated that planters import "improved" breeds of cattle from England (Costello 2022). According to environmental historian Keith Pluymers (2020, 293), the new breeds served as agents of colonization by making land a site for commercial venture, and at the same time, these changes were read as proof that the planters were "fulfilling the civilizing mission." Moreover, increased stock densities and the subsequent enclosure of pastureland encouraged auxiliary markets—in fodder crops, milk, animal hides, tallow, and other animal by-products (Pluymers 2020, 293)—to take root and flourish. It was hoped, too, that improved livestock and commercial pastoralism would encourage the Irish to forsake the Indigenous custom, known as "booleying," of migrating animals to remote mountain pastures in the summer (Costello 2020). Such English writers as Fynes Moryson (1566–1630) described the Gaelic population as rude and primitive, erroneously citing as evidence that they lived like nomads, while the attorney general for Ireland, Sir John Davies (c. 1569–1626), claimed that before plantation the Irish

> would never, to the end of the world, build houses, make townships or villages, or manure or improve the land as it ought to be; therefore it stands neither with Christian policy nor conscience to suffer so good and fruitful a country to lie waste like a wilderness, when his Majesty may lawfully dispose it to such persons as will make a civil plantation thereupon. (cited in Wood 2017, 160)

Informed by an Enlightenment discourse that linked material conditions to moral advancement (Carroll-Burke 2002), planters saw their walled estates and enclosed fields as exemplary sites that would incite a "mimetic response" among the subjugated Gaels (Whelan 1997). This idea was expressed in regulations on a Cork estate owned by Sir Walter Raleigh, which stated that "no tenant belonging to the lands of Mogeely shall henceforth dwell abroad . . . in woods, bogs, glinns and other remote places . . . but shall presently resort and dwell within the town, or depart from those lands. . . . [A]ll shall bring within the castle walls, or town, and shall set their ricks of corn in such places near unto ther castle" (cited in Costello 2022, 297). In general, the planters sought to engineer new relations to the land by constructing roads, walls, fences, dwellings, and towns. In a similar vein, importing better breeds of livestock, planting commercial crops, and reclaiming bogland were seen as instruments of reform and tangible proof that the planters were an edifying and beneficent force.

It is significant, too, that the English referred to themselves as "planters" and their colonies as "plantations" (Greer 2017, 7). From the perspective of the colonizer, imperial culture manifested itself as *praxis*; above all, it was about "writing on the ground a new set of social and spatial relations" (Mbembe 2003, 25–26; cf. Said 1993). Effecting changes at the level of material culture was precisely how the Puritans and Pilgrims of New England secured possession. Patricia Seed (1995) notes that before ownership was recorded in law, it was first registered *on the land*. Building outhouses, erecting homesteads, planting gardens, demarcating boundaries, fencing perimeters—these were the "registers of stability" that established a claim to private, exclusive use (Seed 1995, 18). One of the first laws passed by the Virginia assembly (1623) stated that "every freeman [settler] shall fence in a quarter acre of ground." Fencing was private ownership in *object form*, and the failure of Indigenous communities to enclose ground proved that native plots did not exist. The Puritan lawyer John Winthrop—who was also involved in England's plantation of Ireland (Wood 2017, 159)—wrote, "[T]he Natives in New England, they enclose noe land, neither have they settled habitation, nor any tame cattle to improve their land by." Moreover, removing trees from the realm of nature and repurposing them as palling (fences) or as materials in homes proved the colonists' status as agriculturalists, humans who live by subduing the land and establishing dominion over wild nature. The exogenous cereals introduced by the colonists (wheat, barley, oats, rye), along with a range of root vegetables (parsnips, carrots, turnips, etc.), altered the local ecology, replacing indigenous crops with invasive species that were aligned to the planters' tastes and preferences and were better suited to commodity exchange (Crosby 2003; Scott 1998). European livestock (horses, cattle, sheep, goats, pigs) reproduced quickly, and their collective actions, including excessive grazing, which contributed to soil erosion, trampling crops, consuming stored foods, disturbing wild game, and spreading Old World zoonotic diseases, amounted to what Greer (2017, 261–63) terms a "multispecies assault on the native commons." For Europeans, of course, the introduction of new crop species and the expansion of ranch land was a vital sign that virgin land was being put to productive use.

For Carolyn Merchant (1989, 52), European planters undermined Indigenous lifeways through a series of externally caused "ecological additions and withdrawals." Clearing woodlands and confining crops within enclosed fields and gardens reduced the space in which native trapping and food gathering could operate. An expanding trade in timbers reduced the foraging ground available for such large game as deer, elk, and moose. New protoindustries, such as sawmills, polluted rivers and interrupted watercourses, often affecting the migration routes and breeding practices of marine species that were fished by Indigenous communities. A rapidly expanding fur trade "removed beavers, muskrat, foxes, lynx, bear, and other animals that had supplied Indian meat and pelts" (Merchant 1989, 87). Moreover, the exchange of furs for equipment and utensils (pots, knives, axes) meant that Indigenous communities were soon using technologies that they did not control. "What begun as adaptation and absorption," Merchant tellingly observes (1989, 55), soon "became dependency." Colonization in this sense was a form of "ecologised war" (Sloterdijk 2009, 20). Over time, larger and larger areas of land were rendered inhospitable to subsistence living, and Indigenous communities found themselves trying to reproduce their lives from meager fragments.

At other times or in other colonies, "ecological control" was direct, continuous, and brutal, as was the case on the slave plantation (Beckert 2015; Fraser 2022; Mies and Bennholdt-Thomsen 2009; Wood 2003). To create a series of "sugar islands" in the Caribbean, planters first had to clear the land by slashing brush, burning scrub, and felling trees (Moore 2009). With the ground razed, gangs of transplanted slaves began the work of readying the ground for planting. First manure—in the form of seaweed hauled up from the coast—was applied, and then a second gang of slaves undertook the work of planting, or cane-holing. Uniform square plots were marked out, and holes, approximately two feet long and nine inches deep, were dug and the cane inserted. Once planted, the cane fields had to be weeded, irrigated, kept free of pests (a real problem on monocultures), and vigilantly guarded. To a large degree, the uniqueness of the plantation form was driven by the materiality of the sugar cane plant itself (Mintz 1985). Once harvested, the plant quickly desiccates, and in an exchange economy, where above all production is organized to realize profit, it was vital that the harvested plant was processed at speed (Ogborn 2008; Otter 2020). To make this possible, the planters located the processing mill on the plantation itself—turning the estate into a literal field-factory (Mintz 1985; Moore 2010; Nally 2011)—and they drove their workers at a relentless pace to squeeze every ounce of "white gold" from the harvest. During the harvest season, slaves were expected to work up to ten hours in the field and a further six hours in the mill every other evening for up to five months.

For Sidney Mintz (1985) this unique form of "time discipline" marks the plantation as one of the most ambitious political technologies of the age: here was a regime of planting, harvesting, processing, exporting, and refining that turned a plant into a commodity and the land into a vehicle for capital accumulation. Just as significantly, the plantation form also conjured into being a new, modern regime of labor that *extended* the domain of property to human lives (Bales 2016; Blackburn 1997). Slaves were bought and sold, beaten and brutalized, until their bodies could take no more. "In plantation regimes," writes Sophie Chao (2022, 362), "the fates of uprooted and transplanted humans and plants become strangely intertwined." For Donna Haraway and Anna Tsing (2019), slave plantations are best understood as a violent reconfiguration of land, plants, and people that offered a template for extending the *logos* of mastery and extractivism to all walks of life (cf. Murphy and Schroering 2020). Here, then, we see a land world, comprised of linked metabolisms and entangled agencies, transmuted into a brutally efficient economy of inputs and outputs. Or, put a little differently, the multispecies commons gives way to the extreme simplifications of the "plantationocene" (Barua 2023; Scott 1998).

****

Too often, the process of enclosure has been analyzed from a narrow anthropocentric perspective. Scholars focused on the improvement of waste lands, for example, have had less to say about the destruction of refuge habitats for plants, animals, and people. In a similar vein, the study of land consolidation has had less to say about ecological simplification; work examining the appropriation of the peasantry from the soil (proletarianization) has underplayed the cost of this to actual soils (Foster, Clark, and York 2010; Salazar et al. 2020; Slater and Flaherty 2023); and studies of colonization, plantation, and enslavement have been slow to see these processes as biotic events between people and land (but see Bales 2016). Because the role of extrahuman natures in the formation of colonial capitalism has been underemphasized (Moore 2015; Fraser 2022), scholarship tends to reproduce the Cartesian dualism that partitions "nature" from "society" (Descola 2005). In this way, "forces of nature" are forever masked and mystified as "forces of production" (Moore 2016, 111).

In this brief chapter, I show that there is much to gain from considering the multispecies dimensions of the commons and for taking seriously Aldo Leopold's notion of the "land organism." ["The outstanding scientific discovery of the twentieth century," Leopold writes ([1953] 1993, 146), "is not television, or radio, but rather the complexity of the land organism"]. In part, this analysis is inspired by political ecologists, environmental historians, vital materialists, and more-than-human scholars who have drawn attention to how animals, plants, and people—not to mention a whole cast of microbial actors—exist within webs of relations. However, it is just as important to recognize that forest communities, pastoralists, hunter-gathers, peasants, and Indigenous peoples have also grasped that their lives are inextricably tied up with the lives of others and that taking care of those land relations—by cultivating what Escobar (2020, 126) calls an "ethos of complementarity"—is a fundamental element in the reproduction of their patterns of life. Crucially, the lessons of complementarity were gathered from the land itself. Mutualism, stewardship, restraint, and replenishment—these ideas were gleaned from the land in much the same way that fallen stalks were gleaned from the fringes of common fields.

To the extent that this is true, land remained "embedded" (Polanyi [1941] 2001) in the natural environment and firmly attached to the communities, both human and nonhuman, that lived and toiled on it. Apart from anything else, then, the enclosure of land, in both its metropolitan and colonial forms, was a stark reconfiguration of the *ecology of land relations*. This reconfiguration was enacted through a variety of mechanisms or regimes of extraction. For such scholars as Richard Tawney (1912), Robert Brenner (1976), and Ellen Meiksins Wood (2000; 2017), the development of competitive pressures, particularly the transition to market-mediated leases, created the impetus to consolidate holdings and increase productivity. Increasingly, land was reimagined as an organizing medium for generating economic value. For Carolyn Merchant ([1980] 1990), the arrival of a new mechanistic science, which emphasized the inertness and passivity of matter, provided an additional stimulus for appropriating and exploiting the land organism—trees become fences, plants become crops, animals become livestock, minerals become money. Here the logic of ownership (i.e., the property form) is generalized and becomes a central element in the alienation of land from its common multispecies attachments.

In the colonies, extraeconomic coercion entered much more formally into the process of extractivism as the indigenous commons was violently seized and exploited (Federici 2014; Fraser 2022). To make good their claim to possession, colonial settlers planted the land with commercial crops and improved livestock; they constructed byways and roads, as well as new forms of dwelling; they erected mills that refined nature's gift of wind and water power; and they intervened in watercourses to aid irrigation and supply their own settlements (McNeill 2000). Thus, the settler plantation was not merely a way of laying claim to land; it was also a means of inscribing capitalism on the land itself. In the New World, racialized chattel slavery and simplified monoculture were the solutions to the problem of contracting the energy and time necessary for nature to be made over into commodities. As a field-factory, the plantation captured and enclosed human *and* nonhuman life, turning both into forms of disposable property. Here, then, was a new way to deploy power and "assemble resources" (Richardson and Weszkalnys

2014)—a power that came at the cost of millions of Black lives, not to mention incalculable ecological harms.

In an important essay on the intimacies of place, poet, farmer, and essayist Wendell Berry (2002, 27) writes, "Until we understand what the land is, we are at odds with everything we touch. And to come to that understanding it is necessary, even now, to leave the regions of our conquest—the cleared fields, the towns and cities, the highways—and re-enter the woods." The woods that Berry evokes in this passage are more than merely metaphorical, for the woodland commons have long served, and indeed continue to serve, not only as landscapes of foraging and hunting but also as sites where humans and nonhumans intermingle and where meanings and lessons are found in "every leaf, swarm and downpour" (Jeffs 2022). The forest commons were also, of course, prime sites of enclosure (Thompson 2010); indeed, they feature prominently in Karl Marx's early thinking on the formation of private property (Linebaugh 1981), and they remain vital spaces for contesting the human will to control and exploit nonhuman natures. If, to survive the Anthropocene, "we must once again actively make ourselves more 'like' the environment, not as object, but in the deepest sense of visceral remerging with the earth" (Merchant 2020, 154), then the place to start is the land—not only our woodlands but also our mountains, heaths, moorlands, marshes, and wetlands.

ACKNOWLEDGMENTS

We interexist in our writing lives, too. For their insights and intellectual generosity, I acknowledge and thank Felix Anderl, Olivia Angé, Kevin Bales, Alison Bashford, Lizzie Collingham, Eugene Costello, Inanna Hamati-Ataya, Philip Howell, and Olga Petri.

REFERENCES

Abrahamian, Atossa Araxia, and Denton Ebel. 2018. "Mining the Sky: Meehan Crist, Atossa Araxia Abrahamian, and Denton Ebel on Astrocapitalism." *Logic* 4 (April 1, 2018). https://logicmag.io/scale/meehan-crist-atossa-araxia-abrahamian-and-denton-ebel-on-astrocapitalism/.

Abram, David. (1996) 2017. *The Spell of the Sensuous: Perception and Language in a More-than-Human World.* New York: Vintage.

Bales, Kevin. 2016. *Blood and Earth: Modern Slavery, Ecocide, and the Secret to Saving the World.* New York: Random Books.

Barua, Maan. 2023. "Plantationocene: A Vegetal Geography." *Annals of the American Association of Geographers* 113 (1): 13–29.

Baynes-Rock, Marcus. 2013. "Life and Death in the Multispecies Common." *Social Science Information* 52 (2): 210–27.

Beckert, Sven. 2015. *Empire of Cotton: A Global History.* New York: Vintage Books.

Berry, Wendell. 2002. *The Art of the Commonplace: The Agrarian Essays of Wendell Berry*. Edited by Norman Wirzba. Berkeley, CA: Counterpoint.

Bhandar, Brenna. 2018. *Colonial Lives of Property: Law, Land, and Racial Regimes of Ownership*. Durham, NC: Duke University Press.

Blackburn, Robin. 1997. *The Making of Modern World Slavery: From the Baroque to the Modern*. London: Verso.

Boyd, William. 2001. "Making Meat: Science, Technology, and American Poultry Production." *Technology and Culture* 42 (4): 631–64.

Boyle, James. 2007. "The Second Enclosure Movement." *Renewal: A Journal of Labour Politics* 15 (4): 17–24.

Brenner, Robert. 1976. "Agrarian Class Structure and Economic Development in Pre-Industrial Europe." *Past and Present* 70: 30–75.

Brody, Hugh. 2001. *The Other Side of Eden: Hunter-Gathers, Farmers and the Shaping of the World*. London: Faber and Faber.

Canny, Nicholas. 1976. *The Elizabethan Conquest of Ireland: A Pattern Established.* Sussex, UK: Harvester Press.

Carroll-Burke, Patrick. 2002. "Material Designs: Engineering Cultures and Engineering States, Ireland 1650–1900." *Theory and Society* 31 (1): 75–114.

Chao, Sophie. 2022. "Plantation." *Environmental Humanities* 14 (2): 361–66.

Coccia, Emanuele. 2020. *The Life of Plants: A Metaphysics of Mixture*. Cambridge, UK: Polity.

———. 2021. *Metamorphoses*. Cambridge, UK: Polity.

Costello, Eugene. 2020. *Transhumance and the Making of Ireland's Uplands, 1500–1900*. Woodbridge, UK: Boydell Press.

———. 2022. "Agriculture and the Integration of British Colonial Migrants in Early Modern Ireland." *Journal of Migration History* 8: 291–312.

Cronon, William. 1983. *Changes in the Land: Indians, Colonists and the Ecology of New England.* New York: Hill and Wang.

Crosby, Alfred W. 2003. *The Columbian Exchange: Biological and Cultural Consequences of 1492*. Westport, CT: Praeger.

Davis, Simon J. M., and John V. Beckett. 1999. "Animal Husbandry and Agricultural Improvement: The Archaeological Evidence from Animal Bones and Teeth." *Rural History* 10 (1): 1–17.

Descola, Philippe. 2005. *Beyond Nature and Culture*. Translated by Janet Lloyd. Chicago: University of Chicago Press.

Escobar, Arturo. 2020. *Pluriversal Politics: The Real and the Possible*. Durham, NC: Duke University Press.

Evans, E. Estyn. 1973. *The Personality of Ireland: Habitat, Heritage and History.* Cambridge, UK: Cambridge University Press.

Federici, Silvia. 2014. *Caliban and the Witch: Women, the Body and Primitive Accumulation*. New York: Autonomedia.

Foster, John Bellamy, Brett Clark, and Richard York. 2010. *The Ecological Rift: Capitalism's War on the Earth*. New York: Monthly Review Press.

Fraser, Nancy. 2022. *Cannibal Capitalism: How Our Systems Is Devouring Democracy, Care, and the Planet—and What We Can Do about It*. London: Verso.

Greenblatt, Stephen. 1991. *Marvelous Possessions: The Wonder of the New World*. Chicago: University of Chicago.

Greer, Allan. 2017. *Property and Dispossession: Natives, Empire and Land in Early Modern North America*. Cambridge, UK: Cambridge University Press.

Haraway, Donna. 2016. *Staying with the Trouble: Making Kin in Chthulucene*. Durham, NC: Duke University Press.

Haraway, Donna, and Anna L. Tsing. 2019. "Reflections on the Plantationocene: A Conversation with Donna Haraway and Anna Tsing." Interview by Gregg Mitman. *Edge Effects*, April 18, 2019. https://edgeeffects.net/wp-content/uploads/2019/06/PlantationoceneReflections_Haraway_Tsing.pdf.

Hocart, Richard. 2016. *The Country People of Guernsey and Their Agriculture, 1640–1840*. Guernsey, UK: Taylor Thorne Print.

Hoskins, William George. (1954) 2013. *The Making of the English Landscape*. Dorset, UK: Little Toller Books.

Ingold, Tim. 1993. "The Temporality of the Landscape." *World Archaeology* 25 (2): 152–74.

Isack, H. A., and H.-U. Reyer. 1989. "Honeyguides and Honey Gatherers: Interspecific Communication in a Symbiotic Relationship." *Science* 243 (4896): 1343–46.

Jeffs, Amy. 2022. *Wild: Tales from Early Medieval Britain*. London: Riverun.

Kimmerer, Robin Wall. (2013) 2020. *Braiding Sweetgrass: Indigenous Wisdom, Scientific Knowledge and the Teaching of Plants*. London: Penguin Books.

Kropotkin, Peter. 1902. *Mutual Aid: A Factor of Evolution*. New York: McClure Phillips.

Laslett, Peter, ed. 1960. *Locke: Two Treatises of Government*. Cambridge, UK: Cambridge University Press.

Leopold, Aldo. (1949) 1968. *A Sand County Almanac and Sketches Here and There*. Oxford, UK: Oxford University Press.

———. (1953) 1993. *Round River: From the Journals of Aldo Leopold*. Edited by Luna B. Leopold. Oxford, UK: Oxford University Press.

Li, Tania Murray. 2014. "What Is Land? Assembling a Resource for Global Investment." *Transactions of the Institute of British Geographers* 39 (4): 389–602.

Linebaugh, Peter. 1981. "Karl Marx, the Theft of Wood and Working-Class Composition." In *Crime and Social Justice*, edited by Tony Platt and Paul Takagi, 85–99. London: Palgrave.

———. 2008. *The Magna Carta Manifesto*. Berkeley: University of California Press.

———. 2015. *Stop, Thief! The Commons, Enclosures and Resistance*. Oakland, CA: PM Press.

Linebaugh, Peter, and Marcus Rediker. 2007. *The Many-Headed Hydra: The Hidden History of the Revolutionary Atlantic*. London: Verso.

Margulis, Lynn. 1998. *Symbiotic Planet: A New Look at Evolution*. New York: Basic Books.

Mbembe, Achille. 2003. "Necropolitics." *Public Culture* 15 (1): 11–40.

McDonagh, Briony. 2013. "Making and Breaking Property: Negotiating Enclosure and Common Rights in Sixteenth-Century England." *History Workshop Journal* 76 (1): 32–56.

McNeill, John Robert. 2000. *Something New under the Sun: An Environmental History of the Twentieth Century*. New York: Random House.

Merchant, Carolyn. 1989. *Ecological Revolutions: Nature, Gender and Science in New England.* Chapel Hill: University of North Carolina Press.

———. (1980) 1990. *The Death of Nature: Women, Ecology and the Scientific Revolution*. New York: Harper Row.

———. 2020. *The Anthropocene and the Humanities: From Climate Change to New Age Sustainability*. New Haven, CT: Yale University Press.

Mies, Maria, and Veronika Bennholdt-Thomsen. 2009. *The Subsistence Perspective: Beyond the Globalised Economy*. London: Zed Books.

Mintz, Sidney W. 1985. *Sweetness and Power: The Place of Sugar in Modern History.* New York: Penguin Books.

Moore, Jason W. 2009. "Madeira, Sugar, and the Conquest of Nature in the 'First' Sixteenth Century, Part I: From 'Island of Timber' to Sugar Revolution, 1420–1506." *Review (Fernand Braudel Center)* 32 (4): 345–90.

———. 2010. "Madeira, Sugar, and the Conquest of Nature in the 'First' Sixteenth Century, Part II: From Regional Crisis to Commodity Frontier, 1506–1530." *Review (Fernand Braudel Center)* 33 (1): 1–24.

———. 2015. *Capitalism in the Web of Life*. London: Verso.

———. 2016. "The Rise of Cheap Nature." In *Anthropocene or Capitalocene? Nature History and the Crisis of Capitalism*, edited by Jason W. Moore, 78–115. New York: PM Press.

Murphy, Michael W., and Caitlin Schroering. 2020. "Refiguring the Plantationocene: Racial Capitalism, World-Systems Analysis, and Global Socioecological Transformation." *Journal of World-Systems Research* 26 (2): 400–15.

Nally, David. 2011. "The Biopolitics of Food Provisioning." *Transaction of the Institute of British Geographers* 36 (1): 37–53.

Nally, David, and Gerry Kearns. 2020. "Vegetative States: Potatoes, Affordances and Survival Ecology." *Antipode* 25 (5): 1373–92.

Nichols, Robert. 2020. *Theft Is Property! Dispossession and Critical Theory*. Durham, NC: Duke University Press.

Ochoa, Carlos. 2001. "Universal Gift." In *The Potato Treasure of the Andes: From Agriculture to Culture*, edited by Christine Graves, 122–32. Lima, Peru: International Potato Center.

Ogborn, Miles. 2008. *Global Lives: Britain and the World, 1550–1800.* Cambridge, UK: Cambridge University Press.

Ohlmeyer, Jane. 1998. "'Civilizinge of those Rude Parts': Colonization within Britain and Ireland, 1580s–1640s." In *The Oxford History of the British Empire*. Vol. 1, *The Origins of Empire: British Overseas Enterprise to the Close of the Seventeenth Century*, edited by Nicholas Canny, 124–47. Oxford, UK: Oxford University Press.

Otter, Chris. 2020. *Diet for a Large Planet: Industrial Britain, Food Systems, and World Ecology*. Chicago: University of Chicago Press.

Pluymers, Keith. 2020. "Cow Trials, Climate Change, and the Causes of Violence." *Environmental History* 25: 287–309.

Polanyi, Karl. (1941) 2001. *The Great Transformation: The Political and Economic Origins of Our Times*. Boston: Beacon Press.

Pollan, Michael. 2001. *The Botany of Desire: A Plant's Eye View of the World*. New York: Random House.

Prendergast, Frank. 1997. "The Down Survey of Ireland." *Survey Ireland* 14: 43–52.

Puig de la Bellacasa, María. 2017. *Matters of Care: Speculative Ethics in More than Human Worlds*. Minneapolis: University of Minnesota Press.

Richardson, Tanya, and Gisa Weszkalnys. 2014. "Resource Materialities." *Anthropological Quarterly* 87 (1): 5–30.

Said, Edward W. 1993. *Culture and Imperialism*. New York: Vintage Books.

Salazar, Juan Francisco, Celine Granjou, Matthew Kearns, Anna Krywosynska, and Manuel Tironi, eds. 2020. *Thinking with Soils: Material Politics and Social Theory*. Oxford, UK: Bloomsbury.

Scott, James C. 1976. *The Moral Economy of the Peasant: Rebellion and Subsistence in Southeast Asia.* New Haven, CT: Yale University Press.

———. 1998. *Seeing like a State: How Certain Schemes to Improve the Human Condition Have Failed.* New Haven, CT: Yale University Press.

Schrepfer, Susan R., and Philip Scranton, eds. 2004. *Industrializing Organisms: Introducing Evolutionary History,* New York: Routledge.

Seed, Patricia. 1995. *Ceremonies of Possession in Europe's Conquest of the New World, 1492–1640*. Cambridge, UK: Cambridge University Press.

Slater, Eamonn, and Eoin Flaherty. 2023. "Marx on the Reciprocal Interconnections between the Soil and the Human Body: Ireland and Its Colonialised Metabolic Rifts." *Antipode* 55 (2): 620–42.

Sloterdijk, Peter. 2009. *Terror from the Air*. Frankfurt, Germany: Semiotext(e).

Smyth, William J. 2006. *Map-Making, Landscapes and Memory: A Geography of Colonial and Early Modern Ireland c. 1530–1750*. Cork, Ireland: Cork University Press.

Spooner, David M., and Wilbert L. A. Hetterscheid. 2006. "Origins, Evolution, and Group Classification of Cultivated Potatoes." In *Darwin's Harvest: New Approaches to the Origins, Evolution and Conservation of Crops*, edited by Timothy Motley, Nyree Zerega, and Hugh Cross, 285–307. New York: Columbia University Press.

Squatriti, Paolo. 2013. *Landscape and Change in Early Medieval Italy: Chestnuts, Economy and Culture*. Cambridge, UK: Cambridge University Press.

Tawney, Richard. 1912. *The Agrarian Problem in the Sixteenth-Century*. New York: Burt Franklin.

Thirsk, Joan. 1984. "Patterns of Agriculture in Seventeenth-Century England." In *Seventeenth-Century New England*, edited by David D. Hall and David Grayson Allen, 39–54. Boston: Colonial Society of Massachusetts.

Thompson, Edward P. (1963) 1991. *The Making of the English Working Class*. London: Penguin.

———. 2010. *Customs in Common*. London: Merlin Press.

Whelan, Kevin. 1997. "The Modern Landscape: From Plantation to the Present." In *Atlas of the Irish Rural Landscape*, edited by F. H. A. Aalen, Kevin Whelan, and Matthew Stout, 67–103. Cork, Ireland: University College Cork Press.

Wood, Ellen Meiksins. 2000. "The Agrarian Origins of Capitalism." In *Hungry for Profit: The Agribusiness Threat to Farmers, Food, and the Environment*, edited by Fred Magdoff, John Bellamy Foster, and Frederick H. Buttel, 23–42. New York: Monthly Review Press.

———. 2003. *Empire of Capital.* London: Verso.

———. 2017. *The Origin of Capitalism: A Longer View*. London: Verso.

Wust, Walter H. 2001. "The Potato's Birthplace." In *The Potato Treasure of the Andes: From Agriculture to Culture*, edited by Christine Graves, 42–51. Lima, Peru: International Potato Center.

Zimmerer, Karl S., Hildegardo Córdova-Aguilar, Rafael Mata Olmo, Yolanda Jiménez Olivencia, and Steven J. Vanek. 2017. "Mountain Ecology, Remoteness, and the Rise of Agrobiodiversity: Tracing the Geographic Spaces of Human–Environment Knowledge." *Annals of the American Association of Geographers* 107 (2): 441–55.

Chapter 2

Land as Capital

A Genealogy through the Birth and Development of Economic Thought

Leo Steeds

INTRODUCTION

Increasingly around the world, relations between humans and between humans and the Earth are conditioned by the idea that land is a form of capital. Indeed, so commonplace is this idea that it frequently appears as self-evident, without need of further explanation or investigation. And yet such an understanding of land is historically specific, being both a product and a central characteristic of Western modernity. It is also contingent, its traction hinging on a diverse set of material-discursive practices that reflect and enable such an understanding of land.

Within academia, many critical discussions of land have focused on its "commodification," especially following the work of Polanyi ([1944] 2001). This captures something important about the way in which land is increasingly seen as a kind of alienable asset, especially as opposed to being understood in terms of traditional, cultural, or spiritual relations between certain individuals or communities and specific places. Submitting land to the logic of market-based commerce creates an illusory appearance of fungibility with other kinds of vendible good that belies both the specificity of human relations to place and the broader significance of land as the essential precondition of human subsistence. Yet it is not solely the fact that it is traded that defines the specificity of modern relations to land. This is, as I stress in this chapter, a key factor, both historically and conceptually. But to understand shifting human relations to land today on a range of levels—from the dynamics of land use, ongoing global (dis)appropriation, and the important role of land ownership in distributions of wealth—it is important to acknowledge that the dominant logic governing human-land relations today is not simply that of land as commodity but one that understands land through the conceptual vocabulary of economic theory, as a form of capital.

It is worth stressing that the dominance of the idea of land as capital is one subject to a long and complex development that certainly cannot be reduced to purely theoretical developments in economics or indeed any other body of thought. A fuller account of this phenomenon would have to take into account, among other things, the propagation of private property rights in land across the world via colonialization from the early modern era; ongoing dispossession of various kinds of traditional land users today; the broader suffusion of economic logics into social institutions, especially during the neoliberal period; and particularly the ongoing "financialization" of land (Clapp 2014; Gunnoe 2014). Additionally, the decline of landownership as a sectoral interest distinct from capital ownership means that critical analyses of contemporary capitalism—at least in the global North—have for some time treated land as a form of capital (e.g., Massey and Catalano 1978; Piketty 2014). Nevertheless, the emergence and development of economic rationality, which is the focus here, is a key part of a transformation in relations to land in the modern era, one that in important ways continues to inform dominant cultural attitudes, as well as practices of accounting and governance on a range of levels.

As I show, the emergence of an understanding of land as capital within economic thought was not as straightforward or self-evident as today's common senses might suggest. In the first place, a number of crucial political, legal, cultural, and administrative developments associated with land contributed to providing the conditions of possibility for economic knowledge as a whole, and, in turn, land played a crucial role within economic theory through to the later nineteenth century. However, until this time, land was not considered as a kind of capital. In fact, crucial to economic discourse in this period was that the two were strictly distinguished. It was only later, in the late nineteenth and early twentieth centuries, that this theoretical orthodoxy was challenged and land came to appear to economists as merely one particular species of a much broader field of capital goods, at which point, as critics have complained, land as a concept in its own right ceased to be a key concern of mainstream economic analysis (e.g., Gaffney and Harrison 1994).

Standard narratives in the history of economics literature see this shift as characteristic of a move from a "classical" period of economic thought, commonly seen as spanning the late eighteenth to mid-nineteenth centuries, to the "neoclassical" theory, which today remains the dominant mainstream of economic analysis (e.g., Blaug 1978). The genealogy presented here similarly sees the emergence of neoclassicism in economics as important, marking the conflation of concepts of land and capital. But in contrast to this more narrowly theoretically-focused literature, I suggest that this shift rested on a prior and more fundamental epistemic rupture in understandings of land with the discourses that informed the birth of political economy. This was one that saw the transformation of a set of discourses in which land was considered in terms of an irreducible materiality, as the essential basis of human subsistence, to one in which it was considered much more narrowly in terms of the exchangeable value that it might yield to its owner—that is, in terms of rent. Indeed, it was this transformation, I suggest, that marked the birth of economic knowledge in a recognizably modern form.

In making this argument, my genealogy parallels related claims made by Michel Foucault and Keith Tribe, who both similarly identified a "break" in economic knowledge around the turn of the nineteenth century (Foucault [1966] 2002; Tribe 1978).[1] Foucault's later work is especially significant for the attention it paid to the relationship between forms of knowledge and modern notions of government. As Stuart Elden (2013) has argued, whilst his interpretations of particular thinkers and periods were sometimes misleading, Foucault's emphasis on the significance of new calculative practices, especially the rise of notions of population, remain important for understanding transformations in knowledge in the modern era. Tribe's work, meanwhile, is significant for the extent to which it reads specifically British discourses on private property and improvement as being formally displaced by an emergent discourse of political economy around 1800, an emphasis I echo here.

My genealogy thus draws on both but places the emphasis more squarely on evolving conceptualizations of land. The first section explores changes in political, legal, cultural, and administrative relations to land that were necessary for land to appear as an object of economic analysis and indeed for economic thought to emerge as a body of knowledge. The second section surveys discourses on land and property in the seventeenth and eighteenth centuries through Adam Smith's seminal *The Wealth of Nations*, commonly—if, I suggest, somewhat misleadingly—cited as the founding statement of modern economics. The third section focuses on what I suggest should properly be considered modern economic discourse and changing theoretical apprehensions of land between the early nineteenth and early twentieth centuries.

PRECONDITIONS OF ECONOMIC KNOWLEDGE: PRIVATE PROPERTY IN LAND, A DISCOURSE ON IMPROVEMENT, AND STATISTICS

The understanding of land that was formulated around the 1800s with the emergence of political economy could not have emerged, say, in the 1500s. As I show, economic discourse, such as it arose in the early nineteenth century, was importantly concerned with questions of population and the production of subsistence goods. But it presupposed that the mode of subsistence was one in which production and consumption of the necessaries of life were coordinated exclusively through markets. Even in Britain at the turn of the nineteenth century, this was an abstraction, as significant numbers of traditional subsistence dwellers remained who obtained their subsistence not primarily through markets but rather through working the land directly. And yet the emergence of a market system was clearly sufficiently well established that theorists could take this assumption as a starting point of their analyses.

Essential to both the theory and practice of a market system was that the relationships between individuals involved in agricultural production were regulated by monetary payment. As Tribe (1978, chap. 2) emphasized, this was not the case under feudal systems of land use. European feudalism was characterized by a mode of dependent landholding, in which land was granted to a tenant in exchange for various services, especially military service, in a system that extended up and down the political hierarchy. Within this system, only the king had anything resembling modern notions of ownership in land. His subordinates and their subordinates in turn would merely "hold of" their superior in exchange for specified services. For the majority of individuals at the bottom of this hierarchy, subsistence was gained through a direct relationship with the land, generally organized through systems of shared-use rights. In this context, the term *rent* was used not as it is today, to denote a monetary payment, but rather referred to the obligations of a tenant to their lord.

Developments in England, however, began to challenge this system (Linklater 2014, chap. 1). From the mid-fifteenth century, wool prices across Europe had begun to rise due to the need to clothe fast-growing populations. With well-established export channels, this began to change incentives for English landholders. Until this time, the system of feudal dues in exchange for landholding meant that it had been profitable to have as many tenants as possible on the land. But with the promise of wool profits, lords, as well as better-off tenants, found it increasingly tempting to attempt to remove occupants so small parcels of land could be consolidated (or "engrossed") and enclosed with walls and hedges in order to stock sheep. Indeed, so powerful was this incentive that, as early as the late fifteenth century, whole villages were cleared.

This process unleashed what historian Andro Linklater (2014) termed a *land revolution* that saw the progressive generalization of private property rights in land in the United Kingdom through to the end of the nineteenth century, with land rights becoming a central source of social contestation. The effects were not restricted to Britain, however. Rather, the instantiation of private property rights in land was characteristic of British colonialism, and, indeed their continued propagation around the world continues to be felt today.

The spectacular spread of private property rights in land was of course not only attributable to wool prices. The concentrated stocking of sheep on land had the effect of providing a clear demonstration of the beneficial effects of manuring on soil fertility and the clear potential for increasing the productivity of agriculture. In this context, a characteristically English discourse on improvement emerged. Even by the sixteenth century, the effects on soil fertility were so evident that the terms *manure* and *improvement* had become synonymous (Linklater 2014, 14). Private property thus similarly came to be closely associated with the idea of productivity gains, and indeed, the justification of improvement became an important argument in legal disputes around enclosure.

Through the seventeenth and eighteenth centuries, an extensive literature developed on agricultural improvement, catering to the tastes of a landed gentry whose constitution and interests were changing. Drawing on classical references, seventeenth-century examples were premised on a notion of a household economy, the emphasis being on the relation between the individual laborer and the soil, and stressed in particular the God-given duty of man to cultivate the earth to the highest degree. Whilst more sophisticated examples drew on the language of natural philosophy to reflect on the essence of plants and manures, much of this remained focused on practical aspects of agriculture and into the eighteenth century included advice on such topics as the construction of fences and ditches, practices of surveying, and aligning roads (Tribe 1978, chap. 4).

Tribe, however, identifies a shift in this discourse around the mid-eighteenth century toward an increasing focus on quantifying costs of production and conceptualizing the farm in terms of its preeminent position in a series of exchanges that serve to effect the circulation of wealth among groups in society (Tribe 1978, 66). Among the principal examples of this genre were the works of the prominent agricultural improver Arthur Young, who stressed the need to understand farming as a business and the importance of keeping strict accounts.

It was not only in the discourse improvement that this emphasis on numerical computation was important, however. Work like Young's fitted into a much broader trend toward calculation and quantification from the early modern period. Foucault's work is helpful here. In his later lectures, he connected this trend to the development of modern notions of government. This, he suggested, was irreducibly connected with the emergence of the nation-state and capitalism and was characterized in particular by the incorporation of a diverse range of calculative practices as part of the theory and practice of governing. Emblematic of this, for Foucault, was the emergence of modern demography.

In Britain, such figures as William Petty, John Graunt, and Gregory King pioneered attempts to quantify various aspects of the state's territory. Building on his experience as colonial administrator in Ireland, Petty, for example, sought to enumerate the "souls" to be found within England and Wales and the acreage of land, as well as to make assessments of the availability of various kinds of key subsistence goods. Population was a key concern here. Given the paucity of information, this was the topic of considerable debate. Such declinists as Robert Coke expressed the fear that seventeenth-century England was in decay with its population and thus strength was decreasing. Petty's *Political Arithmetic* answered directly to such arguments, claiming to demonstrate by empirical means that population was in fact increasing.

Nevertheless, methods remained extremely rudimentary. Although also using estimates of numbers of houses, Petty, for example, still made use of estimates of global population based on extrapolation from numbers given by biblical sources. It was only toward the end of the eighteenth century that anything approaching modern demographic methods emerged. It is indicative that among the most important figures in this respect were also prominent improvers. Young, for example, published his own book of *Political Arithmetic* in 1774, which drew on his extensive experience surveying agriculture throughout the country. In Scotland, John Sinclair, credited with the first use of the word *statistics* in the English language, was perhaps the most ardent advocate of the need for improved quantitative apprehension of the country. Sinclair's *Accounts* of the 1790s detailed aspects of geography and topography, population, and agricultural and industrial production in Scotland. He was also instrumental in the establishment in 1793 of the Board of Agriculture in Britain for the promotion of improvement, which began making county-by-county surveys of agricultural production. Increased interest in population culminated in 1801 in the first official census, with subsequent censuses confirming that population was indeed rising.

The period around the turn of the nineteenth century saw a further surge of enclosure. Whereas in earlier periods this had been a piecemeal process, from the seventeenth century, it increasingly had parliamentary support and authorization. By the early nineteenth century, the House of Lords had teams of reporters roving the countryside in search of areas of land that could be enclosed and improved. As historian Edward P. Thompson ([1963] 1982) argued, this process was foundational in *The Making of the English Working Class*, creating a vast body of individuals who no longer had access to land and were therefore forced to seek wage labor for their subsistence. In Scotland, too, such infamous incidents as the Highland Clearances saw the dispossession of traditional land users from great swathes of land. Enclosure was accompanied simultaneously by the infamous Black Act of 1723, which designated severe, often capital punishment for a raft of offenses to property, such as poaching, strengthening increasingly explicit attempts to extinguish traditional forms of land use. As I show in the next section, these developments around land use were essential preconditions for the emergence of economic knowledge.

PRECURSORS OF ECONOMIC THEORY THROUGH ADAM SMITH

Unsurprisingly, ideas of private property and improvement played an important role within discourses on government. The most influential theorist of the era in this respect was John Locke. His *Two Treatises of Government* famously grounded the legitimacy of government in the protection of private property. This theory suggested that private ownership of the Earth was a natural right, historically and conceptually prior to the establishment of any kind of political authority, and that political authority could thus only be justified if it served to secure that right.

The notion of improvement played a key role in Locke's theory. Like the other prominent early modern natural law theorists Hugo Grotius and Samuel von Pufendorf, he began from the biblical proposition that God had given the Earth to man in common and, like them, he was confronted with the task of accounting for the subsequent development of private ownership. Locke's distinctive strategy, however, drew on the peculiarly British discourse on improvement. He argued that, in the state of nature, individuals were justified in appropriating as much land as they could make use of: "As much Land as a Man Tills, Plants, Improves, Cultivates, and can use the Product of, so much is his Property. He by his Labour does, as it were, inclose it from the Common" (Locke [1689] 2017, II.32). *Appropriation* for Locke was thus synonymous with *cultivation* and *improvement*. This allowed him to argue that, by appropriating land, an individual was not in fact diminishing shared resources but rather increasing the "common stock of mankind" (Locke [1689] 2017, II.37).

Implicit within Locke's theory, then, was a utilitarian defense of property rights based on the idea that these served to increase societal productivity. For Locke, this justified private property in land even in situations where appropriation did not leave "enough, and as good" for others (Locke [1689] 2017, II.33). In modern societies, further, this appropriation was not limited by an individual's capacity to consume the product of the land. Rather, well-developed commerce meant that spoilage of the Earth's resources could easily be avoided.

It is easy to see why such a theory might have gained traction in a domestic context where agriculture was becoming increasingly commercialized, land consolidated, and traditional subsistence living in decline. As a number of scholars have noted, it can also be read as justifying colonial disappropriation, especially in North America, a context very familiar to Locke, and which served as a key point of reference for "unimproved" land in the *Two Treatises* (e.g., Arneil 1992).

Another striking aspect of Locke's theory was its consideration of questions of value in relation to land. Part of his argument was that it was "labour," rather than "nature," that "puts the difference of value on every thing" (Locke [1689] 2017, II.40). There was no better example of this, he suggested, than the Native Americans, who, for want of improvement, were "rich in land, and poor in all the comforts of life" (Locke [1689] 2017, II.41). Indeed, he went as far as to say that "of the Products of the Earth useful to the Life of Man, 9/10 are the Effects of labour" (Locke [1689] 2017, II.40).

Locke was not alone in considering the relationship between land and labor in terms of value. Petty's work is again important here. He suggested that,

> all things ought to be valued by two natural Denominations, which is Land and Labour; that is, we ought say, a Ship or garment is worth such a measure of Land, with such another measure of Labour; forasmuch as both Ships and Garments were the creatures of Lands and mens Labours thereupon: This being true, we should be glad to finde out a natural Par between Land and Labour, so as we might express the value by either of them alone, as well or better than by both, and reduce one into the other, as easily and certainly, as we reduce Pence into Pounds. (Petty [1662] 1899, 25)

Within histories of economic thought, Petty is often cited as a key forerunner of modern theoretical economics, posing such a crucial question about the relationship between the value of different inputs to production.

It seems Locke was aware of Petty's work (Locke [1689] 2017, II.27n), and his own theory can be seen as coming down firmly on the side of labor. Indeed, he has sometimes been credited with putting forward a kind of protean labor theory of value. This was not the only possible response to Petty's quandary, however. Writing in the early eighteenth century, Richard Cantillon put forward the somewhat less familiar land theory of value (Brewer 1988). This proposed that, just as raw materials required a certain amount of land for their production, so labor could be understood in terms of the area of land required to produce the subsistence of the laborer. In this way, for Cantillon, thinking in terms of land area provided the "par" that Petty had sought.

Albeit in different ways, Petty, Locke, and Cantillon all considered a process of production in which land's productivity played a key role. Yet all considered this exclusively in terms of a relationship between land and labor. They may have considered accumulated resources that also played a part in production—Locke, for example, talked of how labor was mixed with the land to effect improvement, whilst Cantillon talked of a class of entrepreneurs, entry to which required access to finance in order to fund production. Yet, what these authors did not have that was essential to the emergence of modern economic thought was a theory of capital.

For this, we have to shift the focus temporarily to France. Here, in the late 1750s and 1760s, arose a school that came to be known as physiocracy—literally, the "rule of nature." Heavily influenced by Cantillon and looking enviously at the state of improved agriculture in England, the physiocrats' most famous claim was that land was the original source of all wealth. From this followed a policy program designed to incentivize agricultural development in France. The most well-known theoretical expression of this school of thought came in the form of François Quesnay's *Tableau économique*. This detailed a process of circulation of wealth initiated by the yearly agricultural cycle. Fundamental to this was the idea of advances. Following Cantillon, Quesnay suggested that it was the proprietors of land who annually distribute the country's net product between two other classes—the farmers on the one hand and the manufacturing class on the other. Of these, only the former was deemed productive because they not only reproduced the value of the labor employed in production but also obtained a surplus granted by the natural fertility of the land, which was in turn repaid to the landlords in the form of rent, allowing the cycle to continue.

And yet this was not a theory of capital as such. Agriculture here provided the quintessential example of an activity that required an investment of resources that could be recouped only after a period of time. But the same basic idea could be generalized to account for the systematic consideration of the role of resources beyond land and labor required for a much broader range of forms of human industry. This contribution has often been attributed to Quesnay's pupil and subsequent finance minister of France Anne Robert Jacques Turgot (Schumpeter [1954] 1994, 323). Turgot followed the physiocrats' general diagnosis of France's lackluster agricultural development, suggesting, however, that it was not a restriction of available land area that limited production but rather a lack of capital needed to facilitate production.

This theoretical development provided an essential foundation for the putative founding text of modern economics, Adam Smith's *The Wealth of Nations*. Popular renditions of this text tend to emphasize its focus on modern industry and rehearse its key arguments in the somewhat abstract and distinctly neoliberal terms of the superior allocative efficiency of the "market" over the "state" (Tribe 1999). But this presentation badly distorts the content of the work and its central focus on land.

Smith's work can in many ways be read as picking up key threads of Locke's argument (Hont and Ignatieff 1983). Like Locke's, his argument sought to defend the idea that enclosure and improvement of land were foundational to national wealth and thus that securing property rights was foundational to good government. Whereas Locke had simply stated that private property increases the common stock of mankind, Smith set out to provide a detailed analytical demonstration of exactly why this was so. His approach combined a kind of stadial natural historical account of human subsistence, drawing both on the natural law tradition and contemporary natural historians, with a theory of capital almost certainly derived from Smith's personal acquaintance with the physiocrats (Steeds 2022).

Smith's theory was that the growing prevalence of marketized subsistence relations represented a new stage of societal development—what he termed *commercial society* (Pauchant 2017). The cause for his cautious optimism regarding the prospects of commercial society was that he understood it as engendering the improvement of land, which, in his words, constituted the "greatest of all publick advantages" (Smith [1776] 2014, I.xi.k.12). In the work, he went to great lengths to demonstrate how, in the earlier European agricultural societies of the feudal period, prevailing land tenancy arrangements had systematically thwarted the accumulation of capital in agriculture, forestalling improvement (Smith [1776] 2014, bk. III). This had been further exacerbated by the misguided policy of states who had held back agriculture, especially through paternalist price regulations known as the "grain police" (Hont and Ignatieff 1983).

As much as Smith was interested in prices, there was a crucial material element to his argument. He saw commercial society and the property relations that this entailed as a natural societal development in response to increasing population. But these dynamics also affected agricultural practice. Smith viewed traditional methods of fertilization, which relied on the manure from animals kept for tillage, and the use of night soils from surrounding towns as key limitations of agricultural production. With the growth of population and the progressive enclosure of wastes, however, Smith noted that prices of meat had risen sufficiently to justify for the first time landowners and farmers dedicating areas of land specifically to pasturage. By concentrating animals in a particular area, the key benefit of this was that it provided new opportunities for soil fertilization, and indeed in Scotland, he suggested, this had been the "principal cause of the improvement of the low country" (Smith [1776] 2014, I.xi.k.3).

Smith accorded a special place to agriculture in his theoretical system. Following a very physiocratic line of reasoning, he suggested that here, unlike other forms of industry, "nature labours along with man" (Smith [1776] 2014, II.v.12). For this reason, improvements in the productivity of agriculture formed the backbone of progress in industry more broadly, generating surpluses that could be invested in manufacturing in trade. Smith's prognosis for commercial society, from this perspective, was optimistic: at least in its growth phase, commercial society had the potential to increase societal wealth while also catering to the needs of the poorest in society, especially by ending the recurrent dearths that had plagued early modern societies. At some point, the land area would be "fully peopled" (Smith [1776] 2014, I.ix.14) and a "stationary state" (Smith [1776] 2014, I.viii.24) reached, but this was a sufficiently distant prospect to remain beyond the purview of Smith's analysis.

AFTER SMITH: LAND AS A FACTOR OF PRODUCTION, LAND AS CAPITAL

Common senses among economists have crystallized around the idea that the political economy of the early nineteenth century represented a more or less direct development of the theoretical foundations laid by Smith (e.g., Hollander [1992] 2016; Samuelson 1978). According to this understanding, Smith and his followers represent what is commonly termed a *classical* school of political economy, characterized by its three-factor (land, labor, and capital) analysis. Following Smith, the most prominent member of this school is deemed to be David Ricardo, the most influential of his followers among the political economists of the early nineteenth century. And yet in spite of certain theoretical continuities, I instead follow Tribe and Foucault in seeing Ricardo's work as marking the completion of a radical epistemic break with earlier discourses.

By the turn of the nineteenth century, the population debate had moved on, especially in light of the still (in)famous intervention of the political economist and Anglican reverend Thomas Robert Malthus. While earlier controversies had turned around the fear of depopulation, Malthus introduced a new spectre into this debate—that of *over*population. In his *Essay on the Principle of Population*, first published in 1798, he claimed that population, left unchecked, would tend to increase in a geometric ratio, doubling every twenty-five years, and would thus eventually outstrip food production, which he supposed only to increase in an arithmetic ratio. In the absence of any other factors slowing population growth, population would thus inevitably be subject to the positive checks of privation and death. Indeed, it was partly in response to the alarm caused by Malthus's theory that the official census in Britain was inaugurated in 1801. The second census, conducted in 1811, indeed confirmed the assertion that population was growing.

The Malthusian fear of overpopulation similarly sat at the heart of Ricardo's political economy. In his magnum opus, *The Principles of Political Economy and Taxation*, first published in 1817, he challenged Smith's optimistic view of a rising tide lifting all boats. He suggested that Smith had poorly understood the dynamics of rental prices. The central argument of this work was that, in the absence of international trade in foodstuffs, increasing population would produce a dynamic in which the profits of capital would be progressively eroded by rising rents, advancing the progress of a stationary state.

The key theoretical intervention associated with Ricardo's work is the conception of the rent of land as a differential. In this view, rent could exist in the absence of absolute scarcity as a result of differences in the advantages of location and fertility provided by different pieces of land. The magnitude of this rent, however, was understood to be determined by the productivity of the least favorable land taken into cultivation. It was reasoned that this least favorable land would not generate a rent, since the price fetched for the product of this land would be sufficient only to cover the necessary costs of production—wages and the normal profits of capital. Rents, however, would be generated on superior lands, which amounted to the discrepancy in productivity, above the cost of production. In Ricardo's exposition, this was supported by the idea that land could be imagined to exist in discrete grades of quality (first, second, third, etc.) to which "doses" of labor and capital could be applied. The distressing implication for Ricardo was that, as food production to feed a rising population filled the available land area, profits would be squeezed to zero and the accumulation of capital on which societal progress depended would cease.

Like Smith's, Ricardo's theory treated land, labor, and capital as the three essential constituent parts of a process of agricultural production. But Ricardo radically reconstituted the terrain of analysis by considering these three factors solely in terms of their factor returns—the payment due to each in the process of production—of rent, wages, and profits. It is true that these three factors retained crucial special properties: land's essential qualities were that it was limited in supply and that it was an essential precondition for the provision of foodstuffs; labor, meanwhile—as embodied in the figure of the laborer—consumed foodstuffs and collectively acted as a proxy for population in general, increasing or decreasing in number in response to demand in the labor market. But beyond these assumptions, Ricardo's analysis was conducted entirely in terms of hypothesized price dynamics.

Smith's work had been centrally concerned with issues around property, particularly understood as a kind of mediation of the relationship between humans and the nonhuman world, and around a broad consideration of the materiality of human subsistence. Ricardo's, by contrast, considered land much more narrowly in respect of its place within a system of capitalistic production and no longer in terms of a set of material relations but rather with regard to the revenue that could be derived from land and the system of exchanges of abstract value into which this fitted. Ideas of improvement continued to play a part in Ricardo's theory but not with the centrality they had assumed in Smith's work. Rather than as a set of materialized practices, these were now considered solely in terms of effects on the various factor returns. Ricardo's work can be seen as adopting an accounting perspective, and indeed, the presentation of his theory closely paralleled the tables of accounts presented in contemporary agricultural journals (Morgan 2012, chap. 2).

As Tribe argued, then, the political economy of the early nineteenth century, as epitomized in Ricardo's work, represented a novel discursive formation. This was one in which land appeared as a factor of production within a theorized system of production and distribution. This theoretical system, in its broad outline, persisted until around the turn of the twentieth century. But from the later nineteenth century, the idea of land as a distinct factor of production came increasingly under attack. The so-called marginal revolution in economic theory of the 1860s and 1870s was characterized by arguments in favor of viewing land as a kind of capital. In the words of Léon Walras,

> [L]and laid out as parks and pleasure grounds, both public and private; forest lands; agricultural land growing fruit, vegetables, cereals, fodder and other foodstuffs for man and beast; the ground beneath homes, public buildings, offices, factories, workshops or stores; land used for roads, highways, public squares, canals, railways, and all means of communication. All this land is truly capital. (Walras [1874] 2003, 214)

Meanwhile William Stanley Jevons, one of the other major first-generation marginalists, began to pick away at the category of rent as pertaining solely to land. If rent was conceived as payment for the use of a resource of fixed supply, so his reasoning went, then given that the supply of many or even all capital goods in the short term is essentially fixed, would it not make sense to think in terms of a continuity of rents and quasi-rents? The implication was again that land could be thought of as really a species of a broader field of capital goods. Theoretically at stake, then, was the extent to which rent and profit represented distinct phenomena.

Amongst the first-generation marginalists, however, there was no attempt at a strong theoretical refutation of the idea of land as capital. This is found perhaps most forcefully in the 1890s with the work of John Bates Clark. Clark was responding to the arguments of Henry George, whose insistence that the taxation of land provided potential solutions to a raft of contemporary social issues was gaining worldwide attention and increasing traction (Gaffney and Harrison 1994). His arguments are instructive.

Clark opposed the idea that capital should be regarded as consisting in any particular class of goods. Instead, he suggested that "pure capital" should be understood as a kind of "permanent fund" that "passes through an endless series of outward forms" (Clark 1888, 94), of which land was merely a possible one. He saw it as necessary, however, to give a thorough refutation of George's idea that ownership of land constituted a monopolization of societal wealth. His approach was to distinguish between the various kinds of utility that land provided, suggesting that the term *rent*, as commonly used to refer to the payment made by a tenant to a landlord, failed to convey that this single payment for the use of land should in fact be understood as comprising a set of distinct values relating to the various specific forms of utility provided by land. While Ricardo's theory was premised on the idea that rent constituted a payment for "original and indestructible" powers of the soil (Ricardo [1817] 2004, 67), Clark argued that, in fact, the only aspect of land's utility that could truly be said to be original and indestructible was its physical solidity, which was, in any case, a utility so abundant in the world that it could never be chargeable (Clark 1888, 114).

Whereas Ricardo had used the "original and indestructible" label to refer to the fertility of the soil, Clark's view of land's productive capacities was quite different. He suggested that, in modern societies, land's natural fertility (which could be subject to a monopoly) played a vanishingly small part in the actual productivity of land. Instead, the importance of long-term improvements to the land and of the short-term capital inputs required for agricultural production meant that a large part of land's fertility was not at all natural but rather produced by human industry. Indeed, for Clark, it was even possible to separate conceptually the soil from the land itself:

> The loam is, in a certain way, distinct from the land on which it lies, and is to be regarded rather as a food-creating tool, that wears itself out in imparting to a product the chemical elements that it contains. . . . After the original supply has been reduced, the process of soil manufacture becomes a necessary part of agriculture, and the food-creating qualities of surface loam, like any other product of industry, are worth what they cost. (Clark 1888, 116)

Another kind of utility provided by land was that of place. Clark emphasizes that, to a large extent, this, too, was not an inherent or natural facet of land but was itself reproducible by human labor. In an age when technological developments—above all the railway—had showed their ability to "annihilate distance" (Clark 1888, 115), access to markets was restricted less by any natural attribute of land and more by the state of infrastructural investment. There was, Clark conceded, a residuum of "place utility" based on "literal proximity" that could not be reproduced. This could therefore be said to give to land the "only monopoly value that resides in it" (Clark 1888, 116) but could ultimately account only for a small amount of the value of the rent payment.

Clark's account is striking on a number of levels. But it is the sense of spatiality that is particularly of interest here. In spite of his concession that there existed a residual element of "limited monopoly" (Clark 1888, 116) of place, utility involved in private land ownership, the impetus of the argument was clearly to minimize the significance of this fact, moving away from a concept of land as a portion of an ultimately fixed territorial space. Instead, land was to be conceived overwhelmingly in terms of forms of utility that are not naturally (or indeed societally) given but are made by the labor of individuals; land, that is to say, should be thought of as something "manufactured" (Clark 1888, 136). In this sense, land was seen to have a cost of production, one that ultimately determined the returns due to it. Any problems of limited space, Clark assured the reader, would in fact be dealt with by the tendencies toward the improvement in the productive powers of land and toward an efficient allocation of land's various uses, which are inherent to the forces of the market. The extension of agriculture into new lands, which was at the heart of Ricardo's argument, thus gives way to an emphasis on the intensification of production on lands already in production; accordingly, the "natural" component of land's value simultaneously gives way to a focus on values imparted by human labor and capital (Clark 1888, 129, n. 1).

Clark's theory of the immortality of capital, conceived as distinct from the physicality of worldly things, is striking: "The bodily tissue of capital lives by destruction and replacement; the utility that is the vital essence of it is, in successful industry, perpetual" (Clark 1888, 98). Land, he suggested, is simply one particular form in which a capital can remain indefinitely (Clark 1888, 95).

CONCLUSION

Within economic thought, then, the notion of land as capital arose from a set of debates regarding land's productivity and the extent to which it should be regarded as fundamentally different from other kinds of productive resource.

The turning point, in theoretical terms, came in the later nineteenth century, when the earlier orthodoxy that regarded land and capital as strictly distinct factors of production was overturned. But I suggest that this move was predicated on an earlier and more profound discursive shift that occurred around the turn of the nineteenth century. This was one that established the classical political economy of the early nineteenth century by breaking with an earlier set of discourses around improvement and property, in which land's productivity was considered in material rather than purely monetary terms. I also suggest that these discourses were associated with a broader set of material-discursive developments around, particularly, the development and propagation of private property rights and the development of forms of statistical knowledge. Political economy, such as it emerged in the early nineteenth century, thus built on a much longer history of understanding, measuring, and theorizing land and its productive capacities.

The shifting discourse around land reflected political and cultural developments. Yet, at the same time, it also tracked key changes in agricultural practice. Smith's seminal text, for example, represented a strong faith in the benefits of mixed husbandry on soil fertility, a view that informed a whole theory of societal development. Ricardo's economic theory at the start of the nineteenth century, by contrast, was caught up in debates among landholders and farmers about the relative merits of applying differing proportions of labor and capital to land. Clarke's at the end of the century returned to the problem of soil fertility but addressed this in terms of the cost incurred by the farmer in replacing lost chemical elements, most likely reflecting the rise of chemical fertilizer as an input to the production process.

The view of land as capital, therefore, while commonsense today, has—at least in theoretical terms—emerged from a very specific genealogy. It retains currency due to the ongoing and indeed increasing incorporation of land within circuits of capital. The aim of tracing such a genealogy is not necessarily to reveal hidden truths lurking within the idea of land as capital, but looking at the material-discursive developments that this presupposed, and the debates in which notions of land as capital emerged do perhaps reveal something of the historical specificity of this idea. It invites us to think further about the contingency of this dominant view of land, with its foundations in particular modes of political and economic organization, as well as specific technical and administrative practices that serve to render land legible as a form of capital. Most of all, it invites us to consider the possibilities for thinking about land in other ways.

NOTE

1. This earlier argument about the development of scientific knowledge continued to inform Foucault's (2009) subsequent work on government in *Security, Territory, Population: Lectures at the Collège de France, 1977–1978*.

REFERENCES

Arneil, Barbara. 1992. "John Locke, Natural Law and Colonialism." *History of Political Thought* 13 (4): 587–603.

Blaug, Mark. 1978. *Economic Theory in Retrospect*. Cambridge, UK: Cambridge University Press.

Brewer, Anthony. 1988. "Cantillon and the Land Theory of Value." *History of Political Economy* 20 (1): 1–14. https://doi.org/10.1215/00182702-20-1-1.

Clapp, Jennifer. 2014. "Financialization, Distance and Global Food Politics." *Journal of Peasant Studies* 41 (5): 797–814. https://doi.org/10.1080/03066150.2013.875536.

Clark, John B. 1888. "Capital and Its Earnings." *Publications of the American Economic Association* 3 (2): 9–69.

Elden, Stuart. 2013. "How Should We Do the History of Territory?" *Territory, Politics, Governance* 1 (1): 5–20.

Foucault, Michel. (1966) 2002. *The Order of Things: An Archaeology of the Human Sciences*. London: Routledge.

———. 2009. *Security, Territory, Population: Lectures at the Collège de France, 1977–1978*. Edited by Michel Senellart. Translated by Graham Burchell. New York: Picador.

Gaffney, Mason, and Fred Harrison. 1994. *The Corruption of Economics*. London: Shepheard-Walwyn.

Gunnoe, Andrew. 2014. "The Political Economy of Institutional Landownership: Neorentier Society and the Financialization of Land." *Rural Sociology* 79 (4): 478–504. https://doi.org/10.1111/ruso.12045.

Hollander, Samuel. (1992) 2016. *Classical Economics*. Toronto: University of Toronto Press.

Hont, Istvan, and Michael Ignatieff. 1983. "Needs and Justice in the Wealth of Nations: An Introductory Essay." In *Wealth and Virtue: The Shaping of Political Economy in the Scottish Enlightenment*, edited by Istvan Hont and Michael Ignatieff, 1–44. Cambridge, UK: Cambridge University Press.

Linklater, Andro. 2014. *Owning the Earth: The Transforming History of Land Ownership*. London: Bloomsbury.

Locke, John. (1689) 2017. *Two Treatises of Government*. Translated by Peter Laslett. Cambridge, UK: Cambridge University Press.

Massey, Doreen B., and Alejandrina Catalano. 1978. *Capital and Land: Landownership by Capital in Great Britain*. London: Edward Arnold.

Morgan, Mary S. 2012. *The World in the Model: How Economists Work and Think.* Cambridge, UK: Cambridge University Press.

Pauchant, Thierry C. 2017. "Adam Smith's Four-Stages Theory of Socio-Cultural Evolution." In *The Adam Smith Review*, vol. 9, edited by Fonna Forman, 49–74. London: Routledge.

Petty, William. (1662) 1899. *The Economic Writings of Sir William Petty*. Cambridge, UK: The University Press.

Piketty, Thomas. 2014. *Capital in the Twenty-First Century*. Translated by Arthur Goldhammer. Cambridge, MA: Harvard University Press.

Polanyi, Karl. (1944) 2001. *The Great Transformation: The Political and Economic Origins of Our Times*. Boston: Beacon Press.

Ricardo, David. (1817) 2004. *The Works and Correspondence of David Ricardo.* Vol. 1, *Principles of Political Economy and Taxation*, edited by Piero Sraffa and Maurice Dobb. Indianapolis: Liberty Fund.

Samuelson, Paul A. 1978. "The Canonical Classical Model of Political Economy." *Journal of Economic Literature* 16 (4): 1415–34.

Schumpeter, Joseph A. (1954) 1994. *History of Economic Analysis*. Edited by Elizabeth Boody Schumpeter. Abingdon, UK: Routledge.

Smith, Adam. (1776) 2014. *The Glasgow Edition of the Works and Correspondence of Adam Smith.* Vol. 2, *An Inquiry into the Nature and Causes of the Wealth of Nations*, edited by William B. Todd. Oxford, UK: Oxford University Press.

Steeds, Leo. 2022. "The Social Ecology of Adam Smith: Reconsidering the Intellectual Foundations of Political Economy." *New Political Economy* 27 (1): 132–45. https://doi.org/10.1080/13563467.2021.1926956.

Thompson, Edward P. (1963) 1982. *The Making of the English Working Class.* Harmondsworth, UK: Penguin Books.

Tribe, Keith. 1978. *Land, Labour and Economic Discourse.* London: Routledge.

———. 1999. "Adam Smith: Critical Theorist?" *Journal of Economic Literature* 37 (2): 609–32.

Walras, Léon. (1874) 2003. *Elements of Pure Economics: Or the Theory of Social Wealth*. London: Routledge.

Chapter 3

Of "False Economies" and "Missing Markets"

An Essay in Three Acts

Shailaja Fennell

This chapter reflects on the selection of cereals to achieve food security over the course of the past century. By examining three distinct moments in the trajectory of the Green Revolution—the focus on increasing food grain productivity in Asia in the 1970s, the representation of Africa as a failing agricultural region with a severe hunger problem in the final decade, and the search for new "supergrains" in the early twenty-first century—the chapter interrogates the framing of mainstream economic thinking on grain production. The central argument of this chapter is that a bottom-up research perspective can shed light on why top-down policy design, which is typified by cereal selection, has not resulted in an inclusive agricultural transformation. The chapter makes the case for the adoption of this alternative route to examining models of agricultural production using a participatory approach of identifying agricultural knowledge within farming communities. Based on cataloguing selection mechanisms in each of these three "acts" through records of the narratives and perceptions of researchers in these communities, the chapter makes the important point that the actions and processes of mapping local forms of understanding provide an important opportunity to triangulate knowledge production with the ideas that are put out through scientific inquiry and academic propositions. The lived reality of rural farming communities and how it shapes the identification of risks and values attached to existing production methods are a crucial type of ecological knowledge. The chapter concludes that an ecologically informed and multidisciplinary investigation, drawing across sciences and social sciences, needs to place such community-specific ecological knowledge at the center of its research agenda if it is to achieve sustainable food market systems.

ACT I: AGRICULTURAL PRODUCTIVITY AND ECONOMIC PERFORMANCE

The history of the measurement of agricultural productivity closely approximates the advances in mainstream economics in the twentieth century. The farm studies that were undertaken in the early twentieth century in agricultural stations in Iowa and Texas were to ensure that agricultural production was increased, as well as to keep agricultural prices in check in the United States, and were not strongly linked to economic analysis (Johnson 1963). Indeed, the earlier architects of the US agricultural market, such as W. O. Atwater, regarded it as addressing the need to ensure agricultural food production and adequate nutrition at reasonable prices within the economy (cited in Carpenter 1994). The analysis of supply functions and the use of the technique of decomposition analysis to obtain precise estimates of agricultural productivity using the total factor productivity as the key metric began to dominate agricultural economics from the 1950s (Heady et.al. 1961; OECD 2022).

In the postwar period, there was a large presence of American agricultural scientists in the formulation of and in contributing to the research agenda in professional US agricultural associations, and their high regard for the prime importance of higher yields was a dominant influence in establishing the mandate of international agricultural bodies, such as the Consultative Group on International Agricultural Research (CGIAR).[1] This economic logic created a core calculus of maximizing production that was transferred to key players, both professional agricultural economists at US universities and leading policy makers in US philanthropic funds, in directing research in such bodies as the CGIAR toward selecting methods that focused on producing high-yielding varieties (HYVs) of rice, wheat, and maize (Hopper 2004; Waterhouse 2013). This mandate translated into the backdrop for and the justification of the Green Revolution program to disseminate HYVs across Asia and Africa as a solution to reduce hunger in newly independent colonies in the 1950s and 1960s. The American presence that supported such a research agenda to advance agricultural productivity was not solely based on the identification of objective conditions observed in agricultural sectors in these countries but primarily shaped by Cold War proclivities (Immerwahr 2015).

These seemingly distant geographies across the globe, with very different agrarian traditions from those that were dominant in the United States, are an instance of ahistorical treatment of the economic structures within these countries. The emphasis on agricultural productivity is also built on the pattern of agricultural improvement evident in European, more specifically British, agriculture in decades preceding the Industrial Revolution and regarded as the template against which to measure the state of progress in agrarian environments elsewhere in the world (Fennell 2020).[2] There is also an associated understanding that wide acceptance of low labor productivity in densely populated agrarian regions is attributed to the absence of capitalism in these societies (Kuznets 1966; Lewis 1954).

While it is indeed the case that lack of capital hinders labor productivity in agriculture, it is far too simplistic to regard improvements in agricultural production as solely the result of increasing inputs, such as fertilizer and machinery. Reducing the relationship of the people to the land as the ability to increase labor productivity through increasing inputs has somewhat occluded the extent to which the ecology of a region has a primary influence on the nature of the agricultural production system. The contribution of ecological characteristics in determining the agricultural potential of a region has gathered momentum in the discipline of agrarian history (Bray 1994; Ludden 1999). The shift to examining and emphasizing the relationship between the ecological and societal environments (Gadgil and Guha 1995) also directs the attention to the need to manage natural resources to ensure food production. The growing recognition of agroecological regions also underlines that a focus on technological and demographic processes in a society provides an inadequate basis for understanding the agricultural dynamism of the said society and its region (Martínez-Alier and Muradian 2015). Curry (2022) sets out how the separation of science and social science in understanding agricultural modernization and the associated focus on the improved cultivation of crops has been a key reason for the singular pursuit to advance new agricultural technologies as a solution to agricultural prosperity. This results in a search for technological solutions that push for the identification of crop varieties with the characteristics required for producing the highest yields. This zeroing in on yield from very limited varieties of wheat is a consequence of the adoption of an ideology that regards the new hybrid technology as more productive than the traditional systems of cultivation (Baranski 2022). With a lynchpin of increasing grain yields that guided the launching of the hybrid HYVs of wheat, maize, and rice, termed the Green Revolution, there is little attention accorded to any other relations between humans and land. The inevitability of the Green Revolution option for ensuring food security was built on a platform of agro-industrialization that neglected the other avenues for increasing food production that are more ecologically sound, such as improving mixed cropping systems, improving indigenous seeds, and improving the efficiency of the use of local resources (McMichael 2007). Another shortcoming of the Green Revolution strategy is that it also disregarded the distribution of land ownership across a community, as the core of the model was that of the individual farmer. Social relations were eschewed, and it was the importance of ensuring technical inputs that was prioritized: the need to ensure timely pumping water, and application of fertilizer and pesticides for the success of high-yielding varieties to selected areas. While this strategy successfully raised the productivity of Indian agriculture over the last quarter century, it also had the consequence of reducing the pressure to change agrarian relations, through a more egalitarian system of land ownership through a government programme of land reform. (Gadgil and Guha 1995, 26–28)

The drive to ensure the adoption of these favored few crops as the solution to world hunger was fueled by the institutional interpretation within government and charitable organizations in the United States that there was only one way to ensure that countries in the Third World could escape poverty and hunger (Fennell 2020). This form of thinking completely eschewed any role for the postcolonial possibilities of world making (Getachew 2019), where countries pursue their own approaches to managing agricultural systems. The radical possibility that newly independent countries have their own political, scientific, and community organizations that had the acumen and experience to devise and implement their own policies, including those in the agricultural sector, lies at the core of this concept of world making. Yet this was entirely bypassed by international agricultural organizations that focused on a small number of cereals as a priority strategy to feed the hungry populations who lived in the newly independent countries emerging in the 1950s and 1960s; while well-intentioned, it had unintended consequences for food security in the present century. This is because the high yields that were successfully achieved by the adoption of green technology HYV resulted in farmers moving away from a more diverse set of crops to a small group of crops—rice, wheat, and maize—which account for close to 80 percent of global food consumption in the current decade (FAO 2000). This is a big shift away from the more diverse system of agricultural production that was prominent at the beginning of the twentieth century in developing countries, which produced many minor crops that were locally important but not part of the global value chain (FAO 2007). This exclusion of other crops in pursuing the food needs of populations across the developing world and the singular pursuit of high yields in a few cereal crops (and a very small number of varieties in each crop) has resulted in a plateauing of yields, as well as a greater vulnerability to plant diseases. There has also been an increase in the demand for irrigation and chemical inputs to prevent any further fall in yields in these top three cereals. The uptick in the use of water and chemicals to improve the soil also changed the composition of the land, which in turn reduced its ability to sustain a larger range of plant cultivation. The result is a severe reduction in biodiversity of agricultural production, with the unintended negative consequence that this reduces the likelihood of agricultural sustainability in the twenty-first century (Scherr and McNeely 2008).

My own doctoral research on the cereal trends at provincial level in India and China (1960–1995) showed that the consequences of mindlessly following a strategy of ever-increasing agricultural yields has resulted in unsustainable agricultural strategies by the end of the twentieth century.[3] The false economy of a relentless search for greater land and labor productivity to feed the world's billions through ever-increasing cereal yields had severely adverse implications for the viability of agroecological regions in India and China.[4]

The most striking illustrations that were uncovered were in the case of the northern Indian states of Punjab, Haryana, and Uttar Pradesh, variously labeled as the breadbasket, as well as the rice bowl, of India (Hazell 2009). Here, the conventional Green Revolution story has been of a celebration of high yields and attributed to the comparative advantage of abundant water and ability to purchase fertilizers and pesticides in these northern states in the production of rice, wheat, and maize. This journey is not recognizable as an unmitigated success if one undertakes an examination of growth-instability indices associated with the agricultural performance of Punjab, Haryana, and Uttar Pradesh in the production of these three cereals between the 1960s and the 1990s.[5] While growth rates were exceptionally high in Punjab in the early 1970s (above 10 percent over that decade), there was a high level of instability in the yield, and by the 1990s, growth rates had fallen to less than 5 percent. Uttar Pradesh and Haryana had a more orderly and less dramatic set of trend values than Punjab in food grains, as the lower growth rates were not associated with high instability in yields.

The southern states of India, as a consequence of their geographical features of smaller and narrower river basins due to the igneous and metaphoric geomorphology of the Deccan Plateau, have been regarded as smaller contributors to the national food grain buffer stock. The state of Tamil Nadu, for example, was selected to participate in the Green Revolution program, and while there was a rise in yields in the 1970s, the indices showed high instability in cereal production. During the 1990s, there was a fall in the area and production given over to rice production, despite recording the highest yields in rice production in the country.

The inability of yield trends to explain the pattern of agricultural production is an indication that there are other features of agricultural livelihoods that need to be considered in understanding the operation of cereal crop markets, including the conditions operating in the natural world. These trends are not unique to India alone, as there are equally interesting patterns in China, another major adopter of Green Revolution technologies and, alongside India, ranked among the most populous countries in the world at the end of the twentieth century and regarded as having a significant poor and hungry populace. An examination of the cereal trends in the country between the 1960s and 1990s indicates that there was considerable diversity across the major Chinese provinces contributing to cereal production. The red- and black-earth regions of China were widely recognized as the leading areas in food grain production, with the provinces of Sichuan and Shandong jointly contributing a fifth of the national food grain output at the end of the twentieth century. Sichuan, the largest provincial producer of cereals, showed growth rates of more than 5 percent production in the mid-1980s; Shandong, the second-largest producer, though, continued such growth rates until the end of the 1990s. Instability trends over the entire period were higher in Sichuan than in Shandong, while those of the smaller provinces of Henan and Hebei had high growth rates in the collective period in Chinese agriculture and maintained an acceptable level of increase in the 1980s and 1990s, with a good reduction in instability. This shows that the top performers display very diverse trajectories, and a similar variation is also evident in the southern and southeastern provinces. In the case of the province of Guangdong, there was a strong performance in yield rates, but this did not prevent falling area and production indicators or a rise in the associated instability indices in the last period. The trends in Zhejiang and Jiangxi are more muted in the extremity of change but appear to show the tapering off of growth and middling instability trends.

The dislodgment of the leaders of the agriculture pack in both countries is disconcerting to say the least. The billions who depended almost solely on domestic cereal production in these two countries were likely to find that the surety of the large provincial producers was a thing of the past by the start of the twenty-first century. The evidence that Punjab and Sichuan showed falling growth rates and rising instability by the middle of the 1980s indicates that the promise of the Green Revolution miracle has clearly petered out. Equally, there is little solace in the amazing yields obtained by the smaller southern states and provinces, for the high yields achieved in these areas did not appear to stem the tide of a rapid exit from agriculture, as higher incomes were available in the port-related service-sector livelihoods.

It is clear from this analysis of cereal production that a yield-maximizing approach did not possess the necessary tools to predict future agricultural trends. It also underlines the limitation in the narrow approach of raising cereal yields as a sure way to improve the economic prospects of developing countries, which provides very little insight into the social processes in agriculture. As the traditional rice and wheat bowls are unable to maintain their agricultural levels despite the huge inputs of electricity, fertilizers, and irrigation that are necessary for the HYVs, it points to an underlying unsustainability in HYVs' production over a longer time.

Equally important is the inability of the later winners of the yield race, Tamil Nadu and Guangdong, to ensure increases in the area devoted to rice production in the 1990s. The lack of interest in further investing in the yoke of agriculture was due to the emergence of other forms of livelihoods having relatively easier and plentiful pickings available, and in the case of Tamil Nadu and Guangdong, this was due to the development of extensive navigation and docking facilities. This indicates that, as new labor markets offer better employment opportunities, yield increases do not provide sufficient economic advantages to farmers, who chose new livelihoods over cereal production. The limited understanding of labor markets, particularly how agricultural livelihoods are about more than just achieving record yields, is a significant shortcoming of the agricultural perspective that was prominent in the 1960s.

ACT II: AGRICULTURAL MARKETS AND THE MAKING OF AFRICAN FOOD POLICY

While there was persistent interest in labor-intensive and land-scarce South and Southeast Asia throughout this period, there was a marked difference in the academic analysis of agricultural production conditions in African countries. The academic narrative was that low-labor-density African economies had seen negligible increases in agricultural yields.[6] The primary reason proffered is that there had been a failure to adopt new technologies across the continent (Eicher 2003). There was a distinct shift in the policy interventions in African agriculture at the end of the 1990s, with the first hybrid millet being introduced in 1996. The statistical evidence at the end of the decade shows relatively unchanging shares of land and value added in the agricultural sector (see table 3.1).

The examination of agriculture as solely a matter of material production and its economic contribution to the economy, without any direct reference to the colonial and postcolonial history of the continued denial of land rights, is another example of false economy.[7] By overlooking the importance of recognizing land tenurial rights and its implications for the ability to transform the lives of rural communities (Clover 2003), this narrow economic approach reduces rights to land for the purpose of economic production. It also becomes an acceptable framework to regard land as a resource and devoid of social relationships and cultural values. Consequently, the purpose of accessing land is to maximize the market value of the products that are cultivated by land and labor. There is no acknowledgment of cultural value according to the land or the importance of human and nonhuman interactions on these lands with farming communities.

Table 3.1: Agricultural Land and Agriculture Share of GDP

	Agricultural land (% of land area) *Year*					*Agriculture, value added (% of GDP)* *Year*					
Country	**'95**	**'96**	**'98**	**'00**	**'05**	**'95**	**'96**	**'98**	**'00**	**'05**	**'06**
Angola	46	46	46	46	46	7	7	13	6	8	9
Benin	23	24	28	29	32	34	38	38	37	32	..
Botswana	46	46	46	46	46	4	4	3	2	2	2
Burkina Faso	35	35	36	37	40	35	39	39	29	34	33
Burundi	84	84	88	88	91	48	57	46	40	35	..
Cameroon	20	20	20	20	20	24	24	25	22	20	20
Cape Verde	17	17	18	18	18	14	13	12	12	9	9
Central A.R.	8	8	8	8	8	46	50	53	53	54	55
Chad	38	39	39	39	39	36	39	41	42	21	21
Comoros	73	74	76	78	80	41	41	41	49	51	45
Congo DR	10	10	10	10	10	57	34	47	50	46	46
Congo Rep.	31	31	31	31	31	10	9	11	5	5	4
Cote d'Ivoire	62	62	62	62	64	25	25	24	24	23	23
Equ. Guinea	12	12	12	12	12	52	37	22	10	3	3
Eritrea	73	73	74	75	75	21	18	26	15	23	25
Ethiopia	30	30	31	31	34	57	57	53	50	47	48
Gabon	20	20	20	20	20	8	7	7	6	5	5
Gambia	64	64	68	75	81	30	30	28	36	32	30
Ghana	58	58	62	64	65	39	39	36	35	37	36
Guinea	50	50	50	50	51	19	18	22	20	20	13
Guinea Biss.	54	54	56	58	58	55	58	62	56	60	62
Kenya	48	46	46	47	47	31	31	31	32	27	27
Lesotho	77	77	77	77	77	16	16	17	18	17	16
Liberia	27	27	27	27	27	82	94	79	72	66	55
Madagascar	63	63	66	70	70	27	27	31	29	28	27
Malawi	41	41	42	43	49	30	35	36	40	33	34
Mali	29	30	31	32	32	50	52	46	42	37	37
Mauritania	39	39	39	39	39	37	36	31	28	24	13
Mauritius	56	56	56	56	56	10	10	9	6	6	6
Mayotte	51	51	53	53	53	..	..	..	..	..	..
Mozambique	61	61	61	61	62	35	35	31	24	27	28
Namibia	47	47	47	47	47	12	12	11	11	12	11
Niger	29	29	29	30	30	40	39	43	38	..	..
Nigeria	80	78	77	77	81	..	..	..	..	33	32
Rwanda	60	63	65	68	79	44	47	46	37	39	41
Sao T. and P.	47	47	49	54	59	..	..	..	..	17	..
Senegal	41	41	41	42	43	21	20	19	19	17	15
Seychelles	13	13	13	13	13	4	4	3	3	3	3
Sierra Leone	38	38	38	38	40	43	47	62	58	46	47
Somalia	70	70	70	70	71	..	..	..	..	..	..
South Africa	82	82	82	82	82	4	4	4	3	3	3
Sudan	55	55	56	56	58	39	44	46	42	32	30

Swaziland	78	78	78	81	81	12	14	13	12	9	8
Tanzania	38	38	38	38	39	47	48	45	45	46	45
Togo	61	63	65	67	67	38	41	35	34	44	..
Uganda	62	62	62	62	64	49	45	42	30	27	26
Zambia	32	33	33	34	35	18	18	21	22	22	21
Zimbabwe	36	36	37	38	40	15	22	22	18	19	..

Source: Compiled from World Bank, *World Development Indicators*, 2007.

The shortcomings of the academic literature on agricultural productivity and the severe implications for African agriculture have received extensive treatment at the hands of radical ecological economists and activists on grounds of ignoring issues of livelihoods and sustainability of the natural world (Holt-Giménez and Altieri 2013). The strong influence of conventional economics, with its singular attention on yields, has resulted in reducing food production to a form of economic output. In this formulation, value is accorded solely to the final economic product: that is, the commodity that is sold in national or global supply chains. This formulation also bypasses the richer social dimensions of food within a farming community as well as the processual aspects of food production that are inherent features: from the preparation of land and seed selection through harvesting and sale of agricultural produce (McMichael 2007). The dominance of this narrow conception of food production has hidden costs, as it does not account for the contribution of nature, through patterns of rainfall or other climatic conditions, or the role of ecology, particularly of soils and geomorphology, in ensuring the sustainability of agriculture (Pretty 1995).

The very limited recognition of the unsustainable levels of energy usage in such agricultural practices also generates grave concern. Martínez-Alier (2002) points out that this myopic vision is not restricted to the discipline of agricultural economics but extends to the historical social sciences. He further indicates that the more radical area of "agrarian studies has not considered environmental issues" until the last decade of the twentieth century (Martínez-Alier 2002, 237). By addressing the reluctance of the Marxian tradition to combine political economy with sustainable agriculture, Martínez-Alier calls for recognition of the role of the peasantry in creating a sustainable agriculture. He makes the argument that it is only by bringing together smallholding and ecology and an explicit theorizing around concepts of peasant resistance and moral economy that it is possible to address the limitations of conventional agricultural measurements of productivity and to make explicit the value of an agroecological framework. Martínez-Alier (2002) questions this mainstream practice and interrogates how a historical understanding would interpret the singular pursuit of higher-yield productivity, which does not recognize that this objective has also resulted in a fall in energy efficiency and the reduction in the biodiversity of crops.

There is a follow-through: it does not provide any intellectual space for bringing in the value of alternative/diverse systems of cultivation that might be adopted under different types of land ownership, even though there is evidence from mainstream economic research that policy-induced variations in land rights and their relation to investment in agriculture can change the production mix on the land. For example, Besley (1995) analyzed investment in trees in Ghana; Do and Iyer (2008) studied the impact of specific legal changes in land rights in Vietnam and, in turn, their impact on subsequent agricultural investments in the rural economy, including in terms of perennial crops; Dercon and Ayalew (2007) found a strong causal link between perceived land rights and land allocated to perennial crops, with meaningful economic development.

The focus on the production for the market, using economic tools, is useful in obtaining farm-level data and understanding the technical relationship between inputs and outputs on the farm, but it does not provide a broader ecological perspective on agricultural production (Scoones 2001). A case in point is the wide extent of ecological variation across sub-Saharan Africa that has resulted in very different crop composition across eastern Africa, central Africa, western Africa, and southern Africa, which has not been given much attention. Consequently, the global focus on cereals appears ill placed in sub-Saharan Africa, where such root crops as cassava and yams are as important as cereals, and within cereals, the coarse grains, such as the family of millets, are likely to be the main staple of poor households rather than wheat, rice, or maize.[8] While cereals might be the food crops that ensure the survival of the poor in Asia and Latin America, in sub-Saharan Africa, roots and tubers provide a major source of sustenance, accounting for 20 percent of calories consumed in the region (Rosegrant et al. 2005). Despite the predominance of roots and tubers in the African diet, international agencies have focused on increasing the output and productivity of cereals in Africa (Nweke 2004). This directive is based on a uniform internationally driven technical production approach to agriculture that regards cereal as the primary form of food consumed across the world. The application of such a universalizing principle has been the dominant driver for selecting food commodities to ensure food security across the low-income regions of the world since the 1960s. The seeming contradiction between the large contribution of roots and tubers in African food and the minimal importance accorded by international agencies to roots and tubers and the African share of production in the world is striking: Africa accounts for about 23 percent of the world production of root and tuber crops (FAO 2000).

Furthermore, the diversity of agricultural conditions and therefore the composition of agricultural output vary across regions. While food insecurity is a concern and the Food and Agriculture Organization (FAO) maps show that the highest food imports are needed in Africa to feed the hungry and malnourished, the shortfall is made up by an import of cereals from Europe, North America, and Latin America. This dependence on imported cereals could be replaced by increasing the share of tubers and root crops that already make up the diet of the poor and also form the basis of the livelihoods of smallholder farmers in Africa (Ochieng 2007).

There has been a primary focus on using a market logic of increasing yields, despite the mismatch between global food commodity preferences, food production, and consumption preferences in the African continent. International organizations and policies had followed the Washington Consensus that advocated market-based reform policies of "getting the state out" and "getting prices right" during the 1980s and 1990s and increased the risks and difficulties faced by smallholders (Ponte 2002; United Kingdom Food Group 2008). The insistence on liberalized markets as the appropriate way forward for African agriculture has led to harsher conditions for smallholders, as they have lost subsidies and state support through extension systems but were unable to gain from new market or production opportunities. This misguided policy for improving agricultural output points to the failure among expert finance committees in international organizations to understand that the haste in setting up a cereal value chain to increase commercial production is not devoid of a false economy. Nor did the members of these committees have an in-depth understanding of the different challenges faced by smallholder farmers as a direct result of obstacles to accessing credit on account of missing markets for those below a particular size of landholding.[9]

In the context of the increasing shocks being faced by African economies, there is a push to devise agricultural solutions in institutions located on the continent that build on the participation of farmer communities and are co-created and co-implemented within these spaces (Africa Green Revolution Forum 2021). The Green Revolution for the twenty-first century is to be built around the crops and nutritional practices that are obtained from local food knowledge systems.

ACT III: THE ORPHANING OF MILLETS AND THE LOSS OF ENVIRONMENTAL SUSTAINABILITY

In developing countries, millets were the most common type of cereals cultivated by smallholders in semiarid tropical regions until the halfway mark of the twentieth century. The methods and knowledge of cultivation of these seemingly lesser crops tend to reside among the women in these communities. In India, 40 percent of food production came from millets in the first half of the twentieth century but fell to 10 percent by the end of the century. There was an accompanying devaluation of this group of cereals, which came to be regarded as "coarse grains," considered an inferior food and not a preferred form of consumption commodity in national and international markets. This led to a lack of government support for millets and a disregard for this group of cereals, as well as an erasure of traditional knowledge, as in the case of the community knowledge of millets held by the tribe of Dongria Kondhs in Odisha, India (Aich, Dey, and Roy 2022) and the associated loss of heirloom millet varieties.

It is also important to consider that millets were particularly significant in the crop choices made by small farmers, who preferred stable over unstable seed (as it reduces risk) and crops with greater water stress tolerance that could make the difference between a crop and no crop, as well as a higher return to labor intensity (so that falling back on family labor can yield positive returns). Millets therefore became the default crop to provide a cushion in drought years and a safety net against hunger (Chambers 1974).

While there had been an earlier set of studies conducted in India and East Africa in the 1970s, supported by the World Health Organization (WHO), on how to use community knowledge to improve nutrition among poor communities—by creating weaning foods that used fermented porridges composed of cereal (millet)–legume mixtures and the benefits of incorporating these fermented foods into infant diet (Rajalakshmi and Vanaja 1967)—the lack of support from international agricultural institutions perpetuated the orphan status of millets until the end of the 1990s. It is only over the last two decades that there have been attempts to reduce iron deficiency using the International Crops Research Institute for the Semi-Arid Tropics (ICRISAT) high-iron biofortified pearl millet that provides twice as much iron as modern wheat varieties. Furthermore, though the pathway of enhancing the bioavailability of iron is an established method of dietary manipulation to increase the absorption of iron in the body (Colin et al., 2013), the important potential of millets to improve the nutritive contribution to the lives of women, babies and infants, groups that are recognized as being particularly prone to anemia, remained understudied.

The research that was undertaken in the United Kingdom Research and Innovation (UKRI)–funded TIGR2ESS and MillNETi programs, on working with communities in semiarid regions in eastern and southern India and in East and West Africa, was focused on learning about local farming and the crop choices being made by farmers in the face of water scarcity and increasingly unpredictable rainfall.[10] The objective was to identify locally produced and community-led processes of lactic fermentation of cereals and legumes that use traditional methods of food preparation and preservation. It is a major initiative to address the huge gap in understanding the relationship between millet production and consumption of millets. Millets not having been studied as part of international nutritional studies until the beginning of the twenty-first century (Naylor et al. 2004), this also implied that food-processing methods associated with these less valued set of cereals, such as the nutritive value of fermentation, had not been fully recognized. A half-century of neglect in undertaking systematic analysis of the local knowledge regarding increasing nutritional value in food, as well as increasing the absorption of iron through consumption of these fermented foods, has resulted in an erasure of the intangible value of processes associated with millet production, processing, and sale. Indeed, the missing market is not a direct consequence of smallholders being unable to access international supply chains but an outcome of the international agricultural institutional system discriminating against these crops of the marginalized.[11]

Our research undertook a mapping of the production and consumption of fermented foods created from pearl millet, finger millet, sorghum, or teff through a deep dive into the lives of women. The format of the research design was creating a protocol for a thorough documentation of food (millet) production, cereal fermentation, and food preparation; its consumption by members in the household; and a collection of recipes for key items on the food plates in these communities. This was crucial, as restricting research into the nutritional value of millets would only add to commercial/market value for national and global supply chains, as happened in the case of quinoa, and will result in very limited progress on the creation of functional foods that are readily acceptable to populations (Kumar et al. 2016). In the current context, where there is very limited research on millet-based traditional foods that could improve the nutritional well-being of communities in semiarid tropics and where malnutrition among children and anemia among women are widespread challenges, it is crucial that commercial opportunities are harnessed to improve rural livelihoods.

What is already evident from our research is that there is growing demand for millet, as the health-conscious urban middle classes shift toward more sustainable and nutritious foods, and this change in preferences can prompt the stepping up of millet production by rural communities to meet this growing demand. However, such market-driven incentives would only result in boosting farm income and sustainable agriculture in semiarid regions but would not improve the nutritive value of foods consumed by smallholder farmers, as they sell millets but eat less healthy foods. As millets come to be regarded as a new superfood, given the promise of additional income and market opportunity for these gluten-free and low-glycemic-value crops, the sustainability dimension can only be assured through not falling prey again to false-economy and market-failure fallacies. Millets thrive in semiarid areas on marginal soils, take less water than rice or wheat, and can withstand extreme temperatures of hot or cold. They are poverty or survival crops to which farmers can fall back on in hard times. They can also be very effective in sequestering carbon and limiting greenhouse gases emissions.

Millets are important in Odisha State in India, and research has been underway for the last four years to gather and systematize the knowledge about them that still exists. This involves finding out how people eat millets and mapping the socioeconomic networks associated with the entire millet value chain, which had been largely forgotten by the international development community. The Odisha Chief Minister devised a program around millets to increase famers' income and tackle nutritional deficiency. Yet these crops are not just of regional interest in India: the United Nations has declared 2023 to be the International Year of Millets. Since the COVID-19 pandemic began, children in India and elsewhere have been growing taller because they no longer have school meals and are eating at home instead, where their diet includes millets.[12] A similar shift has also been revealed in other geographies, and our research showed that this shift was also evident in rural communities in the Gambia (Sidebottom et al. 2022). If millet-based foods are prepared and presented in attractive ways, such as in biscuits and similar snacks, children will eat them and so benefit from the relatively slow sugar release. However, millet-based food production presents significant challenges. Considerable force is required, for example, in the manual pounding (usually done by women) of millet grains to make flour. Studies in Ethiopia and the Gambia suggest that, unless this millet processing is appropriately mechanized, it will disappear there.[13]

Until civil society and corporate partners are able to resolve this mechanization problem, our knowledge base will not translate into a viable process that can contribute to sustainable livelihoods. Furthermore, work is needed on all stages in the millet supply chain, not just on one or two, if it is to work better. This requires a multipartner and multidisciplinary effort to prevent a repetition of hastily erected market systems to accumulate significant amounts of millet cereals in local markets that are bound to collapse as a consequence of another bout of false economy.

In Ethiopia, where teff-constituted injera is widely eaten, there is great interest in sorghum and millets because sorghum is used in place of teff when supplies of teff are scarce. In the Gambia, many farmers who grow millet for sale as an urban-middle-class healthy food do not eat it themselves, preferring (polished) rice instead. Does this mean that local knowledge in this case is confined to the marketing aspects only and excludes the health externalities?[14]

The importance of community-level learning between Ethiopia and the Gambia is exemplified by the case of fermented millet. Injera is fermented, and there are several West African–fermented foods made from millets. Fermenting millet increases the bioavailability of iron, important for women and children in areas where anemia is rife. ICRISAT has created a pearl millet biofortified with iron, but getting this into the community requires understanding of the whole system from field to plate: what do rural households eat, what do they sell, and what do they know about the food? Finding ways to improve health and well-being that also create sustainable agriculture requires qualitative and quantitative investigation by dieticians, nutritionists, economists, and medical experts working together.

Betting on millets to create a "sustainable and climate-smart agriculture," which is the chosen language of international organizations, should be replaced by a more transparent accounting framework that begins with examining the direct benefit to agricultural communities that are providing sufficient food and nutrition in the event of climate change–triggered drought by cultivating millets. Rather than returning to another round of Green Revolution thinking with a top-down policy implementation, the TIGR2ESS and MillNETi research programs have adopted a participatory approach of working with communities. By cataloguing the range of millets cultivated by smallholders and explicitly recording their own narratives and perceptions of how the commodity travels across the key segments—production, processing, and marketing—of the commodity value chain, they have recorded the risks through a range of methods: surveys, focus groups, and interviews. It is the lived reality of these communities that becomes the basis for mapping local supply chains, and it is their understanding of how they work the land, with its cultural meanings, that builds a local notion of ecological knowledge that will ascertain what patterns and levels of agricultural productivity these communities are able to achieve and sustain.

CONCLUSION

The acts in this chapter reflect on three distinct moments in the trajectory of the Green Revolution thinking over the past century. The common thread that runs across these acts is the narrow and unflinching focus on increasing food-grain productivity in Asia and Africa, with the objective of reducing poverty and hunger in the low-income regions of the world. The chapter highlights the alarming deficiency in this thinking of international organizations and think tanks, which simplified improving food production to identifying a very small group of cereals (rice, wheat, and maize) and the varieties within each that could produce the highest yields.

The chapter makes the case that such top-down systems have a decided preference for universalizing the improvement of food production to a technical solution so that it is solely about the value of the final commodity in global and national markets. It contrasts this approach with that of a participatory approach of working with and in rural communities to identify agricultural knowledge. The central argument is that the cataloging selection mechanisms in each of these significant acts—of the Green Revolution in Asia in the 1970s, the falling behind of African agriculture in the 1990s, and the search for supergrains of the early twenty-first century—provides an opportunity to explore how hegemonic epistemologies are established in agricultural production systems.

Each of these three acts, through records of the narratives and perceptions of researchers in these communities, shows that there was an incessant race for finding the shortest and often cheapest route to solve the hunger problem, which resulted in the repeated occurrence of false economies. This technical perspective also had deleterious effects on smallholders in rural communities, who in the face of high production risks of commercial crops and the low value of traditional crops, became increasingly excluded from the benefits of cultivating the selected crops by international scientific organizations.

The chapter also identifies that the lived reality of rural communities, both in terms of cultivation of traditional noncereal crops (yams and taros), as well as traditional nutritional practices had not been investigated by these international organizations. Indeed, there was no room for world making, as these organizations regarded these communities as devoid of valuable knowledge on account of their poverty. There was also an erasure of the relationship these farming communities had with the land, as set out in the cultural values to the natural world and their own methods of recording oral forms of information regarding the ecologies within which they resided.

The chapter concludes that an ecologically informed and multidisciplinary investigation drawing across sciences and social sciences needs to place such community-specific ecological knowledge at the center of its research agenda if it is to achieve sustainable food market systems. It also reiterates the importance of identifying the possibility of missing markets and to take onboard that false economies have inimical consequences for the livelihood and nutrition choices available to farmers in low-income countries.

NOTES

1. The Bellagio Conference, funded by the Rockefeller Foundation, was an important venue for the early meetings of CGIAR. The importance of increasing productivity for improved agricultural development was recorded by the Agricultural Development Proceedings of a Conference, April 23–25, 1969 (Rockefeller Foundation 1969).

The CGIAR is an international institution that was set up in 1971 in the wake of growing concerns about food inadequacy in the 1950s and 1960s. The research into wheat, maize, and rice was initially carried out in experimental stations in Latin America and Asia, and there were considerable gains in productivity in both regions, but this success was not witnessed in Africa.

2. There is also an associated approach of regarding the agricultural productivity of a region within the discipline of Marxian economics that has focused on the level of the surplus of the agricultural sector and is at the core of theories of transition from feudalism to capitalism (Dobb 1946; Preobrahzensky 1985).

3. The link between increased yields and the health of the environment has been overlooked in the traditional literature on the Green Revolution (Pingali 2012). This oversight has meant that the misguided policy of pursuing increased food supplies in a very small number of favored cereals has made agriculture more vulnerable to climatic shocks and to pest infestations, which pose a threat to the future sustainability of agriculture.

4. The simple definition of *false economy* is "penny wise, pound foolish." The underlying principle is that focusing on short-term cost cutting, or the cheapest method to get a desired outcome, can have long-term adverse consequences on the creation of an economic product. It is equally true in the case of investments for creating new markets, as there are numerous social costs, often identified as externalities, that do not get calculated into current prices (Leff 1984). These can add up over time and undermine the new market. See Fennell (2003).

5. The Coppock Index was used to measure instability, and it is calculated as the annual average of the yearly percentage deviations from the respective trend values, ignoring the plus and minus signs.

6. Multifactor productivity analysis assessing the impact of the potential determining factors (including science and technology) on agricultural output has shown that in sub-Saharan Africa, research and development (R&D) investment elasticity (i.e., the share of output growth due to R&D) did not exceed 5 percent (Frisvold and Ingram 1995; Thirtle, Hadley, and Townsend 1995) and was often barely significant (Chema, Gilbert, and Roseboom 2003). In contrast, the paper by Craig, Pardey, and Roseboom (1997) revealed the R&D elasticity in the range of 10 percent, and if only developing countries were considered, the R&D elasticity remained as high as 9 percent.

7. In this instance, the false economy arises from the urgency to obtain exports for the colonial mother country and suppression of native and Indigenous rights so as to maximize the amount of land for agricultural commodities that were of high value in Europe. An early example of this was the spice trade.

8. The FAO provides quarterly updates on crop prospects and the food situation that are disaggregated to take into account the major crops in each ecological region in Africa.

9. There has been particular criticism of the *World Bank Development Report 2008: Agriculture for Development* (World Bank 2008), which accurately traced the many problems faced by agriculture but fell short on policies to support the African smallholder (see Oxfam 2007). The formidable obstacles, such as lack of collateral

for being eligible for a loan, that are faced by smallholders in agriculture are largely on account of poorly calculated prices within markets. If the smallholder cannot get cash to invest in the commercial crop for which there is a new market, then they will look for potential income and have to rely on traditional crops for which there is no longer an attractive market price (de Janvry, Fafchamps, and Sadoulet 1991).

10. The research outputs on which this section is built can be found on the TIGR2ESS website at https://tigr2ess.globalfood.cam.ac.uk/.

11. There have been concerns that the case for promotion millets might mirror that of quinoa, which happened a decade earlier. In the case of quinoa, the smallholder farmers who were the primary producers of small-grained seeds that are consumed as an alternative to the major cereals were replaced by large farmers. This is also a case where selection mechanisms for food production have fallen prey to false economies (Alliance Bioversity and CIAT 2013).

12. During the COVID-19 pandemic, international organizations began to take cognizance of the fact that households in rural communities were returning to their traditional food habits of eating millets. ICRISAT has begun to emphasize the renewal of the consumption patterns following in these rural communities and calling for more emphasis of the value of Indigenous nutritional knowledge (Padhee and Kane Potaka 2020).

13. The ICRISAT Sahel Office has also been investigating the role of millets. The evidence that they have obtained shows that, while millets continue to be produced by communities in the Sahel, there is a need to improve production methods and processing techniques (Diallo 2022).

14. See Sidebottom et al. (2022).

REFERENCES

Africa Green Revolution Forum. 2021. "Pathways to Recovery and Resilient Food Systems." Summit report, Africa Green Revolution Forum, Nairobi.

Aich, Amitava, Dipayan Dey, and Arindam Roy, 2022. "Climate Change Resilient Agricultural Practices: A Learning Experience from Indigenous Communities over India." *PLOS Sustain Transform* 1 (7): e0000022. https://doi.org/10.1371/journal.pstr.0000022.

Alliance Bioversity and CIAT. 2013. "Food for Thought on Andean Super Grains." July 2. https://alliancebioversityciat.org/stories/food-thought-andean-super-grains.

Baranski, Marci R. 2022. *The Globalization of Wheat: A Critical History of the Green Revolution*. Pittsburgh, PA: University of Pittsburgh Press.

Besley, Timothy. 1995. "Property Rights and Investment Incentives: Theory and Evidence from Ghana." *Journal of Political Economy* 103 (5): 903–37.

Bray, Francesca. 1994. *The Rice Economies: Technology and Development in Asian Societies*. Berkeley: University of California Press.

Carpenter, Kenneth J. 1994. "The Life and Times of W. O. Atwater (1844–1907)." *Journal of Nutrition* 124 (9): 1707S–14S.

Chambers, Robert. 1974. "Project on Agrarian Change in Rice-Growing Areas of Tamil Nadu and Sri Lanka." Seminar paper, CUPAC Archive, Centre of South Asian Studies, University of Cambridge.

Chema, Sam, Elon Gilbert, and Johannes Roseboom. 2003. "A Review of Key Issues and Recent Experiences in Reforming Agricultural Research in Africa." ISNAR research report 24, ISNAR, the Hague.

Clover, Jenny. 2003. "Food Security in Sub-Saharan Africa." *African Security Review* 12 (1): 5–15.

Colin, Cercamondi, Ines Egli, Evariste Mitchikpe, Felicien Tossou, Christophe Zeder, Joseph Hounhouigan, and Richard Hurrell, 2013. "Total Iron Absorption by Young Women from Iron-Biofortified Pearl Millet Composite Meals Is Double That from Regular Millet Meals but Less than That from Post-Harvest Iron-Fortified Millet Meals." *Journal of Nutrition* 143 (9): 1376–82.

Craig, Barbara, Philip Pardey, and Johannes Roseboom. 1997. "International Productivity Patterns: Accounting for Input Quality, Infrastructure, and Research." *American Journal of Agricultural Economics* 79 (4): 1064–76.

Curry, Helen Anne. 2022. *Endangered Maize: Industrial Agriculture and the Crisis of Extinction*. Berkeley: University of California Press.

de Janvry, Alain, Marcel Fafchamps, and Elisabeth Sadoulet. 1991. "Peasant Household Behaviour with Missing Markets: Some Paradoxes Explained." *Economic Journal* 101 (409): 1400–1417.

Dercon, Stefan, and David Ayalew. 2007. "Land Rights, Power and Trees in Rural Ethiopia." CSAE working paper, University of Oxford, Oxford, UK.

Diallo, Mahamadou. 2022. "Millet, a Food of the Future for the Sahel Region." International Crops Research Institute for the Semi-Arid Tropics. March 22. https://www.icrisat.org/millet-a-food-of-the-future-for-the-sahel-region/.

Do, Quy-Tuan, and Lakshmi Iyer. "Land Titling and Rural Transition in Vietnam." *Economic Development and Cultural Change* 56 (3): 531–79.

Dobb, Maurice. 1946. *Studies in the Development of Capitalism*. London: Routledge.

Eicher, Carl. 2003. "Flashback: Fifty Years of Donor Aid to African Agriculture." Paper presented at the InWEnt, IFPRI, NEPAD, CTA conference Successes in African Agriculture, Pretoria, December 1–3.

FAO. 2000. *The State of Food and Agriculture: Lessons from the Last Fifty Years*. Rome: Food and Agriculture Organization.

———. 2007. *Committee on World Food Security Report, IPC Special Event*. Rome: Food and Agriculture Organization.

Fennell, Shailaja. 2003. "A Study of Agricultural Production at the Level of Household, Community and Region: Long-Term Trends in India and China." PhD diss., University of Cambridge.

———. 2020. "Malthus, Statistics and the State of Indian Agriculture." *Historical Journal* 63 (1): 159–85.

———. 2021. "Poverty in South Asia: An Intellectual History." *Oxford Research Encyclopedia of Asian History*. https://doi.org/10.1093/acrefore/9780190277727.013.308.

Frisvold, George, and Kevin Ingram. 1995. "Sources of Agricultural Productivity Growth and Stagnation in Sub-Saharan Africa." *Agricultural Economics* 13 (1): 51–61.

Gadgil, Madhav, and Ramachandra Guha. 1995. *Ecology and Equity: The Use and Abuse of Nature in Contemporary India*. London: Routledge.

Getachew, Adom. 2019. *Worldmaking after Empire: The Rise and Fall of Self-Determination*. Princeton, NJ: Princeton University Press.

Hazell, Peter. 2009. "The Asian Green Revolution." IFPRI discussion paper 00911.

Heady, Earl O., C. B. Baker, Howard G. Diesslin, Earl Kehrberg, and Sydney Staniforth, eds. 1961. *Agricultural Supply Functions: Estimating Techniques and Interpretations*. Iowa City: Iowa State University Press.

Holt-Giménez, Eric, and Miguel A. Altieri. 2013. "Agroecology, Food Sovereignty, and the New Green Revolution." *Agroecology and Sustainable Food Systems* 37 (1): 90–102.

Hopper, David. 2004. Interview, World Bank Oral Archives, Oral History Program.

Immerwahr, Daniel. 2015. *Thinking Small: The United States and Lure of Community Development*. Cambridge, MA: Harvard University Press.

Johnson, Glenn L. 1963. "Stress on Production Economics." *Australian Journal of Agricultural Economics* 7 (1): 1–15.

Kumar Anil, Mamta Metwal, Sanveen Kaur, Atul K. Gupta, Swati Puranik, Sadhna Singh, Manoj Singh, Supriya Gupta, B. K. Babu, Salej Sood, and Rattan Yadav. 2016. "Nutraceutical Value of Finger Millet [Eleusine coracana (L.) Gaertn.], and Their Improvement Using Omics Approaches." *Frontiers in Plant Science* 7: 1–14. https://doi.org/10.3389/fpls.2016.00934.

Kuznets, Simon. 1966. *Modern Economic Growth: Rate, Structure, and Spread.* New Haven, CT: Yale University Press

Leff, Nathaniel H. 1984. "Externalities, Information Costs, and Social Benefit-Cost Analysis for Economic Development: An Example from Telecommunications." *Economic Development and Cultural Change* 32 (2): 255–76.

Lewis, W. Arthur. 1954. "Economic Development with Unlimited Supplies of Labour." *Manchester School of Economic and Social Studies* 22: 139–91.

Ludden, David. 1999. *The New Cambridge History of India*. Vol. 4, pt. 4, *An Agrarian History of South Asia*. New York: Cambridge University Press.

Martínez-Alier, Joan 2002. *The Environmentalism of the Poor: A Study of Ecological Conflicts and Valuation*. Cheltenham, UK: Edward Elgar

Martínez-Alier, Joan, and Roldan Muradian, eds. 2015. *Handbook of Ecological Economics*. Cheltenham, UK: Edward Elgar.

———. 2007. "Globalization and the Agrarian World." In *The Blackwell Companion to Globalization*, edited by George Ritzer, 216–38. Hoboken, NJ: Blackwell.

Naylor, Rosamund, Walter Falcon, Robert Goodman, Molly Jahn, Theresa Sengooba, Hailu Tefera, and Rebecca Nelson. 2004. "Biotechnology in the Developing World: A Case for Increased Investments in Orphan Crops." *Food Policy* 29: 15–44.

Nweke, Felix. 2004. "New Challenges in the Cassava Transformation in Nigeria and Ghana." Discussion paper no. 118 International Food Policy Research Institute, Washington, DC.

Ochieng, Cosmas Milton Obote. 2007. "Development through Positive Deviance and Its Implications for Economic Policy Making and Public Administration in Africa: The Case of Kenyan Agricultural Development, 1930–2005." *World Development* 35 (3): 454–79.

OECD. 2022. *Insights into the Measurement of Agricultural Total Factor Productivity and the Environment*. Paris: OECD.

Oxfam. 2007. "What Agenda for Agriculture Now?" Oxfam briefing note, October.

Padhee, Arabinda K., and Joanna Kane-Potaka. 2020. "COVID-19 Calls for Renewed Focus on Eating Right and Natural." International Crops Research Institute for the Semi-Arid Tropics. May 24. https://www.icrisat.org/covid-19-calls-for-renewed-focus-on-eating-right-and-natural/.

Pingali, Prabhu L. 2012. "Green Revolution: Impacts, Limits and the Paths Ahead." *PNAS* 109 (31): 12302–8.

Ponte, Stefano. 2002. "The 'Latte Revolution'? Regulation, Markets and Consumption in the Global Coffee Chain." *World Development* 30 (7): 1099–1122.

Preobrahzensky, Evegenii. (1931) 1985. *The Decline of Capitalism*. Translated by Richard Day. Armonk, NY: M. E. Sharpe.

Pretty, Jules N. 1995. *Regenerating Agriculture: Policies and Practice for Sustainability and Self-Reliance*. London: Earthscan.

Rajalakshmi, R., and K. Vanaja. 1967. "Chemical and Biological Evaluation of the Effects of Fermentation on the Nutritive Value of Foods Prepared from Rice and Grams." *British Journal Of Nutrition* 21: 467–73.

Rockefeller Foundation. 1969. *Agricultural Development: Proceedings of a Conference Sponsored by the Rockefeller Foundation, Bellagio, Italy April 23–25, 1969 (Bellagio I)*. Bellagio, Italy: CGIAR. https://cgspace.cgiar.org/handle/10947/153.

Rosegrant, Mark, Sarah Cline, Weibo Li, Timothy Sulser, and Rowena Valmónte-Santos. 2005. "Looking Ahead: Long Term Prospects for Agricultural Development and Food Security, 2020." Discussion paper no. 41, International Food Policy Research Institute, Washington, DC.

Scherr, Sara J., and Jeffrey A. McNeely. 2008. "Biodiversity Conservation and Agricultural Sustainability: Towards a New Paradigm of 'Ecoagriculture' Landscapes." *Philosophical Transactions of the Royal Society B* 363 (1491): 477–94.

Scoones, Ian, ed. 2001. *Dynamics and Diversity: Soil Fertility and Farming Livelihoods in Africa*. London: Earthscan.

Sidebottom, Richard, Solomon Wassie, Carla Cerami, Momodou Jallow, Shailaja Fennell, and Sarah Dalzell. 2022. "A Longitudinal Investigation of Dietary Diversity during the COVID-19 Pandemic in Mandinka Households in Kanifing, Brikama, and the West Kiang Region in the Gambia." *Frontiers in Nutrition* 9: 1–19. https://doi.org/10.3389/fnut.2022.907969.

Siegel, Benjamin. 2018. *Hungry Nation: Food, Famine and the Making of Modern India*. Cambridge, UK: Cambridge University Press.

Thirtle, Colin, David Hadley, and Robert Townsend. 1995. "Policy-Induced Innovation in Sub-Saharan African Agriculture: A Multilateral Malmquist Productivity Index Approach, *Development Policy Review* 13 (4): 323–48.

———. 2008. *Economic Development in Africa, Export Performance Following Trade*

UK Food Group. 2008. *More Aid for African Agriculture: Policy Implications for Small Farmers*. London: UK Food Group. http://www.ukfg.org.uk.

Waterhouse, Amanda Carroll. 2013. *Food and Prosperity: Balancing Technology and Community in Agriculture*. New York: Rockefeller Foundation.

———. 2005. *Managing Agricultural Production Risk: Innovations in Developing Countries.*

———. 2007a. *World Bank Assistance to Agriculture, Independent Evaluation Group.*

———. 2007b. *World Development Indicators*. Washington, DC: World Bank.

———. 2008. *World Development Report 2008: Agriculture for Development*. Washington, DC: World Bank.

PART II

Contesting Land Knowledge through Alternatives

Chapter 4

Stories at "Land's End"

Emplacements and Displacements of Black Women's Land Epistemologies in the Colombian Caribbean

Eloisa Berman-Arévalo

> *How we used to walk these lands. Marisella and Mercedes would walk all the way to Colú and back, selling fish with their bowls on their heads. One day, Marisella and I got lost; I say that was witchcraft or something. We, who are knowers of this land, couldn't find our way out of the bush. I don't know how we ended up in those woods. We saw a white-bearded man taking a bath in a ditch. Next to him was a female dog. When he saw us, he started laughing and laughing nonstop. I know everyone around here, and I had never seen that man. So we started running; we were lost for hours and arrived at night. That was God who brought us back. Imagine us carrying those bowls and stuck in the bush, surrounded by thorns. . . . We, knowers of the land, could not find our way out.*
>
> —Sofía, Paloaltico, June 2015 (author's translation).

This chapter is based on several years of research and collaboration among Afro-descendant communities in Colombia's Caribbean region, particularly in the municipality of Marialabaja in the agrarian mountains of Montes de María. In this historically Afro-campesino territory, born out of centuries of maroonage, rural life has changed dramatically over the past fifty years.[1] Agrarian reform in the late 1960s and 1970s inserted local populations in schemes and logics of agrarian modernization, commercial agriculture, and state recognition as peasants—a class-based category that dismissed Black communities' traditional knowledges, socionatural relations, and territorial dynamics (Berman-Arévalo 2019). Starting in the late 1980s, armed conflict between left-wing guerrillas, right-wing paramilitaries, and the Colombian military generated massive displacements from fields to towns and capital cities, as well as complex and violent negotiations around land tenure that culminated tragically in widespread dispossession and in the installation in the early 2000s of middle- and large-scale palm oil plantations. The latter have expanded at unprecedented rates over the past decades, conditioning rural inhabitants' everyday lives and geographies.[2]

I start with these moments of the region's agrarian history because they are iterations of what Katherine McKittrick (2006, 2011), one of the leading scholars in the field of Black geographies, understands as the "geographic domination" of Black lives. McKittrick's work situates epistemology as a cornerstone for understanding the ongoing project of geographic domination, which manifests materially as the dispossession, displacement, and confinement of Black bodies and spaces. A perspective of transparent space—one that is abstract and pregiven rather than socially constructed and experienced—renders Black people as ungeographic; that is, it is an epistemological perspective that fails to engage the contestations involved in the social construction of space and thereby reproduces domination by invisibilizing the geographic experiences, practices, imaginations, and languages of Black subjects (McKittrick 2006).

The question of how epistemic hierarchies enable the erasure of the geographies of Black life haunts my work. As a geographer who claims to practice critical ethnography with a feminist and decolonial perspective, I am constantly troubled by the impossibility of ethnography escaping its colonial foundations (Simpson 2014; Tuhiwai-Smith 1999). My own research is enabled by social, racial, and geographic privilege as an urban mestiza woman educated in universities of the global North and currently working at a private university in a regional capital. However, although practices of theoretical abstraction and ethnographic translation are unavoidable in academic writing, I believe—like those participating in the project of decolonial geographies—that certain forms of academic knowledge production can contribute to decolonial epistemic-political struggles by creating alternative narratives that "make visible social lives which are . . . rendered un-geographic" (McKittrick 2006, x). This is not disconnected to the broader decolonial project of affirmative refusal of a "racialized political economy of containment, displacement and violence" (Daigle and Ramírez 2019, 80). If the decolonial is a political project that resists gendered and racialized interconnected violences and the mundane and practical ways in which they are reproduced, then to strive for a decolonial academic practice involves naming and dismantling the pervasive violence of epistemic erasure *and* creating alternative narratives where the experiences, knowledges, and politics of subalternized subjects are central.

I am particularly interested in women's everyday stories and storytelling as forms of knowledge making that are deeply political. Narrated through an epistemological register that foregrounds ordinary life, stories may appear as anecdote or gossip, yet they narrate histories, geographies, and racialized and gendered agrarian political economies through the lens of ordinary life events, particularly through gendered everyday practices of care and social reproduction. Women's stories not only express detailed geographic knowledge but, as I argue in this chapter, also configure a politics of claiming land and territory.

Sofía's story at the start of this chapter, which was told in the presence of her two children and three other women, is rich with symbolism and meaning. References to white-bearded men as demons are recurrent in Afro-diasporic oral traditions, often associated with disputed lands, malevolent landowners, and relations of exploitation (Taussig 1980). In turn, her emphasis on being "knowers of the land" not only reinforces the idea that more-than-human forces must be at play for them to lose their way home but also is central to the broader meaning of her story. Her story is a claim of times past. It is humorous and yet nostalgic. It is about the changing conditions of land use, land access, and social relations that make it increasingly difficult for women to walk the land as they used to. In this sense, to claim to be knowers of the land becomes a claim to the land itself, given that this quality can only be realized through walking, using, or *inhabiting* the land (Ingold 2010, 5–6).

As suggested in its title, this chapter is a reflection on the situated nature of land epistemologies, in both a temporal and a geographic sense. I use Tania Murray Li's (2014) notion of "land's end" to refer to a specific spatio-temporal conjuncture in which Black campesino communities are facing the catastrophic effects of more than twenty years of piecemeal dispossession, which has been accompanied by the enclosure of formerly common-use fields, woods and water wells, and increasingly the contamination of soils and water sources. Land's end is also an affective moment marked by a sense of imminent demise of the land and by the uncertainty around the future of life in this place; this emplaced conjuncture makes women's stories of walking and inhabiting the land political actions.

STORIES AS DECOLONIAL EPISTEMOLOGIES

Stories—like space—are not readily available for transparent academic representations. Rather than aiming at making visible preexistent land epistemologies, I use ethnographic writing to cocreate narratives that foreground the geographic knowledge and experience produced by and accountable to the people with whom I work. My contribution to these stories is further to emphasize their decolonial political possibilities as they attempt to keep alive, recreate, and reclaim Black geographic existence in contexts of racialized dispossession.

For more than a decade, Latin American decolonial geographies—both within and outside academia—have emphasized the need to rethink Euro-modern conceptions of land and territory (Halvorsen 2019). Through a fertile dialogue between Latin American critical geography and Indigenous, Afro-descendant, campesino, and feminist social movements in the region, ideas of land and territory have been subject to intense scrutiny and reconceptualization, foregrounding alternative spatial ontologies and epistemologies as a way of decolonizing land and territory, not only conceptually, but also materially (Cabnal 2010; Colectivo Miradas Críticas del Territorio desde el Feminismo 2014; Porto Gonçalves 2002). These alternative traditions of spatial thinking and activism not only decenter capital and the nation-state as reference points but also attempt to subvert spatial rationalities and practices of exclusion and extraction, as well as the exercise of sovereign power. For instance, social movements in the 1990s proposed a concept of territory that articulated a "place-based framework linking history, culture, environment, and social life" (Escobar 2008, 62). Such ways of conceiving land and territory are, for some authors, in fact expressions of alternative ontologies and epistemologies, involving "new forms of signifying our being-in-the-world" (Porto Gonçalves 2002, 227; my translation), which are articulated through the knowledges produced by social movements.

Feminist spatial thinking in the region has expanded the conversation on the epistemologies of land and territory by radically grounding such alternative conceptualizations in the concrete bodies and spaces of ordinary life (Berman-Arévalo 2021; Cabnal 2010; Paredes 2010; Proceso de Comunidades Negras-Equipo Yembé and Gaidepac 2018; Zaragocin 2020). What becomes clear is the inseparability between bodies and territories, the need to understand the body as a fundamental agent in the making of land and territory, and the importance of practices and spaces of social reproduction in shaping the politics of rural space. In what follows, this chapter adds to this conversation by focusing on the emplaced and embodied geographies of knowledge making itself. I draw on Nishnaabeg Indigenous scholar and activist Leanne Simpson's (2014) writings on "Land as Pedagogy," which shift attention to the materialities of land epistemologies and open questions on the political possibilities of alternative land epistemologies in material contexts of dispossession.

Simpson conceives land as the condition of possibility for Indigenous learning to occur. Land is both context and the process of learning itself.

Indigenous epistemology is not only deeply relational, rooted in intersubjective relations between humans and more-than-humans, but it is also clearly grounded in *place*. Developed in the context of ongoing settler colonialism and dispossession, Simpson's work is an invitation to grapple with difficult questions around the relationship between place, land epistemology, and politics. How can we speak of land epistemologies if land is under threat or no longer available? How do land-based epistemologies become a political practice in the face of dispossession? And what is the role of place in shaping the political potential of land epistemologies? In what follows, I reflect on these questions based on a story of a place called Leticia, a village water well that for years was women's favorite gathering place (Berman-Arevalo and Valdivia 2022). In Leticia, the task of fetching water became a time of sociability, laughter, relaxation, and storytelling. Knowledge making in Leticia was an embodied collective practice that was situated in the material, symbolic, affective, and social conditions of a place that was coming to an end.

LETICIA

Against my initial assumptions when I heard women speak about Leticia, Leticia is not a woman but a water well. Its name is symbolic of the relationship between women and the spaces of everyday social reproduction in agrarian settings. As the story goes, many years ago, a woman from the neighboring town of Playón named Leticia discovered the well while harvesting rice in the neighboring fields. After realizing she had forgotten her bucket of water, Leticia walked and walked until she encountered the spring's humid walls. She was so thirsty that she dug and dug until the spring started "crying" crystal-clear waters. Upon her return to Playón, Leticia told others in the community about the well's existence. They decided to name it after the woman who had discovered it with great effort as she walked the land.

Located approximately one kilometer from the village of Paloaltico and surrounded by palm oil plantations, Leticia was clearly under threat. The well lay on lands that had once been claimed by the village's local land-occupation committee, but after the advent of paramilitary violence, the land was claimed by a new landowner, who immediately planted oil palm. The new owner of the lands surrounding Leticia allowed locals to continue using the spring, however it was clear that their presence was unwelcome. Soon after its privatization, fencing was reinforced, and every so often, plantation security guards would leave garbage in its waters to dissuade women from using it. Palm roots then covered the spring's natural walls and dried out its water, which everyone knew must be contaminated by the heavy use of pesticides in surrounding fields. Once measuring two meters in diameter, Leticia was now less than half its original size. The majority of the trees surrounding the well, which women knew were fundamental for its replenishment, had been cut down for the establishment of palm oil trees. It was clear that this important living space of stories and social life would soon disappear.

On my first visit to Leticia, *tía* Luz María, was the lively protagonist of that day's storytelling. Speaking about the place, she told us,

> Imagine, when we first started coming here. It was Eloisa, Margarita, Pocho, a bunch of us young women, cutting creole palm and timber. Not this [industrial] palm, no, but the creole one, the kind that we use for our hair or for making the brooms. Right here is where my dad had his plot, right here in this piece of land we're sitting on! First, he would plant corn, then rice, and more rice. Higher up, he planted plantain. And further on was Carlitos Blanco's plot, then Danielito's. This was amazing. All of this was rice fields. It was real pretty before.

Luz María, now in her sixties, went on to talk about her adventures as a young woman. She and her friends would spend hours in the bush, gathering oil and timber, fishing in the small springs, or cutting rice:

> We were brave. We went anywhere in the bush. We weren't scared of nothin'. . . . That's why one time I was attacked by the African bees, ha ha ha. I was walking with Silvia's son [laughs] and I saw those bees. I tell you, I took off so fast I don't know where I left my sandals. We arrived at a lemon tree, and lemme tell you, I'm lookin' at all those lemons, wondering how I'm gonna reach them and another African bee flies over my head and stings me on the back. Oh man, I'm telling you, I had to spend all night taking out all that sting. . . .
>
> It's not that I didn't like the house, but I liked walking, being out here. . . . When we went out to cut rice, we spent all day here, we really enjoyed it. After two or so in the afternoon, we'd go back home. We went out walking, Aunt Dominga, mama, Francisca, Ida . . . it was a lot of women. We brought our water buckets, our cigarettes, and we talked and talked. Cutting rice was hard work, but we made it fun. We tended a cloth further on by the fields, and the rice we cut, we threw, blum, blum. Then we stepped on it and cleaned it, laughing and talking and telling stories. (Leticia spring, February 2, 2015)

Stories like Luz María's were told at Leticia daily, often in the form of collective conversation. The experience of Leticia's imminent end and the symbolic and material conditions of land in these circumstances shaped the knowledge practices that occurred in and with this place. Here, as in Simpson's work, place was not only an emplaced locale but also a set of social and socionatural relations, where water—the material basis of life itself—was entangled with gendered sociabilities and knowledges and sedimented layers of racialized dispossession.

Placing land epistemologies in Leticia allows us to reflect on epistemologies as collective political practices that are configured in relation to the concrete yet multidimensional and multitemporal conditions of place. Leticia brings to the fore the importance of considering the materiality of contamination, erosion, or enclosure, as this materiality (as part of the land itself) participates in relational knowledge making. Leticia's dire physical conditions were constant reference points in stories, as women complained about its drying waters and speculated about future alternatives for accessing clean water. Materiality was a crass reminder that dispossession—although piecemeal and everyday—is a matter of physical survival. Further, the experience of collectively witnessing the slow death of a place that was so central for both physical survival and women's everyday social life imbued stories in Leticia with an affective dimension marked by anguish and uncertainty and, at the same time, by joy and nostalgia, as women evoked memories of walking the land.

Symbolically, Leticia had been the possibility of creating cracks of Black social life within a territorial regime that was based on its erasure, exclusion, and expulsion. For Black women in particular, it was also the possibility of experiencing care and social reproduction as practices of freedom, nurturance, enjoyment, and collective knowledge making (hooks 1991). At the same time, its demise materialized the layered oppressions that enabled its current state: structural racism and its epistemic erasures; the devaluation of Black life; and the impossibility of being heard. It is against this backdrop that stories decidedly repositioned women as geographic agents with epistemic authority. The constant references to being knowers and walkers of the land reflected a particular political stance toward the current situation. As argued by geographer Carolyn Finney, writing from an African American context, emplaced stories of land were a way of saying, "We were there," and "We are here now" (Finney 2014, 55).

Finally, land epistemologies in Leticia conjugated multiple and entangled temporalities: histories of racialized dispossession written on the land; an evocation of a past of land-based social life; the slowness of the well's death; and a sense of uncertainty about the future. These different temporalities operated simultaneously and shaped the contents, the form, and the epistemological register of stories.

As I have argued before (Berman-Arévalo 2018), in the context of the spatial exclusions brought about by current agro-capitalist expansion, stories become profoundly *territorial*. Stories in Leticia recognized the well as a disputed territory and made Leticia a site of Black women's territoriality. On the one hand, they revealed the ways in which women's everyday practices produced alternative territories by inhabiting land through everyday movements, socialities, and agrarian practices, symbolically and materially transforming spaces where dominant territorial regimes would otherwise limit local spatial agencies. On the other hand, stories themselves produced territory. Stories inscribed women's personal histories onto contemporary spaces of exclusion. Through the epistemological register of the ordinary, this threatened space was inscribed with the familiar, thereby enabling women to claim protagonism as geographic agents and to reclaim Leticia as their own. In this sense, stories were live spatial-political practices that shaped collective political subjectivities and granted political meaning to space. Thus, through storytelling practices performed by "knowers of the land," land acquired cultural, personal, *and* political meanings.

THE END OF LETICIA AND THE QUESTION OF DISPLACED LAND EPISTEMOLOGIES

Toward the end of 2015, I was informed that Leticia had disappeared. While women's stories had preemptively responded to its imminent demise, what followed after its physical disappearance was silence. The silence could be interpreted as a sign of passivity or acquiescence, as people grew accustomed to injustice and loss. Surely, an ex post facto reaction was limited, among other things, by the disappearance of the well, as it was itself a *place* of politics (Berman-Arévalo and Valdivia 2022). Rather than suggesting a tragic end to land-based epistemologies and politics, Leticia's end opens important questions and invites creative political alternatives. What happens to land epistemologies—and to their politics—when the places of knowledge making are no longer available?

Here, Leanne Simpson (2014) offers important insights. Simpson's work is not only a statement on the centrality of land for Nishnaabeg intelligence. She also offers a political horizon for what she calls *cultural resurgence* based on the recreation of the conditions within which Indigenous learning occurred. She is writing in the context of the very real effects of settler colonial dispossession, which implies that many Indigenous peoples live in urban settings and away from their stolen lands. Under these conditions, recreating Indigenous land epistemologies requires challenging settler colonial-spatial ontologies that fix place onto a location and dissect, in her words, "our territories and our bodies into reserve/city or rural/urban dichotomies" (Simpson 2014, 23). Place here is understood *expansively*, for the land is inseparable from the context of family, community, and relations (L. Simpson 2014, 7), and it is by recreating the latter that it becomes possible to in turn recreate emplaced epistemologies (even in urban contexts) while reclaiming stolen lands.

Simpson opens political avenues, which are not free of challenges. In the case of Black campesino communities, these challenges are related to the importance of material places in enabling sociabilities and relations; these places must be recreated and reimagined under current conditions. This is in fact occurring, as kitchens or backyards gain more importance for women's sociabilities and knowledge sharing. The second, perhaps more difficult, challenge has to do with the fact that, as Verónica Gago (2020) writes, agrarian extractivism must be understood in an *expansive* sense. It is not only physical resources that are extracted but also communal relations and collective solidarities (Gago 2020). This is particularly true in communities recently enrolled in agrarian capitalism under increasingly precarious relations of labor and land. Despite these challenges, women in the community are actively recreating places and practices of collective work and solidarity; while the effects of precarity and dispossession make everyday life increasingly challenging, stories of life with the land continue to be told, resisting displacement while suffering its effects.

Decolonial geographers Michelle Daigle and Margaret Ramírez (2019) propose the idea of "constellations" as a spatial concept that highlights the interconnected character of ongoing decolonial struggles. Constellations, they write, "are in formation all around us, re-envisioning and re-embodying a politics of place by interweaving spatial practices of resistance, refusal and liberation" (Daigle and Ramírez 2019). In the case of Black communities in Montes de María, the recreation of place-based land epistemologies increasingly entails this creative reconstruction of a politics of place. This is a multisite process that involves individuals now living in urban settings; others living in the village with little access to land; others who—with great effort—manage to still walk the land; and a set of external actors, like academics and nongovernmental organization representatives who also participate in these struggles. The role of academics is particularly relevant precisely because of its potential to call attention to land-based knowledge practices and propose epistemic conversations in which Black campesino knowledges are engaged as political, theoretical, and transformative practices. I end with a short story on how my own knowledge production entered into a productive constellation in formation through cyberspace.

A couple weeks ago, I was tagged on three posts made by my friend Duváń on his Facebook page. Duván, twenty-four, is from Paloaltico. He was able to study audiovisual production in the state capital, Cartagena, and currently lives in a regional city on Colombia's Caribbean coast, though he visits his hometown regularly. He and I are members of a collective that thinks through questions of land, culture, and social justice in Marialabaja. To my surprise, Duván had posted excerpts of an article published in 2019 where I discussed Black refusal to state-led agrarian reform in the 1970s. Based largely on the memories and knowledge of village elders, I had refuted the widespread idea that locals had rejected land titling based on their ignorance and their docility.

Duván's grandfather and great-grandmother were quoted extensively in the excerpts posted on his Facebook page; perhaps for this reason, and because he understood the article's political purpose, he also tagged his eight siblings and cousins in his posts. I am unsure of what happened next, but I assume at the very least that they read and commented on it. This minor cyberevent may seem inconsequential, yet it speaks of how academia participates in the translation of place-based land epistemologies. These translations can become politically productive conversations that can travel and be reemplaced as they reach younger generations through cyberspace. These, too, are the contemporary emplacements and displacements of land epistemologies whose politics can be rerouted to support the struggle for Black land, territory, and rural life itself.

CONCLUSION

This chapter situates the epistemologies of land in the concrete spatial-temporal conjuncture of Leticia, a dying water well surrounded by agro-industrial oil palm plantations in the Colombian Caribbean. Based on the recreation of women's stories told at the well itself, the chapter discusses the political purchase of Black women's storytelling as counternarratives to the colonial and ongoing epistemic erasure of Black spatialities. At the same time, it stresses the importance of taking seriously the materialities of epistemological practices as they shape the content and the politics of women's narratives of land and territory. In the case of Leticia, the precarity of contamination and erosion, the sense of the well's imminent death, and the material and symbolic importance of unstoppable oil palm encroachment imbued stories with particular epistemological politics: stories became a way of grappling with an uncertain future and claiming a sense of territorial agency and epistemic authority in the context of racialized dispossession.

The land epistemologies discussed in the chapter are not only primordially ways of *representing* land but also the situated material, social, and symbolic relationships that shape a subject's knowledge-making practices through and about land. In this sense, this chapter is an invitation to take seriously the spatialities and materialities of land epistemologies and to think about the politics of emplaced knowledges in the context of globalized capitalist dispossession. If emplacing land stories is central for reclaiming Black geographic agency and decolonizing academic narratives on rural space, current global conditions push community members, scholars, practitioners, and activists to collectively find ways of re-placing land epistemologies in ways that are politically conducive to the material and symbolic struggle for land justice.

NOTES

1. Translated as "peasant," the contemporary notion of campesino in the Latin American context extends beyond a class-based analysis; rather it constitutes a flexible identity category that generally expresses an intergenerational relationship with the land, nature, and family and community agriculture, as well as rural life (Forero Álvarez 2002; Lederach 2017), and whose territorialities, subjectivities, and political repertoires are in permanent construction (Hoffman 2016; Ojeda and González 2018).

2. The municipality of Marialabaja has one of the highest rates of expansion of oil palm plantations in the country (Fedepalma 2011). Between 2001 and 2012, the area planted in oil palm plantations in Marialabaja grew by 1.35 percent, expanding from 570 hectares in 2001 to 8,310 hectares in 2012 (Secretaría de Agricultura de Bolívar 2012), while the national rate of growth for the same period was 174 percent (Fedepalma 2011). By 2015, this area had almost doubled to 11,022 hectares.

REFERENCES

Berman-Arévalo, Eloisa. 2018. "Making Space in the 'Territorial Cracks': Afro-Campesino Politics of Land and Territory in the Colombian Caribbean." PhD diss., University of North Carolina at Chapel Hill.

———. 2019. "El 'fracaso ruinoso' de la reforma agraria en clave de negridad: comunidades afrocampesinas y reconocimiento liberal en Montes de María, Colombia." *Memorias: Revista Digital de Historia y Arqueología desde el Caribe* 37: 117–49. https://doi.org/10.14482/memor.37.986.105.

———. 2021. "Geografías Negras del Arroz en el Caribe Colombiano: *Tongueo* y Cuerpo Territorio 'en las grietas' de la modernización agrícola." *Latin American and Caribbean Ethnic Studies*: 1–19. https://doi.org/10.1080/17442222.2021.2009638.

Berman-Arévalo, Eloisa, and Gabriela Valdivia. 2022. "The rhythms of 'acostumbrarse': Noticing quiet hydro-politics in Colombia's Caribbean coast."*Environment and Planning D: Society and Space* 40 (5): 483–461. https://journals.sagepub.com/doi/abs/10.1177/02637758221118571

Cabnal, Lorena. 2010. *Feminismos Diversos: El Feminismo Comunitario*. Madrid: ACSUR—Las Segovias.

Colectivo Miradas Críticas del Territorio desde el Feminismo. 2014. *La Vida en el Centro y el Crudo Bajo Tierra: El Yasuní en Clave Feminista*. Quito, Ecuador: Colectivo Miradas Críticas del Territorio desde el Feminismo.

Daigle, Michelle, and Margaret Marietta Ramírez. 2019. "Decolonial Geographies." In *Keywords in Radical Geography: Antipode at 50*, edited by the Antipode Editorial Collective, 78–84. Hoboken, NJ: Wiley Blackwell.

Escobar, Arturo. 2008. *Territories of Difference: Place, Movements, Life, Redes*. Durham, NC: Duke University Press.

Finney, Carolyn. 2014. *Black Faces, White Spaces: Reimagining the Relationship of African Americans to the Great Outdoors*. Chapel Hill: University of North Carolina Press.

Forero Álvarez, Jaime. 2002. *La Economía Campesina Colombiana, 1990–2001*. Bogotá, Colombia: Instituto Latinoamericano de Servicios Legales Alternativos.

Gago, Verónica. 2020. *Feminist International: How to Change Everything*. Translated by Liz Mason-Deese. London: Verso.

Halvorsen, Sam. 2019. "Decolonising Territory: Dialogues with Latin American Knowledges and Grassroots Strategies." *Progress in Human Geography* 43 (5): 790–814. https://doi.org/10.1177/0309132518777623.

hooks, bell. 1991. *Homeplace: A Site of Resistance*. London: Turnaround.

Ingold, Tim. 2010. *Bringing Things Back to Life: Creative Entanglements in a World of Materials*. NCRM working paper, Realities/Morgan Centre, University of Manchester, Manchester, UK. http://eprints.ncrm.ac.uk/1306/.

Lederach, Angela J. 2017. "'The *Campesino* Was Born for the *Campo*': A Multispecies Approach to Territorial Peace in Colombia." *American Anthropologist* 119 (4): 589–602.

Li, Tania Murray. 2014. *Land's End: Capitalist Relations on an Indigenous Frontier*. Durham, NC: Duke University Press.

McKittrick, Katherine. 2006. *Demonic Grounds: Black Women and the Cartographies of Struggle*. Minneapolis: University of Minnesota Press.

———. 2011. "On Plantations, Prisons, and a Black Sense of Place." *Social and Cultural Geography* 12 (8): 947–63. https://doi.org/10.1080/14649365.2011.624280.

Paredes, Julieta. 2010. *Hilando Fino desde el Feminismo Comunitario*. La Paz: Creative Commons.

Porto Gonçalves, Carlos Walter. 2002. "Da Geografia ás Geo-grafias: Um Mundo em Busca de Novas Territorialidades." In *La Guerra Infinita: Hegemonía y Terror Mundial*, compiled by Ana Esther Ceceña and Emir Sader, 217–56. Buenos Aires: CLACSO.

Proceso de Comunidades Negras-Equipo Yembé and Gaidepac. 2018. *Ubuntu: Una Invitación para Comprender la Acción Política, Cultural y Ecológica de las Resistencias Afroandina y Afropacífica*. Buenos Aires: CLACSO. https://doi.org/10.2307/j.ctvn5tznb.

Simpson, Audra. 2014. *Mohawk Interruptus: Political Life across the Borders of Settler States*. Durham, NC: Duke University Press.

Simpson, Leanne. 2014. "Land as Pedagogy: Nishnaabeg Intelligence and Rebellious Transformation." *Decolonization: Indigeneity, Education and Society* 3 (3): 1–25.

Taussig, Michael. 1980. *The Devil and Commodity Fetishism in South America*. Chapel Hill: University of North Carolina Press.

Tuhiwai-Smith, Linda. 1999. *Decolonizing Methodologies: Research and Indigenous Peoples*. London: Zed Books.

Zaragocin, Sofía. 2020. "La Geopolítica del Útero: Hacia una Geopolítica Feminista Decolonial en Espacios de Muerte Lenta." In *Cuerpos, Territorios y*

Feminismos: Compilación Latinoamericana de Teorías, Metodologías y Prácticas Políticas, edited by Delmy Tania Cruz Hernández and Manuel Bayón Jiménez, 83–99. Quito, Ecuador: Abya-Yala, Instituto de Estudios Ecologistas del Tercer Mundo, Bajo Tierra Ediciones, and Libertad Bajo Palabra.

Chapter 5

What's in a Land Grab?

Knowing Dispossession and Land in Southeast Europe

Katarina Kušić

In 2018, the Agricultural Combine Belgrade (Poljoprivredni kombinat Beograd, PKB) was sold after a decade of debates around its privatization. The sale controversially included more than 17,000 hectares of agricultural land that PKB was using. It was a part of a larger set of investments by the United Arab Emirates in Serbia that, besides the notorious Belgrade Waterfront, included the defense industries, an airline, and agriculture.[1] All of these were criticized for lack of transparency and corruption. Investigative journalists questioned the process in which state land that cannot be sold legally was transformed into PKB ownership and then privatized (Stanković 2021). Former employees and pensioners are still contesting the lack of payment for their own earned shares, and the state stepped in to accommodate the diverse requests through similarly nontransparent payments (Kušić and Lazić 2022). Despite these manifold issues, the sale was concluded legally and definitively. Both the working conditions and animal welfare at the farms have been criticized in national media. The people I spoke to told me of generational attachments to this land that was taken from the swamp and turned into a shining example of Yugoslav agricultural modernism: peasants moved here from all over Yugoslavia to become workers, and it is not uncommon for three generations in a family to have lived in and from PKB employment.

In Bosnia and Herzegovina in 2017 and 2018, women from nearby villages occupied a bridge in Kruščica for more than five hundred days and successfully stopped the development of two small hydropower plants. This was part of a larger Balkan mobilization against hydropower developments that endanger river flows and landscapes and dramatically change local communities. A diverse constellation of local actors, "[f]rom Bulgarian fishermen to Montenegrin cyclists, Albanian villagers, and Serbian mountaineers" (Rajković 2020), were joined by both international nongovernmental organizations (NGOs) and global brands like Patagonia to save the "Blue Heart of Europe."[2] The role of the European Union in the process of hydropower development in Bosnia and Herzegovina and the Balkans more broadly is ambiguous. It was the European Green Deal that served as a catalyst for development of hydro as green energy, and it was the European Bank for Reconstruction and Development (alongside other foreign banks operating in the region) that funded the initiatives. Paradoxically, it is also EU regulation—especially in the case of Serbia, which holds a candidate status—that is seen as a tool of resistance and perhaps the only way of stopping the developments long term (Pešić and Vukelić 2022).

These protests gave rise to what Ivan Rajković refers to as "ecopopulist universality" in the Balkan mountains and beyond: an insurrection that rallies around the environment as a sort of a "hypersubject" or "flawed universality" and brings together people who are differently incorporated into the dynamics of green capitalism (Rajković 2022a, 2022b). The same universality was present in the more recent (2022) mobilizations against Rio Tinto's plans for lithium mining in Serbia. In these mobilizations, land generally and agricultural land specifically feature prominently. In a letter to Porfirije, the patriarch of the Serbian Orthodox Church, Bojana Novaković, actor and one of the coordinators of *Marš sa Drine*, the organization mobilizing against mining plans, wrote, "[C]ommitting a crime against nature, [against] those who take care of it and produce food to feed our compatriots, is a terrible sin" (*Danas* 2022). Agricultural land and those working it thus become sacred—a peculiar position in a region where *seljak* (peasant) is still considered an effective insult of a state of mind rather than a marker of a mode of production or a biography wedded to a rural space.

In the very different rural setting of Lubenice on the island of Cres in Croatia, people have been protesting, on a smaller scale, the development of a glamping site since the first plans reached the local community in 2020.[3] At a meeting in November 2020, where the developers were invited to present their plans to those concerned, people arrived from other villages on the island, from the regional centers, and from the capital. They worried about pressures on the village infrastructure—parking and the sewage system—and argued for keeping "that one thing" that brings tourists—Lubenice as it is now—intact.[4] During my short visit in 2021, the situation was unclear: several houses were already sold to the investors; the cable car that would connect the hillside with the beach was confirmed to indeed exist in the zoning plans; and there were fears and speculations about possible Russian sources of the capital for the investment. In this debate, agriculture and the sheep that provided for the community prior to tourism are seen as both a development opportunity and a hardship that marks those living on the island.

These seemingly unrelated events point to land and the diverse political, ecological, and socioeconomic relations that turn it into a contested site. While not all these contestations are framed around environmental issues—the sale of PKB did not mobilize green activists, and the damage of the proposed glamping site in Lubenice is seen as hurting particular visions of heritage—they all happen around land: relations between humans and soils that turn particular coordinates into property that can be owned, a resource that can be used, and an object of policy that can be governed. It can also be said that all these events are about the control of land and different forms of dispossession. Some, like the PKB sale, fit the concept of land grabbing traditionally understood, while others move through lines that are less clear-cut. In this chapter, I argue that understanding the political, economic, and ecological consequences of these transformations requires turning our attention on both these dimensions—land and dispossession—as objects of knowing.

In the first section, I re-visit the concept of land grabbing and investigate how it can help us better understand changing land relations in the Balkans and ways in which this space can contribute to further development of the concept. While the concept of land grabbing is not easily defined and usually depends on criteria like foreign origin of the capital or size of the investment, here I build on a looser understanding of it as "capturing control of extended tracts of land" (van der Ploeg, Franco, and Borras 2015, 152). I do not argue that traditionally understood land grabbing captures all the dynamics mentioned previously, as some obviously do not even directly involve agricultural land. But I show how the fact of land being on the move, whether toward a concentrated model of farming fit for the EU Common Agricultural Policy (CAP) or touristification, can be illuminated by the concept (and the literature born out of it) and help develop it further. This section highlights the productive possibilities of the land-grab lens. In activist and policy discussion, it may help articulate an alternative and inclusionary vision for development. In scholarly work, it can both benefit from and add to a more nuanced understanding of some of the binaries that usually structure land-grabbing and investment narratives.

Even though the concept of land grabbing can help us understand these events better, great potential also lies beyond its epistemological frames. In the second section of the chapter, I argue for expanding our view in two ways. I first use Alexander Vorbrugg's (2019) work to consider different analytics of *dispossession*. This reorientation moves away from spectacular dispossession that land-grabbing literature and activism deal with, and pays attention to the slow decay so prevalent in postsocialist rural spaces. And second, I draw on my ongoing work on relational understanding of land in Southeast Europe to similarly consider different dimensions of *land* (Kušić 2022a). This section connects studies of land grabbing with the broader efforts to understand the ever-changing relations between humans and their environments. I thus discuss technologies and built environments, different forms of human and more-than-human community making, and varied knowledges and practices that reside in and on land. In these two moves—thinking with and beyond the concept of land grabbing—land emerges not only as a matter of subsistence and market relations but also as a site of social and more-than-human life.

WHAT'S IN A LAND GRAB?

Using land grabbing as a concept in policy, activism, and scholarly work creates a particular metanarrative. Activists use it as a "stable concept for strategic purposes, creating significant impact and attention for the problems raised" (Goetz 2021, 351). The scholarly debate, however, "revolves around deconstruction and decentring of the meta-narrative" (Goetz 2021, 351). This metanarrative, however, did not 'stick' in Southeast Europe, as land grabbing did not become a rallying cry of activists nor a focus of researchers working in or on Southeast Europe.[5] Even when protests against hydropower development and lithium extraction gained wide traction and ushered in what is increasingly recognized as a new era of environmental activism in the region, they remained separate from processes that concentrated agricultural land and reshaped ownership relations in the last three decades.

Cases from Serbia are routinely included in the large Land Matrix and GRAIN databases and reports. Milenko Srećković, activist and researcher, made important inroads in early 2010s by connecting issues of land sale and privatization in Serbia to transnational peasant struggles through La Vía Campesina.[6] A strong peasant movement, however, did not emerge. Large acquisitions in Serbia—especially those conducted under the auspices of the deal with the United Arab Emirates—brought farmers to the streets, but they did not attract attention of civil society (outside of farmers' associations) or urban activists who have the resources to connect them further to transnational social movements and governance. While quick "killer facts" (Oya 2013) can be problematic when inaccurate or unconfirmed, the relative silence around the attempts to create them in the Yugoslav space is confounding.[7]

In addition to being an opportunity for political mobilization, land grabbing as a conceptual lens might also be able to frame existing contestation in more progressive terms. East Europe is habitually described as an important part of the global move to exclusionary populism, where environment, agriculture, and land come together. In Hungary, for example, rural and agricultural issues are framed in a binary way: either as a part of global environmentalism or in exclusionary politics that romanticize the homeland, which needs defending (Lubarda 2020). In my own research on land grabbing in Serbia, I found that some participants who were a part of the initial mobilization around land ownership in the early 2010s went on to join or implicitly support far-right options in Serbia. This tension in frames through which investment dynamics are understood is discussed at length in relation to the antilithium protests in Serbia. Some call for the Left to lead and suppress the right-wing political options that increasingly hijack the resistance to the investment plans (Kojanić 2022), while others see the new alliances as an opportunity for the Left to not only lead but also learn (Rajković 2022a, 2022b). The land-grabbing framework here presents a possibility for *political* action in deciding how the dramatic crises of today will be understood and mobilized.

In parallel to the lack of concern for land grabbing in mainstream media and political organizing, significant attention of researchers also did not materialize. While the phenomenon is recognized in local academic publications (Šljukić and Šljukić 2019), in-depth studies are nonexistent. Parramore and Webb (2021), for example, "reject the neoliberal Balkan land grab hypothesis" by self-admittedly focusing on urban contexts exclusively, although the literature they refer to comes primarily from cases of agricultural and rural land acquisitions. Their conclusion that EU policies are not related to land grabs is indicative of a narrow understanding of effects that includes only direct policies and ignores the larger and less direct impact of the European Union on land markets.[8] Others, like Mandacı and Tutan (2018), while adding a valuable historical perspective, suffer the same problems as "early" land-grab studies described by Carlos Oya (2013). They lack complex data and ultimately reproduce tropes of big versus small and domestic versus foreign that plague the land-grab literature more broadly and do not fit the contexts in Serbia and the Yugoslav space.

These cases from the Balkans also help complicate the metanarrative of land grabbing. For example, they cannot be explained through the narrative of weak states and powerful investors, but they offer a window into the complex interplay of the local state and elites and transnational and international capital (see Wolford et al. 2013). The privatization of PKB to Al Dahra did not require only state approval but also the convoluted machinations that turned land that was until then only *used* by PKB into its property available for sale (Stanković 2021). The meeting point of Gulf capital and local enthusiasm for it can only be understood when seen as both a technique of validation for local elites that rely on narratives of "good investors" bringing prosperity (Kušić 2022b; Prelec 2020) and a further restructuring of global markets in which "non-Western" actors take prominent roles (Bartlett et al. 2017; Todorova 2018).

The role of international actors is similarly complex. For example, the European Union considers agricultural land a national issue and does not include it in the vast bundle of legislative changes completed during the accession period (besides forbidding any restrictions that would prevent the free movement of capital).[9] Yet it is abundantly clear that the European Union, or CAP's per-hectare payments more precisely, makes agricultural land an EU issue: the rise in land prices, the disappearance of small producers, and the competition in the single market have profoundly reshaped new member states that do not fit the EU "family farm" model, often helping land concentration and land grabbing (Franco and Borras 2013; van der Ploeg, Franco, and Borras 2015).

Outside agriculture as well, EU policies move alongside and within global capital markets: the proposed mines that would replace fields in western Serbia in search of lithium can only be understood through Serbia's semiperipheral position in the global economy. The plans themselves are an embodiment of "ecological imperialism" that would bring ore necessary for the green transition to the European Union's doorstep and that is sustained by international law (Matković 2022). This positioning complicates the north-south division through which international politics are commonly understood (see Müller 2020) and can contribute to more nuanced discussions of land grabbing and ecological economics "from the margins" (see Hanaček et al. 2020).

In addition to states and elites, these examples build onto increasingly sophisticated understandings of the complexities of responses and resistances to land deals. Based on her work in Ukraine, Mamonova (2015) shows how local responses to land grabbing do not fit the binaries of the land-grabbing framework: local residents do not *inherently* oppose land deals; they are able to coexist with industrial agriculture in a myriad of ways; and when they do oppose land acquisitions, they are more motivated by personal interests than concerns for the peasant way of life, land and food sovereignty, or ecological matters. Similar dynamics can be observed in the Yugoslav cases, as well, not least due to some similarities in the (post)socialist experiences.

WHAT'S BESIDES THE LAND GRAB?

So far, I have argued that the land-grabbing concept is productive in the context of land politics transformations in the Yugoslav space in two ways: (1) as a lens that can help better understand these dynamics and articulate their political importance and (2) as a concept that can be further fruitfully developed by thinking about it from this space. But the epistemological potential of land also pushes against the boundaries of this concept. In this section, I thus propose different ways to extend understandings of its constitutive parts: dispossession and land.

Rethinking Dispossession

Vorbrugg (2019) draws on observations from Russia to reconceptualize rural dispossession. In discussions of land grabbing (and critical agrarian studies more generally), dispossession has specific conceptual underpinnings: "Dispossession here is about land, manifests itself through eventful grabs, and is particularly critical because of farmland's existential role for rural livelihoods" (Vorbrugg 2019, 4). In contrast, Vorbrugg found that dispossession is not always about land but about a variety of "supporting and sustaining relations" in processes of "slow, silent and creeping deterioration" (Vorbrugg 2019, 1026). This leads him to reconceptualize dispossession toward "dispersed dispossession" consisting of four analytical dimensions: objects, modes, subjectivities, and temporalities. In Yugoslav rural spaces, spectacular dispossessions that would fill the websites of NGOs working against land grabbing are similarly lacking. But the slow decay is always there.

In an expanded understanding of dispossession, the *objects* of analyses go beyond farmland because owning or using farmland is often not the primary or the most important issue (Vorbrugg 2019, 1022–23). In the case of PKB, the workers never *owned* the land to begin with—as is the case with Ukrainian and Russian contexts. And beyond issues of ownership, other objects appear: the "products" of socialist agricultural combines and enterprises are not limited to monetary rewards or subsistence, as they provided "extended everyday life" for its employees and the wider community (Djokić, Milovanović, and Ristić Trajković 2020, 451). These institutions were not just employers but also "represented the orbits of the entire social life of the majority of the population" (Radenković and Solar 2018, 165). This everyday life is dramatically reconfigured when combines are sold, but it has also been reshaped by decades of postsocialist restructuring that paved the way for privatizations to be concluded.

Vorbrugg's second analytical dimension is the different *modes* through which dispersed dispossession functions. Here, he focuses on two particular postsocialist processes that can be observed in the Yugoslav space, as well: "[t]he disintegration of structures and infrastructures necessary for the realisation of resource potential, and the historic devaluation and structural disadvantage of the entire agricultural and rural sphere" (Vorbrugg 2019, 1023). While these dynamics in Yugoslavia have been addressed in writing (Diković 2014, 2021; Naumović 2013; Obad 2021; Thiemann 2014, 2017,

2020), there are also processes that do not just erase value but also reconfigure it in ways that profoundly change land relations.

On Cres, for example, the resistance to the glamping development was shaped by the fact that the village—as well as the island and the broader region—depends on tourism. In never-ending conversations about revitalization and the urgency of "saving the village from depopulation," it is difficult to imagine any kind of development that would be outside of tourism.[10] In such a context, might not (more) sustainable tourism—as the glamping project presents itself to be—be the answer? What might be the role of peasants, or small-scale food productions more generally, in such a system? Moreover, value can be reconfigured in the process of resisting land grabbing. The village of Topli Do in Serbia—one of the early successes of the movement against hydropower—rebranded itself as an ecotourist destination and refrained from shaping the struggle for the rivers further (Rajković 2022a). Researchers interested in making sense of land on the move thus have to account for not only the value lost in the agricultural sphere but also how the sale of land changes and forms new class and identity lines.

The third analytical dimension of dispersed dispossession points to the *subjectivities of those who were supposedly* "independent and unharmed subjects" before the grab (Vorbrugg 2019, 1025). Across postsocialist Eurasia, the figure of a peasant is more complex than usually imagined: the distinctions between rural and semiurban producers are blurred to say the least, and they live alongside large farms, often in symbioses with them (Mamonova 2015; Visser et al. 2019; Visser, Kuns, and Jehlička 2021). Many residents are guided by their own interests rather than ecological or political ideals when they do contest land sales. A challenge for researchers is to refrain from dismissing these acts as selling out or falling prey to false consciousness and theorize ways in which complex political subjecthoods are engaged by land deals that reach from group to transnational politics (see Rajković 2022a, 2022b).

And finally, dispersed dispossession points to different *temporalities*: instead of spectacle or a singular act that can be pinpointed, we encounter slow processes of change (Vorbrugg 2019, 1025–26). In the Yugoslav case, these are shaped by both the failures and successes of socialism. Many families who participate in these processes—whether as landowners or as laborers—have bitter histories of collectivization and rebellion against it (Bokovoy 1998). Others are stories of successes of socialist egalitarianism and development. Analyses of this late stage of transition that the region now finds itself in thus cannot rely on spectacle but must tease apart the long-lasting echoes of historical processes, driven both by socialism and the restoration of capitalism.

Rethinking Land

Scholars rarely engage with land conceptually on its own. Instead, we turn it into concepts like land grabbing, land markets, or land reforms. When authors do engage with it conceptually, they often refer to its materiality—it is fixed in quantity and location (Akram-Lodhi 2021, 72). Here I suggest three dimensions of land that can be investigated to expand our understandings of land: (1) technologies and built environments, (2) different forms of human and more-than-human community making, and (3) varied knowledges and practices that reside in and on land.

First, while we often imagine land in romanticized and romanticizing images of fertile-because-pristine landscapes, both land itself and our engagement with it are mediated through specific technologies. Whether these are the tools that helped drain the swamp that made the PKB fields, the batteries that need lithium safely stashed away in the composite mineral jadarite (that the Rio Tinto mining company compared to kryptonite) in western Serbia, or the pipes in which Balkan rivers are imagined flowing, rural landscapes are sites of modernism shaped by politics and ideologies. Investigating how those visions emerge and how they are enacted is crucial for understanding how land comes to be through a series of social relations. Understanding these relations can serve as a starting point for untangling the changes in land markets and prying open the visions of development that underlie them.

This also connects with the processes of dispersed dispossession discussed earlier. In addition to everyday lives, agricultural combines and enterprises in Yugoslavia also organized landscape, natural and built environments. Agricultural combines generally and PKB especially served as "spatial, social, economic and environmental and political entit[ies]" (Djokić, Milovanović, and Ristić Trajković 2020, 19). PKB shaped urban planning in and around Belgrade on multiple levels: not only in draining the swamp that became farmland but also in intimately affecting the urban development of Belgrade throughout its life. Controlling PKB, then, implies a role that far surpasses anything possibly imagined in neoliberal market narratives. With only these two examples in mind—how PKB shaped individual and social realities and how it participated in reshaping rural and urban landscapes—the urgency of going beyond land as a sole object of dispossession in these dynamics becomes dramatically visible.

Second, land is a site of community making. The idea that land grabs destroy communities is almost a given, yet there is surprisingly little about how those communities come to be and how they change in land-grabbing narratives. Yugoslavia is a dramatic example of the intricate ways in which ethnic belonging depends on territory (Leutloff-Grandits 2003, 2016) and ways in which landscapes can become sites of painful memories (Schäuble

2014). A most obvious question is how those ethnic relations are reconfigured in the changing land relations and vice versa. For example, my interlocutors in the ethnically mixed region of Vojvodina, where most large agricultural land acquisitions happen in Serbia, were clear about land markets working through ethnic lines. Do these established trends change with the introduction of new actors—both East and West?

Importantly, ideas of community and subjecthood should not be confined to ethnic territory (as is too often the case with scholarship on Yugoslavia). Azra Hromadžić (2022) wrote about ways in which the river Una in Bosnia and Herzegovina and its unique "sociality and materiality—its structure, smell, sounds, rock, and riverine worlds" make the town residents who they are. Moreover, in times of war, the river became a place of community making by allowing "swimmers to destabilize boundaries of their own person, to expose themselves to other swimmers, to move in sync, to coappear, and to 'stick' to each other" (Hromadžić 2022, 6). A river—and the land that makes its shores—then becomes a site of sociality beyond the human, where identities and unexpected experiences are forged. Instead of dispossession and suffering, we can thus stay open to rurality as spaces of joy and community making, not only to understand the present, but also to find strategies for alternative futures.

Third, both technologies and communities imply specific knowledge practices and traditions. The relationships to environments in East Europe are increasingly understood through the lens of quiet sustainability—"practices that result in beneficial environmental or social outcomes, that do not relate directly or indirectly to market transactions, and that are not represented by the practitioners as relating directly to environmental or sustainability goals" (Smith and Jehlička 2013, 155). Famously, these are practices of growing, preserving, and sharing food that are so common across postsocialist Eurasia and the global South. They remain misunderstood in the geopolitics of knowledge production that see them as remnants of obsolete traditions or by-products of (post)socialist hardships (Ančić, Domazet, and Župarić-Iljić 2019; Hanaček et al. 2020; Jehlička 2021; Jehlička, Ančić et al. 2021; Jehlička, Grīviņš et al. 2020). Another example are different practices of the commons—like the Eko Gajna pasturing community in Croatia that has survived centuries. In these experiments, longer histories—both socialist and presocialist—are brought together to respond to contemporary and future problems (Tomašević et al. 2018). What other types of quiet sustainability can be found in human-soil relations? Do these relations change in cases of land acquisitions? Can the articulation of resistance to land grabs serve as an impetus for excavating and preserving those practices? These are only some of the questions that can be posed within and around land grabs and the relations that make them.

CONCLUSION

This chapter looks at the potential and limitations of investigating the changing landscapes of control over land in Yugoslavia through the land-grabbing lens. I first note how the concept is productive in political action and in complicating the binaries that plague research on land grabs around the world. In the second section, I show how the concepts of dispossession and land can be expanded into new research agendas that investigate life on and with land. In pointing to dimensions of land that are not easily known through the land-grab framework, I am not so much providing an overview or critique of topics and blind spots of the now vast literature on land grabs (Edelman, Oya, and Borras 2013; Goetz 2021; Oya 2013; Vorbrugg 2019). Instead, I used the short examples in the introduction to offer possibly productive ways of knowing land (that is being grabbed) differently.

This serves a twofold purpose. First, if we are to understand the dynamics and consequences of land grabs, then we should understand what is at stake when *land* is grabbed. At stake are not just resources, markets, and subsistence but also ways of life—both social and more-than-human. While such considerations of land are more common in contexts of Indigenous communities and cosmologies that explicitly relate to landscapes, the absence of straightforwardly alternative cosmologies should not preclude researching land in multiple dimensions in diverse geographical areas, including postsocialist Eurasia. Spaces that are threatened or fall victim to various forms of grabbing are also sites where the multiplicity of the social life of soil can be observed and its entanglements with more-than-human relations made visible.

And second, such a broadening is also a move toward epistemic justice. While the conceptual broadening of dispossession is an undeniably productive way of thinking about rural change and land relations this entails, it remains bound to an image of rurality broadly as a space of suffering. Of course, rural spaces—especially in postsocialist countries—have been sites of dispersed (and spectacular) dispossession that continues to the present day. They are, however, also sites of life, knowledge, and creativity. This is not to romanticize (again) the peasant way of life or the bucolic landscapes supposedly found in rural areas but to encourage new ways of knowing land and the relations that make it.

NOTES

1. This relates to the controversial development of the Sava Riverbank in downtown Belgrade that was heavily protested (see Matković and Ivković 2018).

2. *Blue Heart* (Caillouette 2018), a film produced by Patagonia (clothing brand) that includes the story of defending Kruščica, is available online.

3. This relatively recent form of tourism combines glamour and comfort with camping and thus taps into both tourism and sustainability as key pillars of future tourism development.

4. The video of the meeting where the project was presented to the community was available online; now a copy is with me.

5. Of course, there are notable exceptions of both activists and researchers who engaged with the concept. I return to them throughout the text.

6. The Land Matrix Database monitors large-scale land acquisitions (LSLA-a). You can find the open-access platform at https://landmatrix.org.

GRAIN is an international nonprofit organization supporting farmers and social movement struggles for just and sustainable food systems. You can see some of their work on land at https://grain.org/en/category/537.

In June 2012, Freedom Fight (Pokret za slobodu) organized a conference with regional activists and representatives of La Vía Campesina (see Srećković and Bogićević 2013). For a more recent take on issues of food sovereignty in Serbia, see the publication prepared by Ama Center, *Food Sovereignty in Serbian Context: Food Production System Critical Analysis Framework* (Petrović 2019). For a reflection on some limitations of the food sovereignty movement in postsocialist Europe, see Hajdu and Mamonova (2020) on Romania, Visser et al. (2015) on Russia, and Mamonova (2018) on Ukraine.

7. A notable exception here is Branislav Gulan, journalist and activist who has been publicizing dramatic figures on agricultural land in Vojvodina for decades, to very little effect.

8. For their Bosnia and Herzegovina case study, Buroj Ozone, a much more comprehensive and illuminating treatment of EU presence is provided by Mirna Pedalo (2020).

9. In practice, this means that most member states then develop additional legislature to "discourage" foreign acquisition of agricultural land through non-nationality requirements: place of residence, experience of production, and so on (Roebeling et al. 2021).

10. In the most recent population census, Lubenice famously had only three residents. This, of course, does not account for the seasonality of life on the Adriatic islands. Winter 2021–2022 was notable in that it was the first winter where no one stayed in the village, with the old woman who persisted the longest admitting that she needed the help of her family and moved to another town on the island for the winter. In 2021, the story of the "last three residents" ran on national TV as the "saddest story of the day" (RTL 2021).

REFERENCES

Akram-Lodhi, A. H. 2021. "Land." In *Handbook of Critical Agrarian Studies*, edited by A. H. Akram-Lodhi, Kristina Dietz, Bettina Engels, and Ben M. McKay, 72–79. Cheltenham, UK: Edward Elgar. https://doi.org/10.4337/9781788972468.

Ančić, Branko, Mladen Domazet, and Drago Župarić-Iljić. 2019. "'For My Health and for My Friends': Exploring Motivation, Sharing, Environmentalism, Resilience and Class Structure of Food Self-Provisioning." *Geoforum* 106: 68–77. https://doi.org/10.1016/j.geoforum.2019.07.018.

Bartlett, Will, James Ker-Lindsay, Kristian Alexander, and Tena Prelec. 2017. "The UAE as an Emerging Actor in the Western Balkans: The Case of Strategic Investment in Serbia." *Journal of Arabian Studies* 7 (1): 94–112. https://doi.org/10.1080/21534764.2017.1322753.

Bokovoy, Melissa K. 1998. *Peasants and Communists: Politics and Ideology in the Yugoslav Countryside, 1941–1953*. Pittsburgh, PA: University of Pittsburgh Press.

Caillouette, Briton, dir. 2018. *Blue Heart*. Documentary. Patagonia. https://www.youtube.com/watch?v=OhmHByZ0Xd8.

Danas. 2022. "Bojana Novaković pisala Patrijarhu Porfiriju: Sačuvajte Crkvu i podržite narod koji odbija da proda imovinu." March 21, 2022. https://www.danas.rs/vesti/drustvo/bojana-novakovic-pisala-patrijarhu-porfiriju-sacuvajte-crkvu-i-podrzite-narod-koji-odbija-da-proda-imovinu-riotinto/.

Diković, Jovana. 2014. "Neither Peasant, nor Farmer: Transformations of Agriculture in Serbia after 2000." *Martor: Revue d'Anthropologie du Musée du Paysan Roumain* 19: 149–62.

———. 2021. "What Is Not Known about Rural Development? Village Experiences from Serbia." In *Politics and the Environment in Eastern Europe*, edited by Eszter Krasznai Kovács, 261–82. Cambridge, UK: Open Book.

Djokić, Vladan, Aleksandra Milovanović, and Jelena Ristić Trajković. 2020. "The Textuality of the Modernist Rural Landscape: Belgrade Agricultural Combine (PKB) as a Driver of the Urban Development of Third Belgrade." *Land* 9 (11): 1–24. https://doi.org/10.3390/land9110452.

Edelman, Marc, Carlos Oya, and Saturnino M. Borras. 2013. "Global Land Grabs: Historical Processes, Theoretical and Methodological Implications and Current Trajectories." *Third World Quarterly* 34 (9): 1517–31. https://doi.org/10.1080/01436597.2013.850190.

Franco, Jennifer, and Saturnino M. Borras, eds. 2013. *Land Concentration, Land Grabbing and People's Struggles in Europe*. Amsterdam: Transnational Institute.

Goetz, Ariane. 2021. "Land Grabs." In *Handbook of Critical Agrarian Studies*, edited by A. H. Akram-Lodhi, Kristina Dietz, Bettina Engels, and Ben M. McKay, 346–57. Cheltenham, UK: Edward Elgar. https://doi.org/10.4337/9781788972468.

Hajdu, Anna, and Natalia Mamonova. 2020. "Prospects of Agrarian Populism and Food Sovereignty Movement in Post-Socialist Romania." *Sociologia Ruralis* 60 (4): 880–904. https://doi.org/10.1111/soru.12301.

Hanaček, Ksenija, Brototi Roy, Sofia Avila, and Giorgos Kallis. 2020. "Ecological Economics and Degrowth: Proposing a Future Research Agenda from the

Margins." *Ecological Economics* 169: 106495. https://doi.org/10.1016/j.ecolecon.2019.106495.

Hromadžić, Azra. 2022. "Life in an Age of Death: War and the River in Bosnia and Herzegovina." *American Anthropologist* 124 (2): 263–78. https://doi.org/10.1111/aman.13710.

Jehlička, Petr. 2021. "Eastern Europe and the Geography of Knowledge Production: The Case of the Invisible Gardener." *Progress in Human Geography* 45 (5): 1218–36.

Jehlička, Petr, Branko Ančić, Petr Daněk, and Mladen Domazet. 2021. "Beyond Hardship and Joy: Framing Home Gardening on Insights from the European Semi-Periphery." *Geoforum* 126: 150–58. https://doi.org/10.1016/j.geoforum.2021.05.018.

Jehlička, Petr, Miķelis Grīviņš, Oane Visser, and Bálint Balázs. 2020. "Thinking Food like an East European: A Critical Reflection on the Framing of Food Systems." *Journal of Rural Studies* 76: 286–95. https://doi.org/10.1016/j.jrurstud.2020.04.015.

Kojanić, Ognjen. 2022. "Environmental Issues Spark Large-Scale Protests in Serbia." *LeftEast* (blog). January 31, 2022. https://lefteast.org/environmental-issues-spark-large-scale-protests-in-serbia/.

Kušić, Katarina. 2022a. "Land and Human-Soil Relations in Southeast Europe." *Connections: A Journal for Historians and Area Specialists*: 1–13.

———. 2022b. "Lessons for the 'Green' Transition: Learning from Cooperatives in Former Yugoslavia." *Le Club de Mediapart* (blog). February 18, 2022. https://blogs.mediapart.fr/berliner-gazette/blog/180222/lessons-green-transition-learning-cooperatives-former-yugoslavia.

Kušić, Katarina, and Sladjana Lazić. 2022. "Land on the Move: Inequality and Consolidation of Agricultural Land in Serbia." *LeftEast* (blog). March 11, 2022. https://lefteast.org/land-on-the-move-inequality-and-consolidation-of-agricultural-land-in-serbia/.

Leutloff-Grandits, Carolin. 2003. "Coping with Economic Devastation: Agriculture in Post-War Knin, Croatia." In *The Postsocialist Agrarian Question: Property Relations and the Rural Condition*, edited by Chris Hann, 143–70. Münster, Germany: LIT.

———. 2016. "Post-Dayton Ethnic Engineering in Croatia through the Lenses of Property Issues and Social Transformations." *Journal of Genocide Research* 18 (4): 485–502. https://doi.org/10.1080/14623528.2016.1230299.

Lubarda, Balša. 2020. "'Homeland Farming' or 'Rural Emancipation'? The Discursive Overlap between Populist and Green Parties in Hungary." *Sociologia Ruralis* 60 (4): 810–32. https://doi.org/10.1111/soru.12289.

Mamonova, Natalia. 2015. "Resistance or Adaptation? Ukrainian Peasants' Responses to Large-Scale Land Acquisitions." *Journal of Peasant Studies* 42 (3–4): 607–34. https://doi.org/10.1080/03066150.2014.993320.

———. 2018. "Patriotism and Food Sovereignty: Changes in the Social Imaginary of Small-Scale Farming in Post-Euromaidan Ukraine: Patriotism and Food Sovereignty." *Sociologia Ruralis* 58 (1): 190–212. https://doi.org/10.1111/soru.12188.

Mandacı, Nazif, and Mehmet Ufuk Tutan. 2018. "Global Land Grab and the Balkans: Continuity and Changes in a Unique Historical Context." *Journal of Balkan and Near Eastern Studies* 20 (3): 230–50. https://doi.org/10.1080/19448953.2018.1379754.

Matković, Aleksandar. 2022. "Why a New Form of Ecological Imperialism Is Developing in the Balkans." *Le Club de Mediapart* (blog). February 17, 2022. https://blogs.mediapart.fr/berliner-gazette/blog/170222/why-new-form-ecological-imperialism-developing-balkans.

Matković, Aleksandar, and Marjan Ivković. 2018. "Neoliberal Instrumentalism and the Fight against It: The 'We Won't Let Belgrade D(r)Own' Movement." *East European Politics* 34 (1): 27–38.

Müller, Martin. 2020. "In Search of the Global East: Thinking between North and South." *Geopolitics* 25 (3): 734–55. https://doi.org/10.1080/14650045.2018.1477757.

Naumović, Slobodan. 2013. *Fields of Paradox: Three Case Studies on the Europeanisation of Agriculture in Serbia*. Belgrade, Serbia: University of Belgrade, Faculty of Philosophy, SGC.

Obad, Orlanda. 2021. *Socioekonomske Nejednakosti Na Relaciji Selo-Grad [Socioeconomic Inequalities in the City-Village Relation]*. Zagreb, Croatia: Institut za etnologiju i folkloristiku.

Oya, Carlos. 2013. "Methodological Reflections on 'Land Grab' Databases and the 'Land Grab' Literature 'Rush.'" *Journal of Peasant Studies* 40 (3): 503–20. https://doi.org/10.1080/03066150.2013.799465.

Parramore, Sean, and Jonathan Webb. 2021. "Rejecting the Neoliberal Balkan Land Grab Hypothesis: The Absence of the EU's Transformative Power in Land Use Governance in Bosnia and Serbia." *Journal of Balkan and Near Eastern Studies* 23 (2): 358–77. https://doi.org/10.1080/19448953.2020.1867804.

Pedalo, Mirna. 2020. "The Gulf in Bosnia and Herzegovina: An (Un)intentional Consequence of Peace." *Journal of Architecture* 25 (2): 166–85. https://www.doi.org/10.1080/13602365.2020.1733338.

Pešić, Jelena, and Jelisaveta Vukelić. 2022. "Europeanisation from Below at the Semi-Periphery: The Movement against Small Hydropower Plants in Serbia." *Sociologija* 64 (1): 5–27. https://doi.org/10.2298/SOC2201005P.

Petrović, Saša. 2019. *Food Sovereignty in Serbian Context: Food Production System Critical Analysis Framework*. Translated by Dragan Jonić. Belgrade, Serbia: Ama, Center for the Care of People and Nature.

Prelec, Tena. 2020. "'Our Brothers,' 'Our Saviours': The Importance of Chinese Investment for the Serbian Government's Narrative of Economic Rebound." Policy paper, Prague Security Studies Institute, Prague, Czech Republic.

Radenković, Ivan, and Maja Solar. 2018. "From Arable Land through Socialist Industrialisation to the Dinner Table and Social Life." In *We Have Built Cities for You: On the Contradictions of Yugoslav Socialism*, edited by Vida Knežević and Marko Miletić, 155–68. Belgrade, Serbia: Center CZKD, Center for Cultural Decontamination.

Rajković, Ivan. 2020. "Rivers to the People: Ecopopulist Universality in the Balkan Mountains." Society for Cultural Anthropology. March 24, 2020. https://culanth.org/fieldsights/rivers-to-the-people-ecopopulist-universality-in-the-balkan-mountains.

———. 2022a. "The People against Rio Tinto: Three Ecopopulist Lessons for the Balkan Left." *LeftEast* (blog). April 19, 2022. https://lefteast.org/people-against-rio-tinto-three-ecopopulist-lessons/.

———. 2022b. "'Serbia Is (Not) for Sale': On Lithium, Hunger and Other Betrayals." *LeftEast* (blog). March 16, 2022. https://lefteast.org/serbia-is-not-for-sale-on-lithium-hunger-and-other-betrayals/.

Roebeling, Peter, Pavel Ciaian, Liesbet Vranken, and Ewa Tabeau. 2021. "Agricultural Land Market Regulations in the EU Member States." JRC technical report, Publications Office of the European Union, Luxembourg. https://op.europa.eu/publication/manifestation_identifier/PUB_KJNA30838ENN.

RTL. 2021. "RTL Direkt iz Lubenica na Cresu, imaju točno tri stanovnika: Nisam mislio da bih mogao biti baš zadnji . . . " *Danas*, September 17, 2021. https://www.rtl.hr/vijesti/hrvatska/rtl-direkt-iz-lubenica-na-cresu-imaju-tocno-tri-stanovnika-nisam-mislio-da-bih-mogao-biti-bas-zadnji-lubenican-c0ce0da8-b9f4-11ec-b53f-0242ac13001a.

Schäuble, Michaela. 2014. *Narrating Victimhood: Gender, Religion and the Making of Place in Post-War Croatia*. New York: Berghahn.

Šljukić, S., and M. Šljukić. 2019. "Sociological Aspects of the Transformation of Agrarian Structure of Serbia in 1990–2018." *RUDN Journal of Sociology* 19 (2): 235–43. https://doi.org/10.22363/2313-2272-2019-19-2-235-243.

Smith, Joe, and Petr Jehlička. 2013. "Quiet Sustainability: Fertile Lessons from Europe's Productive Gardeners." *Journal of Rural Studies* 32 (October): 148–57. https://doi.org/10.1016/j.jrurstud.2013.05.002.

Srećković, Milenko, and Vladimir Bogićević. 2013. *Borba Za Budućnost: Ka Balkanskom Pokretu Otpora: Otpor Deindustrijalizaciji i Otimanju Zemlje* (*The Fight for Future: Toward a Balkan Movement of Resistances: Resisting Deindustrialisation and Land-Grabbing*). Belgrade, Serbia: Freedom Fight [Pokret za slobodu].

Stanković, Brankica, dir. 2021. *Prodaja*. Three-episode series. Insajder. https://insajder.net/arhiva/tema/insajder-o-privatizaciji-pkb-a-prodaja-emisija.

Thiemann, André. 2014. "'It Was the Least Painful to Go into Greenhouse Production': The Moral Appreciation of Social Security in Post-Socialist Serbia." *Contemporary Southeastern Europe* 1 (2): 23–41.

———. 2017. "Shrinking Capitalism, 'Milky Ways,' and the Moral Appreciation of Serbia's 'Living Village.'" *Glasnik Etnografskog Instituta* 65 (2): 387–402. https://doi.org/10.2298/GEI1702387T.

———. 2020. "The Red Gold of Serbia: A Historical Ethnography of Serbian Raspberry Production for the Global Market." *Vienna Working Papers in Ethnography* 10: 1–34.

Todorova, Miglena S. 2018. "Foreign Investment Inflows to Former Socialist Countries in the Balkans: Mapping Global Capitalism." *Interventions* 20 (6): 814–31. https://doi.org/10.1080/1369801X.2018.1492953.

Tomašević, Tomislav, Vedran Horvat, Alma Midžić, Ivana Dragšić, and Miodrag Dakić. 2018. *Commons in South East Europe: Case of Croatia, Bosnia and Herzegovina and Macedonia*. Zagreb, Croatia: Institute for Political Ecology.

van der Ploeg, Jan Douwe, Jennifer C. Franco, and Saturnino M. Borras. 2015. "Land Concentration and Land Grabbing in Europe: A Preliminary Analysis." *Canadian Journal of Development Studies* (*Revue canadienne d'études du développement*) 36 (2): 147–62. https://doi.org/10.1080/02255189.2015.1027673.

Visser, Oane, Stefan Dorondel, Petr Jehlička, and Max Spoor. 2019. "Post-Socialist Smallholders: Silence, Resistance and Alternatives." *Canadian Journal of Development Studies* (*Revue canadienne d'études du développement*) 40 (4): 499–510. https://doi.org/10.1080/02255189.2019.1688649.

Visser, Oane, Brian Kuns, and Petr Jehlička. 2021. "Beyond Confrontation: Silent Growers, Symbiosis and Subtle Peasantness in Post-Socialist Eurasia." In *Handbook of Critical Agrarian Studies*, edited by A. H. Akram-Lodhi, Kristina Dietz, Bettina Engels, and Ben M. McKay, 305–15. Cheltenham, UK: Edward Elgar. https://doi.org/10.4337/9781788972468.

Visser, Oane, Natalia Mamonova, Max Spoor, and Alexander Nikulin. 2015. "'Quiet Food Sovereignty' as Food Sovereignty without a Movement? Insights from Post-Socialist Russia." *Globalizations* 12 (4): 513–28. https://doi.org/10.1080/14747731.2015.1005968.

Vorbrugg, Alexander. 2019. "Not about Land, Not Quite a Grab: Dispersed Dispossession in Rural Russia." *Antipode* 51 (3): 1011–31. https://doi.org/10.1111/anti.12523.

Wolford, Wendy, Saturnino M. Borras, Ruth Hall, Ian Scoones, and Benjamin White, eds. 2013. *Governing Global Land Deals: The Role of the State in the Rush for Land*. Chichester, UK: Wiley-Blackwell.

Chapter 6

Land in Courts

Registers of Memory, Sovereignty, and Justice

Sakshi

Land, like law, is versatile. It is a register for a multitude of relationalities, ontologies, and multispecies living. Among other things, land embodies justice, sovereignty, and kinship and, as a consequence, becomes an epicenter for understanding what justice means in material terms. In its multiple legal iterations, the land also becomes the embodiment of sovereignty and jurisdiction. In her book *Grounded Authority*, Shiri Pasternak (2017) argues that land becomes a mode through which we understand "how authority is established, exercised, and contested in settler colonies." The land holds diverse meanings in its everyday operations: it is a means of production, capital, a space for governance, a place scripted with emotions and memories, a place of violent dispossession and occupation. The law and the land are often reduced to their regulatory relationships where they converge. However, there is a more-than-juridical role for both that remains to be explored and understood. Especially in the contexts of Indigenous land claims and environmental litigation, land assumes many forms as it progresses through the filters of law and justice. Land is not limited to physical territory but also extends to water, natural resources, Indigeneity, cultural representations, and knowledge forms within and outside of litigation.

This chapter looks at the intricate ways in which courts encounter more than juridical articulations of land in Indigenous environmental litigation. I analyze two recent cases before settler courts of Australia that adjudicate on the environment and incommensurable loss of land. I develop three frames encapsulating sovereignty, intergenerational justice, and memory to contextualize the cases and advance an argument for a radical reform of environmental jurisprudence that addresses present and past wrongs against First Nations.

LAND AS PLACE OF KNOWLEDGE PRODUCTION

The prevailing Western legal theories have scarcely engaged with Indigenous cosmologies and worldviews. The knowledge forms at the foundation of legal processes are still steeped in Western epistemologies and ontologies (Borrows 2002). A substantial body of work that exists in relation to land claims and native title in Australia go as far as determining claims over the territory without addressing the attendant violence of dispossession and loss. The rigid construction of legal claims emerges from the Western legal doctrines that cleave land away from its more-than-human relationships to facilitate the doctrines of dominion, possession, ownership, commons, and so on (Attwood 2020). Although the genealogy of settler laws suggests that they have been devised to address the native title or land claims, it is unproductive for courts to hold onto these unhelpful frameworks in the context of increasing environmental claims that raise entangled questions of intergenerational harm, cultural heritage, and Indigenous sovereignty.

Leanne Simpson (2014) terms the Indigenous relation to place as "land-based pedagogy." Simpson works her way through Canada's Nishnaabeg community knowledge forms and values associated with the land to illustrate how the landscape remains core to the love, compassion, and understanding within the community (Simpson 2017). Land replaces settler education and morality, thereby becoming the governing force for First Nations' relationship with the living beings (for instance, how hunting must be carried on) and natural resources (what trees can be chopped and when can maple syrup be extracted), among others (Simpson 2014).

Simpson argues that land is both the context and the process: "Indigenous education is not Indigenous or education from within our intellectual practices unless it comes through the land, unless it occurs in an Indigenous context using Indigenous processes" (Simpson 2014). To recreate the education, one needs to recreate the conditions in which the elements were learned and not just the contents or the processes. This formulation makes up for what is lacking in the Western pedagogy. It also subtracts the coercion and authority embedded in the property relations (Simpson 2014). In the Indigenous philosophies, land becomes a material that teaches Indigenous modes of existence and a conduit that passes on community knowledge across generations. The integrity of the land is, therefore, vital for their continuing identity formation and maintenance (Winter 2020). Sandy Grande (2004) illustrates the "educative" and decolonizing potential of the land in Native American social and political thought by terming it the *Red Pedagogy*.

Acknowledgment of the multiplicity of roles land can play is ineluctably central to Indigenous environmental justice in courts. First Nations have built and cherished their cultural and material relationships to land since time immemorial. The existing environmental justice movements spearheaded by the Indigenous peoples also involve the protection of sacred sites and burial grounds that stand in the way of industrial expansion, developmental projects, and other extractive enterprises. Schlosberg and Carruthers (2010) recognise the centrality of land to Indigenous survival in North America. They argue that the vulnerability of the land to contamination and dumping projects interferes severely with the ability of the communities to sustainably interact with the land and maintain the practices, ceremonies, and beliefs linked to the place. Their case study of the decision in *Navajo Nation v. US Forest Service* (*Navajo Nation*) is a telling example of how environmental cases with the potential to articulate Indigenous environmental justice forego that opportunity by sidelining Indigenous perspectives as irrelevant. In *Navajo Nation*, the community objected to the operations of the ski resort, especially to its plans to reclaim the sewage water and use it in the making of artificial snow for the resort. Schlosberg and Carruthers analyze the judgment's reluctance to recognize certain practices as religious or spiritual under the Religious Freedom Restoration Act and also its failure to treat them as vital for the continuity of the community. Such a judicial disregard marginalises Indigenous retelling of what constitutes environmental harm and denies the recognition and respect for the Indigenous voice.

LAND AND INDIGENOUS RELATIONSHIPS IN AUSTRALIA

Indigenous peoples' relationship with the land is not alien to the idea of environmental stewardship or management. Caring for the Country in Australia testifies to the reciprocal relationship between First Nations and the land, representing all the entangled environmental relationships. "If you look after the Country, the Country will look after you" is a principle around which the social and political lives of the communities are organized (Griffiths and Kinnane 2011). The power to manage land and its resources is a natural extension of the demands of self-governance. Indigenous land has remained a "sentient participant" in Australian Indigenous environmentalisms (Weir, Stacey, and Youngetob 2011). These environmentalisms draw from the values of listening and voicing Indigenous knowledge forms in everyday processes of participation and recognition, such as the heritage consultation.[1] A firm belief in *Caring for the Country* as a philosophy for remedying environmental injustices perpetrated by the settler colony is one of the reasons a separation between the land rights movement and Indigenous environmental litigation in Australia is challenging. Land as pedagogy in Australia echoes the sentiments of the Standing Rock historic preservation officer on why she cannot forget the Whitestone massacre while thinking of the pipeline proposed to cut through the reservation area:

> The U.S. government is wiping out our most important cultural and spiritual areas. And as it erases our footprint from the world, it erases us as a people. These sites must be protected, or our world will end, it is that simple. Our young people have a right to know who they are. They have a right to language, to culture, to tradition. The way they learn these things is through connection to our lands and our history . . . If we allow an oil company to dig through and destroy our histories, our ancestors, our hearts and souls as a people, is that not genocide? (quoted in Allard 2016)

Environmental jurisprudence in a settler nation is an exercise in reading against the grain. In Australia, the field of land rights has been predominantly occupied by native title litigation. It may even have provided courts with an opportunity to avoid the notions of conflicting sovereignties within settler spaces. Nevertheless, the looming sense of planetary collapse and the ongoing environmental crises tear apart the previous conceptions of the remit of the law as much as they compel one to revisit the idea of litigation being a technical process of adjudication. The courts of law are driven to rethink their place as courts of justice and make space in the juridical realm to resist the structures of the settler-colonial state. Australian jurist Julius Stone speaks about concealed references—a principle that is necessary for the determination of legal goals but the nature of which is more than the issue at hand, relevant precedents, or applicable principles. For Stone (1966), "[t]he very amplitude of the house of jurisprudence means of course that what goes on under its roofs has great potential meanings for many urgent and practical questions of the day. This is so even for stable and peaceful times; all the more for our time of turbulent dynamic movement and confrontation."

Land plays a transformative role in thinking about the novelty of Indigenous environmental justice as a segue from doctrinal environmental litigation to a more holistic justice-oriented jurisprudence. Land is a form of open textured evidence, reinforcing Indigenous claims for self-determination, cultural integrity, and Indigeneity. While Indigenous scholarship has explored the many worlds of their existence, being/kinship, sovereignty, and more-than-human relationships, how one melds the Indigenous knowledge forms with settler juridical spaces is a difficult question. Nonetheless, courts in Australia in recent decades have created avenues to break the imperviousness of the law to respond to the novelty of environmental claims and, in turn, have extended constructive recognition to Indigenous voices.

THREE FRAMES

Three critical frames form the backdrop for understanding Australian Indigenous environmental jurisprudence. The three frames capture what theorizing land and place-based identities mean in the legal sense; these are:

1. **Land as Memory and Pedagogy:** Land functions as a register that holds and cultivates Indigenous cosmologies and worldviews. In effect, it reflects not only the precolonial identity formation through the land but also the gradual corrosive effects of settler colonialism and extractivism. Hence the register becomes a reference point for evaluating the cultural and environmental loss endured by the progress of extractive and settler capitalism.
2. **Land as Justice:** The movement for decolonization is nothing but an expression of the "land back." Unless there is an opportunity for confronting the truth about Indigenous dispossession and erasure, there is little hope for reconciliation and repatriation. The present environmental harms or the disproportionate impact of climate change is not a singular event. Indigeneity draws its existence from the past and is handed over to the future. A disruption in these processes suggests that the harm from environmental destruction is unquantifiable and continues to extend to the future generation unless the settler violence at the root of such destructions is addressed.
3. **Land as Sovereignty:** Multiple sovereignties coexist where the structure of settler colonialism cannot be entirely eliminated. While most of the transformation in the sovereignty question awaits constitutional action [e.g., the Uluru Statement from the Heart in Australia that demands constitutional recognition of the Indigenous voice (Markham and Sanders 2020)], there is a partial preconstitutional action that can be enabled through courts. These possibilities are specifically manifested in environmental litigations that encounter both colonial and extractive violence. Juridical spaces often have the ability to recognize plural sovereignties, privilege Indigenous voices, and seek evidence in Indigenous epistemologies and legal systems to resolve the unjustness, blind spots, and inadequacies of the settler law.

In the following section, I discuss the case laws from Australia where land remains central to the contemporary juridical transformation, even as the settler state remains intact. The discussion entails the traces of the three frames. However, these frames are expected to fulfill a more complex role than being some formulaic rule against which each judgment must be tested. The three frames may be used as exploratory tools while thinking about the courts and the cases discussed in the next segment.

CLIMATE LITIGATION AND INDIGENOUS ENVIRONMENTAL JUSTICE

While *Mabo v. Queensland* was the defining case of native title jurisprudence in Australia, recognizing the concept of native title in common law depending on the nature and character of Indigenous occupation, little has been contributed to the expansion and consolidation of Indigenous rights within the juridical spaces since then. However, the recent spate of climate litigation and cases against mining corporations has brought a shift in judicial attitudes. Although one must be cautious about generalizing on the basis of the environmental jurisprudence of the specialist courts, the impact of specific environmental litigation on Indigenous rights has been significant.

Gloucester Resources Limited v. Minister for Planning (2019) illuminates a body of case laws emblematic of anticoal jurisprudence. It also effectively captures the field occupied by what is denominated as essentially an *extractivism versus environment* binary. In *Gloucester Resources* (2019), Gloucester Resources Limited (GRL) made an application for the operation of the Rocky Hill open-cut coal mine. The minister for planning refused the consent, and the matter came before the New South Wales Land and Environment Court (NSWLEC) as merits review. Chief Justice Brian J. Preston determined that the application must be refused, thereby elevating *Gloucester Resources* into one of the prominent climate change cases in recent times. Because it was a merits review, where the facts may be considered afresh, the case delved into the social, economic, and environmental impacts of the Rocky Hill project in detail. Preston considered the cost-benefit analysis of the open-cut mine before rejecting the application. The decision considered four broad categories of impacts that weighed against the mining project:

1. Visual impact
2. Social impact—extending to a sense of place, community, and place relations

3. Impact on climate change—engaging with intergenerational and inter-community impacts
4. Economic impacts

The case is a fine specimen of environmental litigation. Preston provided an extraordinary opportunity to hear evidence from Aboriginal elders to understand the social impacts of the mine. The ministerial submission before the Court recognized that the environmental and social impact assessment provided by GRL was highly inadequate. The latter also ignored the Aboriginal perspectives on the Gloucester Valley, which was a place of great cultural and spiritual significance. Rebecca Lawrence and others authored the ministerial expert report on the social impact of the mine, whereas Hedda Askland submitted the expert report on social impact on behalf of the second respondent, the Groundswell Gloucester Organisation. The Askland report gives a detailed account of Aboriginals' relation to the place and how the exclusion of their voice has injured their sense of community and belonging (Askland 2018). The report also identifies what such exclusion means for Aboriginal people and the sense of justice. To quote one of the elders interviewed in the report, the "lack of recognition of Aboriginal heritage, ontology and epistemology incites a decolonial [sic] process which, in Sarah's words, 'mimics the historical relationship between government and our People—relegate, move and dismiss'" (Askland 2018, para. 86; cited in *Gloucester Resources* 2019, para. 344).

Askland emphasizes that the Country holds a spiritual value to the people; hence, it is both a sacred entity and a cultural heritage. The impending loss of the Country creates an incommensurable sense of loss to the Indigenous community living on the land. In the process, the report also calls to question the minister's uncontested acceptance of GRL's submission that the place was of low research potential and no educational or aesthetic value.

The judgment used the Askland report extensively to understand why the social impact is experienced differently for Indigenous communities and amplifies their loss. Besides, Preston invited independent testimonies from Aboriginal elders to demonstrate what the Indigenous land, specifically the Gloucester Valley, meant to them and their communities. Preston concluded that the GRL's expert evidence was inadequate to capture the impact of the mine on how the First Nations would relate to the land. The judgment accepted the elders' testimony to infer that the value of the land increases when one accounts for how Indigenous identities rely on it (*Gloucester Resources* 2019, paras. 120–21). It emphasized that the Aboriginal cultural heritage is not embedded in a specific piece of land but landscape as a whole (*Gloucester Resources* 2019, para. 346). Throughout the judgment, Preston referred to and included the Aboriginal voice in every factor vital to the decision, such as visual amenities, social impact, cultural heritage, connection to land, and sense of place (*Gloucester Resources* 2019, para. 345). The judgment also considered the past violence of settlement, which erased and ruptured collective memories, as it was significant in understanding how the open-cut mine might affect future knowledge (*Gloucester Resources*, paras. 348–51). In the voice of elder Kim Eveleigh,

> We are the Aboriginal people of this land, so don't you dare ignore us, pay attention and listen as this is our Spiritual connection to our land, we the Gooreengai people belong to the Significant Buckan Valley in Gloucester it is our past, present, and future. If you allow it to be destroyed, you cannot fix it. Stop it before it begins. Everything from our Ancestors has been removed. All we have left is our Dreaming of our land. (*Gloucester Resources* 2019, para. 121)

Solastalgia, or a sense of despair arising from loss of place and ecology, found a prominent place in the judgment.[2] Preston heavily relied on the concept of solastalgia even in his earlier judgments, such as Bulga Mibrodale Progress Association v. Minister for Planning and Warkworth Mining (2013), to highlight the fact that the social impact of mining may be undermined in robotic impact assessment processes (*Bulga Mibrodale*, para. 404). In Gloucester Resources (2019), Preston discussed the idea of solastalgia to stress how Indigenous people have greater emotional connection to land and environment. The NSWLEC had previous records of making room for Aboriginal testimonies and concerns, even when they are seemingly marginal to the issue. The Court in Milne v. Minister for Planning and Amr (2007), which dealt with the social impact of the expansion of marina, called for testimonies from Aboriginal elders to remedy the exclusion of impact assessment on cultural heritage. In the final decision to refuse the permit, Presiding Judge Jayne Jagot found that the impact on Aboriginal heritage and traditional activities, among other issues, was more significant than the promised economic benefits.

In Gloucester Resources (2019), the Court made the best use of its power to review to bring the Indigenous voice to the forefront. Through a repeated emphasis on Indigenous cultural heritage and spiritual connection to the land as key elements that may be harmed by the coal mine, the Court enabled meaningful participation and recognition of Indigenous concerns. While participation and effective control in decision making must be done through consultation in impact assessments, the Court steps in to remedy the absence retrospectively.

NORTHERN TERRITORY V. GRIFFITHS AND ORS (TIMBER CREEK)

Northern Territory v. Griffiths and Ors (*Timber Creek* 2017) was hailed for the unexpected recognition of intangible values in compensating land claims. While we must be mindful of the fact *Timber Creek* is a native title decision, the materials available through the claims and the judgment surpass the usual confines of native title litigation. The questions considered in the *Timber Creek* decision, such as treatment of the loss of land, spiritual connection to the land, and judicial responses to categories of losses that have so far remained unexamined, are contemporary and have wide-ranging consequences to the future of Indigenous and environmental rights jurisprudence. The judgment concerned itself with a sense of disconnect with the land and loss of Indigenous sovereignty in the environmental contexts. The *Timber Creek* decision had three tiers of litigation. At the trial stage, a single judge bench of Federal Court consisting of Justice John Mansfield considered the matter. It was later appealed and considered by the Full Federal Court (FCAFC), which upheld the trial court decision. Subsequently, the decision of the FCAFC was appealed in the High Court. The High Court partially upheld the decision of the FCAFC while retaining the new category of "spiritual losses" and the amount awarded by the trial court concerning such category intact.

Ngaliwurru and Nungali People (henceforth "the claim group") had obtained a favorable native title determination of the Timber Creek land in 2007 (*Griffiths v. Northern Territory* 2006). Between 1980 and 1996, the Northern Territory had made fifty-three grants of tenures and public works contracts in Timber Creek. Most of them involved the compulsory acquisition of land that were said to have impaired or extinguished native title rights and interests held by the claim group. Therefore, a claim for compensation was made under S.51 of the Native Title Act 1993 (NTA) along with Schedule 2 of the Land Acquisition Act 1978 (LAA).[3] The claim group contended that the compensation must include

1. The value of the land to be determined according to the criteria in rule 2(a) (market value). It would presume that the interest acquired was on a freehold estate. Similarly, the date of acquisition was the date of validation of the Act.
2. Interest on economic compensation.
3. Loss or diminution of connection or traditional attachment to the land and intangible disadvantages of loss of rights to live on and gain

spiritual and material sustenance from the land, with the adaptation of the criteria in rules 2(b) (special value) and 9 (intangible loss).

ECONOMIC COMPENSATION

Mansfield set off by addressing the question of economic loss and the attendant compensation claim. There were two aspects of economic compensation contested by the parties: the first aspect concerned the date of assessment; the second, the nature of the assessment. The Northern Territory government argued that the compensation should be evaluated from the date of determination of native title (i.e., 2006) instead of compulsory acquisition of the land that lasted between 1980 and 1996. It also argued that the value of the land should be less than the market value of freehold, as the native title land was inalienable and could only be subject to exclusive possession (*Timber Creek* 2017, paras. 47–48). The claim group contended that the native-title recognition was a mere recognition of the title, whereas they had exercised control and customary relationship with the land long before such recognition (*Timber Creek* 2017, paras. 7–31). They also urged that the value of assessment should be market value, as inalienability of native title land did not mean that there was no power to relinquish their rights over the land. They could always do so by surrendering the title [*Timber Creek* 2017, para. 175, clause (e)].

Mansfield resorted to a series of precedents, including *Native Title Act Case* (1995) and *Jango v. Northern Territory* (2007), which had implications for the applicability and operations of NTA. The plurality of judicial opinions in both the *Native Title Case* and *Jango v. Northern Territory* held that the past act by the state is a linchpin for the operation of NTA. The compensable act was determined from the point when Indigenous rights, usufructuary or otherwise, were denied to the title holders and not merely from the point such rights were recognized (*Timber Creek* 2017, paras. 122–31). Mansfield in *Timber Creek* relied on these ideas of exclusivity and permanence to advance the idea of justness in compensating native title land. Therefore, the date of extinguishment of the right by the validating act was held relevant for the assessment of the compensation. Mansfield clarified the point of justness further in the segment where the decision considered the tangible worth of the native title land. The decision attributed greater importance to negotiation value, or the value at which native title holders would be willing to surrender the title and value of the territory, which would reflect the importance of the land to the Aboriginal community (*Timber Creek* 2017, paras. 200, 210–21).

Although, for the sake of assessment, it would be the market value that was vital, Mansfield considered other forms in which native title land can be assessed and valued. He reiterated that the compensation should be determined based on what the native title group lost after the acquisition and not merely on what the purchaser was willing to pay for the freehold title (*Timber Creek* 2017, paras. 220–21). The decision revisited the idea that Aboriginal communities have lived on the land for a long and uninterrupted period and acknowledged that this period, however tempestuous and conflict ridden, did not diminish the value of Indigenous connection to the Country (*Timber Creek* 2017, para. 364). While the settlers may have disrupted the connection with the land and later involved the Aboriginal communities in new forms of exploitative economic structures, the judgment emphasised only the connection to the Country. The decision held that "it would be erroneous to treat the nature of their original interests in land as other than the equivalent of freehold and the economic value of those interests as other than the equivalent of freehold interests" (*Timber Creek* 2017, para. 214).

SPIRITUAL LOSS—SOLATIUM

The second significant part of the decision dealt with the intangible loss or the noneconomic loss. The decision was at its innovative best in creating a category of "spiritual loss" to capture noneconomic losses, unfamiliar to the native title jurisprudence in the past. Mansfield engaged in an illuminating discussion by clarifying what would be an appropriate term to encapsulate the loss in the specific context of this case. The discussion in the judgment may be summarized as follows: the said compensation cannot be termed as a special value, as it does not recognize any of the property rights that are within a communal bundle (*Timber Creek* 2017, paras. 297–98). Such recognition may amount to double compensation, and that is not the intention of the court (*Timber Creek* 2017, para. 297). Instead, he proposed that this compensation would be called a "solatium." The applicants had only submitted two elements of the noneconomic or intangible loss without specifying an amount that could compensate their alleged loss. These were (1) the diminution or disruption in the traditional attachment to Country and (2) the loss of rights to live on and gain spiritual and material sustenance from the land (*Timber Creek* 2017, para. 295).

In the following discussion on categorization and discussion of noneconomic losses, Mansfield revisited the historical disconnect suffered by the Aboriginal people with respect to their land. Drawing from the evidence of the claimants, he contended that the Aboriginal dispossession and noneconomic loss had been "incremental and cumulative" (*Timber Creek* 2017, para. 324). While settler colonialism had displaced the communities from their primal relationship with the land, they were subsequently integrated as laborers in the cattle station (*Timber Creek* 2017, para. 24). However, they witnessed a continuing erosion of Song lines and Dreaming sites, which now constituted the category of intangible loss. The judgment relied on the testimony of elders and of anthropologists equally to determine the spiritual connection and loss endured by the community.

The complexity of the decision laid in arriving at a sum of compensation. The judge identified that the compensation amount must, at the very least, reflect the loss of communal native title and collective-ownership rights (*Timber Creek* 2017, para. 371). These rights were not restricted to a patch of land or an isolated geographical area but were as pervasive as the Dreaming. More importantly, the judgment recognised the intergenerational consequences of the damage. It stated that the losses would continue to be experienced in the future by the generations that depend on continuity of land and Dreaming sites for their cultural and spiritual education.

Finally, Justice Mansfield stated the three factors that ascertained the solatium:

1. First, the construction of the water tank as a part of the developmental activities on the land, which destroyed the Dreaming site, caused immense grief and sense of loss to the Aboriginal community.
2. Second, since it is not a particular site but an entire landscape that is harmed, it is difficult to carry on spiritual activities on the land.
3. Third, cultural connection and belongingness to the land is harmed. Furthermore, again, its effects cannot be insulated on a stretch of land and must be understood as affecting the whole landscape (*Timber Creek* 2017, paras. 374–84).

In a critical observation summing up all the compensation awarded, Mansfield obliquely recognised the responsibility of courts to regard native title land with the significance they deserved:

> I accept that the component awarded for solatium should be assessed having regard to the communal native and collective ownership of the native title rights and interests. It must reflect the loss or diminution of traditional attachment to land arising from the extinguishment or impairment in question (rather than from earlier or subsequent events or effects), and it must be assessed having regard to the non-exclusive nature of the native title rights and interests in question. So much is not contentious. The process required is a complex, but essentially an intuitive, one. As the Territory pointed out, the compensation must be assessed having regard to the spiritual and usufructuary significance and area of the land affected, but relative to other lands that remained available to the Claim Group for the exercise of the native title rights and interests. (*Timber Creek* 2017, paras. 301–2)

As expected of settler courts, neither the NSWLEC nor the Federal Court deliberated on Indigenous sovereignty explicitly. A traditional legal theorist may even argue that such consideration is irrelevant to the adjudication of the issue. However, the Indigenous voice and relationship to the land, which are central to the two cases, are aspects of plural sovereignties. Where Indigenous sovereignty must coexist with the state sovereignty, constructive recognition of Indigenous voice and land relationships are indispensable for a just outcome.

CONCLUSION

Through litigation and adjudication, the concept of land—with all its meanings, implications, and embodiments—provides an opportunity for the juridical spaces to learn and engage with Indigenous knowledge and cosmologies. While express disavowal of state sovereignty is difficult to accomplish without violating the separation of power, the idea of justice is about how to do things differently even when the settler state has not been dismantled. The specialist environmental court of New South Wales and the Federal Court in *Timber Creek* (2017) were operating within the rigid positivist culture and cannot be singled out as instances of judicial overreach. The judges in these cases extended the remit of their inquiry and judicial powers to ask questions that were ignored for a long time. These judgments push the constitutional limits without disrupting the existing structures, delving into how expansively the constructs of justice may be stretched to accommodate present claims. Only when juridical spaces understand land broadly, in all its depths and relations to Indigenous communities, can the birth of such radical environmental jurisprudence be possible.

This chapter looks at how Indigenous connection to the land has become relevant in Australia's new wave of climate and land-rights litigation. By inviting Indigenous knowledge and cosmologies to the juridical space, Australian courts have created opportunities for more expansive ways of thinking about and framing justice. Invariably, such a process involves a constructive recognition of the Indigenous voice. Often, courts are ill equipped for this task, especially when no explicit laws or constitutional provisions are available to subtend the process. However, both *Gloucester Resource* (2019) and *Timber Creek* (2017) decisions show that understanding land as a register of cultural memory, sovereignty, and intergenerational justice is illuminating. Such an understanding makes room for Indigenous voices in the juridical spaces and propels the environmental and Indigenous-rights jurisprudence within settler institutions, thereby providing a meaningful opportunity to transition toward Indigenous environmental justice.

NOTES

1. See the Aboriginal and Torres Strait Islander Heritage Protection Act 1984 (Cth; ATSIHP Act), the Protection of Movable Cultural Heritage Act 1986 (Cth), and Truscott (1997).

2. A term coined by Australian anthropologist Glenn Albrecht and that is referred to in Askland (2018, para. 106).

3. NTA 1993, S.51: Criteria for determining compensation

Just compensation

1. Subject to subsection (3), the entitlement to compensation under Division 2, 2A, 2B, 3 or 4 is an entitlement on just terms to compensate the native title holders for any loss, diminution, impairment or other effect of the act on their native title rights and interests.

Acquisition under compulsory acquisition law

2. If the act is the compulsory acquisition of all or any of the native title rights and interests of the native title holders, the court, person or body making the determination of compensation on just terms may, subject to subsections (5) to (8), in doing so have regard to any principles or criteria for determining compensation set out in the law under which the compulsory acquisition takes place.

Compensation where similar compensable interest test satisfied

3. If:
    a. the act is not the compulsory acquisition of all or any of the native title rights and interests; and
    b. the similar compensable interest test is satisfied in relation to the act; the court, person or body making the determination of compensation must, subject to subsections (5) to (8), in doing so apply any principles or criteria for determining compensation (whether or not on just terms) set out in the law mentioned in section 240 (which defines *similar compensable interest test*).

Compensation not covered by subsection (2) or (3)

4. If:
    a. neither subsection (2) nor (3) applies; and
    b. there is a compulsory acquisition law for the Commonwealth (if the act giving rise to the entitlement is attributable to the Commonwealth) or for the State or Territory to which the act is attributable; the court, person or body making the determination of compensation on just terms may, subject to subsections (5) to (8), in doing so have regard to any principles or criteria set out in that law for determining compensation.

Monetary compensation

5. Subject to subsection (6), the compensation may only consist of the payment of money.

Requests for non-monetary compensation

6. If the person claiming to be entitled to the compensation requests that the whole or part of the compensation should consist of the transfer of property or the provision of goods or services, the court, person or body:

a. must consider the request; and
b. may, instead of determining the whole or any part of the compensation, recommend that the person liable to give the compensation should, within a specified period, transfer property or provide goods or services in accordance with the recommendation.

Where recommendation not complied with

7. If the person does not transfer the property or provide the goods or services in accordance with the recommendation, the person claiming to be entitled to the compensation may request the court, person or body to determine instead that the whole or the part of the compensation concerned is to consist of the payment of money.

Where recommendation complied with

8. If the person does transfer the property or provide the goods or services in accordance with the recommendation, the transfer of the property or provision of the goods or services constitutes full compensation for the act, and the entitlement to it is taken to have been determined in accordance with this Division.

REFERENCES

Allard, Ladonna Brave Bull. 2016. "Why the Founder of Standing Rock Sioux Camp Can't Forget the Whitestone Massacre." *Yes! Magazine*, September 3, 2016. http://www.yesmagazine.org/people-power/why-the-founder-of-standing-rock-sioux-camp cantforget-the-whitestone-massacre-20160903.

Askland, Hedda. 2018. "Expert Witness Report on Social Impacts." Witness statement, June 14.

Attwood, Bain. 2020. *Empire and the Making of Native Title: Sovereignty, Property and Indigenous People*. Cambridge, UK: Cambridge University Press.

Borrows, John. 2002. *Recovering Canada: The Resurgence of Indigenous Law.* Toronto: University of Toronto Press.

Bulga Mibrodale Progress Association v. Minister for Planning and Warkworth Mining. 2013. NSWLEC 48.

Gloucester Resources Limited v. Minister for Planning. 2019. NSWLEC 7.

Grande, Sandy. 2004. *Red Pedagogy: Native American Social and Political Thought.* New York: Rowman and Littlefield.

Griffiths, Sharon, and Stephen Kinnane. 2011. Kimberley Aboriginal Caring for Country Plan. Halls Creek, Australia: Kimberley Language Resource Centre.

Griffiths v. Northern Territory. 2006. 165 FCR 391.

Jango v. Northern Territory. 2007. 159 FCR 53.

Mabo v. Queensland. 1992. HCA 23.

Markham, Francis, and Will Sanders. 2020. "Support for a Constitutionally Enshrined First Nations Voice to Parliament: Evidence from Opinion Research since 2017." Working paper no. 138/2020, Centre for Aboriginal Economic Policy Research, Australian National University, Canberra.

Milne v. Minister for Planning and Amr. 2007. NSWLEC 66.

Native Title Act Case. 1995. 183 CLR 373.

Navajo Nation v. United States Forest Serv. 2008. Opposition no. 08–846. https://www.justice.gov/osg/brief/navajo-nation-v-united-states-forest-serv-opposition.

Northern Territory v. Griffiths and Ors (Timber Creek). 2017. FCAFC 106.

Pasternak, Shiri. 2017. *Grounded Authority: The Algonquins of Barriere Lake against the State*. Minneapolis: University of Minnesota Press.

Schlosberg, David, and David Carruthers. 2010. "Indigenous Struggles, Environmental Justice, and Community Capabilities." *Global Environmental Politics* 10 (4): 12–35.

Simpson, Leanne. 2014. "Land as Pedagogy: Nishnaabeg Intelligence and Rebellious Transformation." *Decolonization: Indigeneity, Education and Society* 3 (3): 1–25.

———. 2017. *As We Have Always Done: Indigenous Freedom through Radical Resistance*. Minneapolis: University of Minnesota Press.

Stone, Julius. 1966. *Social Dimensions of Law and Justice*. Stanford, CA: Stanford University Press.

Truscott, Marilyn. 1997. *Draft Guidelines for the Protection, Management and Use of Aboriginal and Torres Strait Islander Cultural Heritage Places: Heritage Places: Past, Present and Future*. Canberra, Australia: Department of Communications and the Arts.

Weir, Jessica K., Claire Stacey, and Kara Youngetob. 2011. *The Benefits Associated with Caring for Country*. Canberra: Australian Institute of Aboriginal and Torres Strait Islander Studies. https://aiatsis.gov.au/sites/default/files/research_pub/benefits-cfc_0_3.pdf.

Winter, Christine Jill. 2020. "Does Time Colonise Intergenerational Environmental Justice Theory?" *Environmental Politics* 29 (2): 278–96.

PART III

Knowing and Unknowing Land

Chapter 7

Knowing and Unknowing the Countryside

Epistemological Implications of Rural Social Policy in Zambia

Anna Wolkenhauer

INTRODUCTION: AGRICULTURAL POLICY AS AN EPISTEMIC SITE

Governments and international organizations have rediscovered the African countryside. It plays a key role in sustainable development discourses, in concerns about global food (in)security and the accelerating competition for land, and in debates about the future of agriculture. Agriculture had been somewhat forgotten by international organizations but became the topic of the World Bank's *World Development Report 2008* and has been identified as a key sector in the African Union's Comprehensive African Agricultural Development Programme (CAADP) of 2003. Agricultural input subsidies in particular have become a priority of several African governments (Sitko, Burke, and Jayne 2018). This new attention occurs against a background of the historical marginalization of rural areas that began in the colonial period (Amin 1972) and was further entrenched during the high time of neoliberal adjustment reforms in the 1990s (Chang 2009). With the new attention to agricultural and rural social policy, some of that marginalization is now being overcome (Wolkenhauer 2020).[1] What has been less understood so far are the epistemological implications of this new concern with agriculture. After having fallen off political radars, how is the countryside made known through the new agricultural policies?

This chapter starts with the argument that the new agricultural policies have become a central site for getting to know the countryside. They constitute certainly not the only but one important field where epistemological foundations are created, which in turn exert significant effects through informing political choices. Knowledge plays a big role in critical agrarian debates, too, where it is often said that local knowledges need to become more influential. To zoom in on epistemological processes hence can help to understand dynamics of inclusion and exclusion as the place of land and rural people in our present capitalist order is defined. While agricultural policies are government driven, they are deeply embedded in transnational processes of reimagining rural futures and of making social policy. While the field of global social policy is not inattentive to the role of knowledge—studying, for instance, its diffusion (Kuhlmann et al. 2020), its tendency for quantification (Berten and Leisering 2017), or the terminologies it builds on (Béland and Petersen 2017)—the epistemological effects of internationalized rural policies on the identities and roles of rural people and the land need more attention.

Critical policy studies alert us to the fact that policies are not neutral procedures but create identities and categories of people who are "to be governed" (Wedel et al. 2005, 30). Policies are not just based on knowledge generated in a separate sphere but themselves also have epistemological implications. Freeman and Sturdy (2014) suggest a differentiation between three forms, or phases, of knowledge: embodied, inscribed, and enacted. Embodied knowledge refers to knowledge produced by the subtle learning that occurs through experience, such as that of a policy administrator or service recipient, and includes tacit and nonverbal forms of knowing (Freeman and Sturdy 2014, 8–10). It is mobile to the extent that human bodies are mobile, and it tends to be updated on a continuous basis. Inscribed knowledge is more lasting—it is conserved in text, pictures, measuring instruments, or artifacts. It is not only more stable than embodied knowledge but also more mobile: by making things comparable across time and space, it "provide[s] a means of standardising how we come to know the world" (Freeman and Sturdy 2014, 11). Last, when enacted, knowledge leaves the state of latency. Only by acting upon what we know do we put this knowledge to effect, and reversely, only by knowing things do our actions become meaningful (Freeman and Sturdy 2014, 12). This threefold distinction is revisited later because it helps to understand dynamics of exclusion and inclusion within epistemic practices.

This chapter draws on field research in Zambia conducted between 2016 and 2018 to trace some of the epistemological implications of recent agricultural discourse and policies. Zambia was a British colony until 1964, largely resembling what Amin (1972) called a "labour reserve economy." This meant that its rural areas were purposefully depleted of resources in order to force people to work in the copper-mining areas and on commercial farms that were run by White settlers (Amin 1972). African farming in more remote areas was for the most part discouraged, even though that changed slightly after World War II, when 'welfare' and 'development' became colonial concerns. Due to its unequal insertion into the global economy and Zambia's high dependence on world market prices for copper, even after independence, there were limits to what the government could do to remedy this inequality. Instead, the center-periphery divide became further entrenched because, after a decade of favorable conditions, the country faced economic crises that lasted until the end of the century. While having been at its core an economic phenomenon (large urban-rural inequalities), the center-periphery divide also translated into political inequality (lack of influence on political centers) and ultimately became mirrored in a bifurcated and lopsided social policy system (Mhone 2004; Wolkenhauer 2022).

This is the background against which, in the early 2000s, new rural social policies were initiated by the state: most importantly, a subsidy scheme for smallholders, the Farmer Input Support Programme (FISP). This is a scheme that provides farmers who cultivate up to five hectares of land with highly subsidized seed and fertilizer, administered by the Ministry of Agriculture and partly implemented with the help of an electronic voucher (Government of the Republic of Zambia 2016a, 2016b). While being a government initiative, it is embedded in a transnational context. First, Zambia receives considerable amounts of international loans and credit, and international financial institutions have always been strongly shaping economic and other policies. Second, various donors and UN agencies are involved in the larger social-protection initiative of the country that includes also other new interventions, like a cash transfer. While being less closely involved in the implementation of FISP than, for instance, in the implementation of the cash transfer, these policies are often treated in conjunction when discussing overall spending decisions and rural poverty reduction. Third, in line with the larger trend toward evidence-based policy making, researchers have been studying the countryside to find out if and how FISP works, and many of them are funded by international organizations or have links with international research centers. Last, the Zambian government has looked to similar policies in neighboring countries, such as the Malawian smallholder subsidy scheme and the Kenyan e-voucher, for designing its own programs.

The epistemological exploration of the countryside is thus a transnational process with many actors. In the following, I first demonstrate that and how rural people and places are epistemologically reconnected through recent social policy discourse and practice. I then trace some practices through which this knowledge of the countryside arises in order to understand better how some truths and not others get to be accepted.

RECONNECTING THE RURAL

Social policies in present-day Zambia are meant to contribute to a socio-economic transformation that "leaves no one behind" (Government of the Republic of Zambia 2017, 4). Historically, Zambia had followed an ideology of Humanism that was formulated by its postindependence president Kenneth Kaunda, who ruled the country from 1964 until 1991. Humanism combined socialist values and strategies with principles of African traditional societies and the recognition of each individual person's well-being (Kaunda 1968), and Zambia forged strong links to socialist countries during the Cold War (Ghodsee 2019). My interviewees from ministries often framed the current developmental strategies, such as what is captured in national development plans and the country's overall *Vision 2030* (Government of Zambia 2006), as part of an ongoing transition away from humanism toward capitalism (Wolkenhauer 2020). In this transition, social policies play an important role in making growth inclusive. The country's seventh *National Development Plan*, for instance, describes the intricate connection between economic growth and poverty reduction, which calls for social protection policies (Government of the Republic of Zambia 2017, 87). After development planning was abandoned in the 1980s and 1990s, these initiatives are forging new discursive links between the center and peripheries: that is, between those who are already part of the growth process and those who are yet to be included. Given the aforementioned geographical bias of economic and state activities toward the urban centers, this ultimately translates into a deeper integration of remote rural areas.

Rural areas play an important role in the new social policy discourse not just because poverty is predominantly rural but also because they are made out to host a lot of untapped wealth in the form of natural resources and fertile land. This also explains the new attention paid to agricultural development that is meant to form a central part of the country's strategy for economic diversification. Agriculture has been identified as a priority sector by the government, which reflects the global trend spelled out previously (New Partnership for Africa's Development 2003; World Bank 2007). A former public-sector worker in Chipata exclaimed to me on August 18, 2017, "There's nothing that we do not have as a natural resource in Zambia which cannot make farmers move." And an official in the Ministry of Community Development and Social Services in Lusaka moreover explained on March 30, 2017, "Whichever direction you take in Zambia, you find that something could be a resource that could be converted into money." The new developmental and social aspirations of the country are thus based on the untapped potential of its resources; even remote areas provide cause for hope.

Food production and hence FISP, the input subsidy, are perceived to fulfill two aims at once: (1) contribute to economic growth by stimulating the agricultural sector and (2) reduce poverty. Agriculture in general is seen as a core component of economic diversification: that is, of the move away from an overreliance on copper exports (Government of the Republic of Zambia 2017, 65). At the same time, it is viewed as an effective avenue to poverty reduction. The *Second National Agricultural Policy* aims to "promote competitiveness, stimulate efficiency, increased productivity and profitability in the agriculture sector" and "thus contribute effectively to attaining food and nutrition security, employment creation, increased incomes and reduced rural poverty" (Government of the Republic of Zambia 2016c, 8). My interviewee from one of the international financial institutions in Lusaka confirmed on February 5, 2018, the double role: "So the two reasons why we really need agricultural development is, one, start creating the surpluses that allow the economy to shift over to nonagricultural activities to do other things and, second, to start providing income to the people in the rural areas." In fact, the twofold hope placed in agriculture reflects the thinking about this sector in global-development discourse that has increasingly focused on poverty reduction (Shaw 2009, 71–76).

But while there might have been an overall shift globally that blurs economic transformation with the much narrower vision of poverty reduction, the conception of rural people as poor but also (potentially) productive can already be found in Zambia throughout earlier periods (Scott 1995, 2). Kaunda (1969), too, emphasized that the state was supposed to support agricultural production in order to enable people to help themselves and their communities. So rather than creating new rural identities, the rediscovery of the countryside through new agricultural policies entails the reaffirmation of an older dual role. In the following section, I trace some of the epistemic practices that bring this dual role about in the present policy discourse.

PROCESSES OF KNOWING AND UNKNOWING

The introduction of various new programmes under Zambia's *National Social Protection Policy* (Government of the Republic of Zambia 2014) has ushered in a growing interest in getting to know the needs of the people they are supposed to address, as well as the effectiveness of these interventions. While a lot of embodied knowledge is created through the daily implementation of social programs by local officers, another form of knowledge stems from the proliferating studies carried out by professional researchers. This is a case of a much wider trend toward results- and evidence-based policy making that has increasingly defined what counts as valid knowledge and what does not (Eyben 2013; Wolkenhauer 2023). In the Zambian context, national and international researchers undertake impact evaluations and programme assessments in order to plan, review, and improve interventions like FISP. Such research hence plays an important role in the epistemological reconnect that happens in the wake of the new social policies. While it contributes to a better knowledge of remote areas and life worlds, the knowledge that results is shaped by the logics structuring the research itself. These have implications for how identities and relationships are perceived and thus, ultimately shape possibilities for action.

Methodologies structure the ways in which we get to know the countryside in the course of rural social policy research. Perhaps unsurprisingly, agricultural economists play an important role in advising governments and in the academic discussions about agricultural schemes. In Zambia, to give an example, one think tank has a prominent position in public discourse, the Indaba Agricultural Policy and Research Institute (IAPRI). IAPRI not only conducts its own research but also is often chosen as the local partner for foreign researchers and donor organizations and receives external funding from them. It was founded in 2011, emerging out of a research project funded by the United States Agency for International Development (USAID) and Michigan State University, not least because the planning department in the Ministry of Agriculture was insufficient

IAPRI's studies are produced by a team of mostly economists, under the leadership of an executive director who is a former chief executive officer of the Food Reserve Agency (a parastatal institution), former member of Parliament, and former deputy minister of agriculture. IAPRI's connections with the Ministry of Agriculture are hence well developed. The institute has been closely monitoring FISP, its effects on smallholders, poverty levels, and maize production, and it has been involved in a reform process that saw the introduction of an electronic voucher card (Resnick and Mason 2016). IAPRI researchers also prominently shape what is academically known about rural areas in Zambia, featuring in various publications spanning themes like local livelihoods (Matenga and Hichaambwa 2017) and land rights (Sitko, Burke, and Jayne 2018).

Policy evaluations are predominantly based on quantitative methodologies, even if with a qualitative component, as recipients are surveyed and social and economic indicators are measured. The rise in the use of randomized controlled trials (RCTs), which gained a lot of attention with the 2019 Nobel Prize in Economics, epitomizes this trend (de Souza Leão and Eyal 2019). In Zambia, RCTs were, for instance, used in evaluations of the social cash transfer that found—among other things—the productive effects of cash (much in line with previously described overlaps between poverty reduction and production) and was an important political lever for scaling up the cash transfer (Quarles van Ufford et al. 2016). While being praised as the gold standard for evaluations by some, it was seriously critiqued by others for, for example, depoliticized conceptions of empowerment or a neglect of history and context (Kabeer 2020). Research like this contributes to the economization of the social, where state-society relations, policy making, and individual human subjects are increasingly governed by economistic rationales (Madra and Adaman 2013), which also come to shape our common perceptions of African countrysides.

Whether using RCTs or other quantitative methods, evaluations tend to be based on deductive research designs where questions, key concepts, and expected answers are defined at the outset. In an insightful anthropology of public health, Biruk (2018, 60) has described how survey research undertaken in rural Malawi with standardized interview grids led to a twisting of responses to fit predetermined codes. While impact evaluations can and often do leave room for open-ended discussions, too, some contextual detail inevitably needs to be sacrificed in the course of calculating overall tendencies. Equally inevitably, quantitative studies need to work with existing definitions and categories from national or international agencies, such as *household*, *poverty*, and *vulnerability*. Such studies are therefore not the place where epistemological contestation could take place by engaging in deeper reflections about the meaning of *poverty* and *wealth*. Previously defined (and necessarily contingent) categories and identities are thereby further reified.

What also shines through in studying rural areas in Zambia is the dominance of applied research for solutions to problems rather than building and discussing concepts and theories. For obvious reasons, policy makers are interested more in how to make programmes effective than in opening discussions on what it means to be rural or how human identities are affected by capitalist rationalities. Given the underfunding of African universities, such policy-relevant research, often funded by external agencies, has long dominated the research landscape. Universities, however, could be the place for devising future visions, "decolonizing minds," and critically engaging with received wisdoms (Mamdani 2007), something that policy papers cannot deliver.

Besides reproducing certain categories and identities, rural social policy research also builds on and reiterates accepted readings of Zambian history. For similar reasons as stated earlier, policy evaluations are not the place to engage in deep studies of historical sources. Often, history features in the "Background" section of a report or evaluation, either beginning at the inception of a given program or at an earlier point, in an attempt to contextualize present policies. A 2018 World Bank publication, for instance, that discusses ways of reducing risk and increasing resilience for smallholders devotes a few pages to the historical background of agricultural policies in Zambia, discussing national and international influences on the sector (Braimoh et al. 2018, 7–11). This policy discourse is not completely ahistorical, yet the types of questions that are asked of history remain somewhat limited. Such background paragraphs do not usually address the historical marginalization and injustice that rural people have experienced since the colonial era. Nor are historical experiences taken seriously for informing policy choices.

In the World Bank example, the "History" section reiterates several phases in Zambian history, including the structural adjustment reforms of the 1990s, which—stated in this report—negatively affected rural production and livelihoods. What is not mentioned, though, is the important social role that the cooperative movement had played during much of the Kaunda era for rural people and how many of the social problems addressed today were exacerbated by cutting the funding to cooperative structures during the 1990s. In a way, then, history literally remains in the background; it is not explored in more detail for possible solutions that might have existed in the past. A more thorough engagement with the complex histories of state-driven agricultural development and the hostile international context that these interventions faced might have led to slightly different conceptions of the transformation from Humanism to capitalism that is not so unidirectional after all. It could also broaden the understanding of what needs to change in order to achieve the envisaged transformation.

The partial reading of history leads to situations where policy reforms are based more on universal theories of change than actual historical experiences. For instance, the introduction in FISP of an electronic voucher card and, connected to this, the intended reliance of smallholders on private agro-dealers rather than on state delivery of seed and fertilizer have encountered several difficulties. Even though presenting itself as a much-needed remedy to several problems that FISP had encountered, the e-voucher reform shifted rather than resolved many of these problems (now, for instance, smallholders were not waiting in vain for state deliveries but were waiting in vain for agro-dealers to set up shop). The mixed success of the reform, which had been strongly endorsed by donors and IAPRI but not initially the Ministry of Agriculture itself, was then explained away as "teething problems." This hopeful narrative seemed unimpressed by earlier experiences with private agro-dealers, who had, after the sector's liberalization in the 1990s, not provided the hoped-for rural infrastructure for farmers, either (Chiwele, Muyatwa-Sipula, and Kalinda 1996, 11). To rely on the private sector once again seemed to be driven more by the skepticism toward state employees than by a realistic assessment of the availability and accessibility of private dealers in remote places. In both cases, regarding the lack of space for situational detail, as well as the partial representation of history, one might speak of unknowing rather than knowing the countryside.

Last, the fact that policies are informed by inscribed knowledge like research findings and program evaluations entails a degree of depoliticization. As indicated in the introduction, the initial economic disconnect between centers and peripheries has long had mutually reinforcing effects with a political disconnect, in that social groups in rural areas are less politically influential (Mhone 1982). This bias is not only reflected in the stronger position of industrial trade unions compared to farmers' groups but also within the agricultural sector itself. The main farmers' union has its origin in the European commercial settler farmers' bureau, and although it has since evolved and efforts have been undertaken to also include smallholders, the union is still widely perceived to be biased toward bigger farmers. For historical reasons, the latter tend to be located in the country's more accessible central areas. Policies for smallholder farmers, such as FISP, in contrast, are made on their behalf from the top down and are informed more by research findings and negotiations at the center than as a response to organized political demands (Wolkenhauer 2020). In the technocratic policy making that results, debates are narrowed around questions of how to fine-tune policies to make them more effective. As Voß and Freeman (2016, 4) spell out, technocratic governance "is worked out in competition for epistemic authority, rather than in the probings, conflicts, and corroborations of political mobilisation and public debate." And in this competition, those with the most refined measurement techniques and more highly recognized academic degrees possess more epistemic authority. In sum, if neoliberalism is a way of governing through knowledge (Bacevic 2019), then political contestation would have to address this knowledge production itself.

CONCLUSION: DIVERSIFYING KNOWLEDGES

Why does all this matter? How roles, identities, and responsibilities are being inscribed in how we know rural people and places through agricultural policies has material effects. This knowledge provides the basis for political decisions—about state services, land reforms, and not least international aid. This chapter provides a brief description of the place that rural people and places are assigned in recent, transnationalised Zambian social policy discourse and traces some epistemic practices that enable this discursive order. One of the main conclusions is a methodological one: rethinking and contesting accepted futures of the rural cannot happen in the economistic knowledge that pervades political and a lot of academic discourse.

Different forms of knowing, importantly those resulting from lived experience, need to become more influential in shaping policies and common perceptions. Historical context and theoretical reflections could open the space for thinking about transformations in the countryside in ways that provide real alternatives to, instead of a fine-tuning of, the present order. Knowledge production can then become a site for political contestation. Last, an awareness of the importance of knowledge in shaping social policies also entails an imperative to rethink our own place in this apparatus as academics. Given the intricate connections between policy and academic research on rural places, more self-reflexivity is needed about the performative effects of our own epistemic practices.

NOTE

1. Because of high rural-urban inequality and rural poverty levels, interventions targeted at improving agricultural output are located at the blurred boundary of economic (agricultural) and social policy.

REFERENCES

Amin, Samir. 1972. "Underdevelopment and Dependence in Black Africa: Origins and Contemporary Forms." *Journal of Modern African Studies* 10 (4): 503–24.

Bacevic, Jana. 2019. "Knowing Neoliberalism." *Social Epistemology* 33 (4): 380–92.

Béland, Daniel, and Klaus Petersen. 2017. "Exploring Social Policy Ideas and Language." In *Handbook of European Social Policy*, edited by Patricia Kennett and Noemi Lendvai-Bainton, 15–28. Cheltenham, UK: Edward Elgar.

Berten, John, and Lutz Leisering. 2017. "Social Policy by Numbers: How International Organisations Construct Global Policy Proposals." *International Journal of Social Welfare* 26 (2): 151–67.

Biruk, Crystal. 2018. *Cooking Data: Culture and Politics in an African Research World*. Durham, NC: Duke University Press.

Braimoh, Ademola, Alex Mwanakasale, Antony Chapoto, Rhoda Rubaiza, Brian Chisanga, Ngao Mubanga, Paul Samboko, Asa Hoglund Giertz, and Grace Obuya. 2018. *Increasing Agricultural Resilience through Better Risk Management in Zambia*. Washington, DC: World Bank.

Chang, Ha-Joon. 2009. "Rethinking Public Policy in Agriculture: Lessons from History, Distant and Recent." *Journal of Peasant Studies* 36 (3): 477–515.

Chiwele, Dennis K., Pumulo Muyatwa-Sipula, and Henrietta Kalinda. 1996. *Private Sector Response to Agricultural Marketing Liberalisation in Zambia: A Case Study of Eastern Province Maize Markets*. Uppsala, Sweden: Nordiska Afrikainstitutet.

de Souza Leão, Luciana, and Gil Eyal. 2019. "The Rise of Randomized Controlled Trials (RCTs) in International Development in Historical Perspective." *Theory and Society* 48: 383–418.

Eyben, Rosalind. 2013. "Uncovering the Politics of 'Evidence' and 'Results': A Framing Paper for Development Practitioners." Paper prepared for the Politics of Evidence Conference, Institute of Development Studies, Brighton, UK, April 23–24.

Freeman, Richard, and Steve Sturdy. 2014. "Introduction: Knowledge in Policy—Embodied, Inscribed, Enacted." In *Knowledge in Policy: Embodied, Inscribed, Enacted*, edited by Richard Freeman and Steve Sturdy, 1–18. Bristol, UK: Bristol University Press.

Ghodsee, Kristen. 2019. *Second World, Second Sex: Socialist Women's Activism and Global Solidarity during the Cold War*. Durham, NC: Duke University Press.

Government of the Republic of Zambia. 2006. *Vision 2030*. Lusaka: Government of the Republic of Zambia.

———. 2014. *National Social Protection Policy*. Lusaka: Government of the Republic of Zambia.

———. 2016a. *Electronic Voucher Implementation Manual 2016/17 Agricultural Season*. Lusaka: Government of the Republic of Zambia.

———. 2016b. *FISP Implementation Manual 2016/17*. Lusaka: Government of the Republic of Zambia.

———. 2016c. *Second National Agricultural Policy*. Lusaka: Government of the Republic of Zambia.

———. 2017. *7 National Development Plan 2017–2021*. Lusaka: Government of the Republic of Zambia.

Kabeer, Naila. 2020. "Women's Empowerment and Economic Development: A Feminist Critique of Storytelling Practices in 'Randomista' Economics." *Feminist Economics* 26 (2): 1–26.

Kaunda, Kenneth. 1968. *Humanism in Zambia and a Guide to Its Implementation*. Lusaka: Zambia Information Services.

———. 1969. "Humanism in Zambia." In *After Mulungushi: The Economics of Zambian Humanism*, edited by Bastiaan de Gaay Fortman, 9–33. Nairobi, Kenya: East African Publishing House.

Kuhlmann, Johanna, Delia González de Reufels, Klaus Schlichte, and Frank Nullmeier. 2020. "How Social Policy Travels: A Refined Model of Diffusion." *Global Social Policy* 20 (1): 80–96.

Madra, Yahya M., and Fikret Adaman. 2013. "Neoliberal Reason and Its Forms: De-Politicisation through Economisation." *Antipode* 46 (3): 691–716.

Mamdani, Mahmood. 2007. *Scholars in the Marketplace: The Dilemmas of Neo-Liberal Reform at Makerere University, 1989–2005*. Kampala, Uganda: Fountain.

Matenga, Chrispin R., and Munguzwe Hichaambwa. 2017. "Impacts of Land and Agricultural Commercialisation on Local Livelihoods in Zambia: Evidence from Three Models." *Journal of Peasant Studies* 44 (3): 574–93.

Mhone, Guy. 1982. *The Political Economy of a Dual Labor Market in Africa: The Copper Industry and Dependency in Zambia, 1929–1969*. Madison, WI: Fairleigh Dickinson University Press.

———. 2004. "Historical Trajectories of Social Policy in Post-Colonial Africa: The Case of Zambia." In *Social Policy in a Development Context*, edited by Thandika Mkandawire, 308–37. New York: Palgrave Macmillan.

New Partnership for Africa's Development. 2003. *Comprehensive Africa Agriculture Development Programme*. Midrand, South Africa: New Partnership for Africa's Development.

Quarles van Ufford, Paul, Charlotte Harland, Stanfield Michelo, Gelson Tembo, Kelley Toole, and Denis Wood. 2016. "The Role of Impact Evaluation in the Evolution of Zambia's Cash Transfer Programme." In *From Evidence to Action: The Story of Cash Transfers and Impact Evaluation in Sub Saharan Africa*, edited by Benjamin Davis, Sudhanshu Handa, Nicola Hypher, Natalia Winder Rossi, Paul Winters, and Jennifer Yablonski, 197–225. Oxford, UK: Oxford University Press.

Resnick, Danielle, and Nicole M. Mason. 2016. *What Drives Input Subsidy Policy Reform? The Case of Zambia, 2002–2016*. IFPRI discussion paper 1572, International Food Policy Research Institute, Washington, DC.

Scott, Guy. 1995. "Agricultural Transformation in Zambia: Past Experience and Future Prospects." Paper presented at the Workshop on Agricultural Transformation in Africa, Abidjan, Côte d'Ivoire, September 26–29.

Shaw, D. John. 2009. *Global Food and Agricultural Institutions*. London: Routledge.

Sitko, Nicholas J., William J. Burke, and T. S. Jayne. 2018. "The Quiet Rise of Large-Scale Trading Firms in East and Southern Africa." *Journal of Development Studies* 54 (5): 895–914. https://www.doi.org/10.1080/00220388.2018.1430773.

Voß, Jan-Peter, and Richard Freeman. 2016. "Introduction: Knowing Governance." In *Knowing Governance: The Epistemic Construction of Political Order*, edited by Jan-Peter Voß and Richard Freeman, 1–33. London: Palgrave Macmillan.

Wedel, Janine R., Cris Shore, Gregory Feldman, and Stacy Lathrop. 2005. "Toward an Anthropology of Public Policy." *Annals of the American Academy of Political and Social Science* 600 (1): 30–51.

Wolkenhauer, Anna. 2020. "State Formation after Retrenchment: Social Policy in Zambia." Unpublished PhD diss., University of Bremen, Germany.

———. 2022. "The Colonial Legacies of Copper Dependence: Inequality and Bifurcated Social Protection in Zambia." In *International Impacts on Social Policy: Short Histories in a Global Perspective*, edited by Frank Nullmeier, Delia González de Reufels, and Herbert Obinger, 119–30. Cham, Switzerland: Palgrave Macmillan.

———. 2023. "Neoliberalism, Social Policy, and the State: Searching for the Transformative Potential of Zambia's Social Cash Transfer." *Canadian Journal of Development Studies* (*Revue canadienne d'études du développement*): 1–17.

World Bank. 2007. *World Development Report 2008: Agriculture for Development*. Washington, DC: World Bank Group.

Chapter 8

On the European Union's Epistemologies of Soils' Resourcefulness, or

Why Land and Soil Are Not the Same

Maarten Meijer

There has been a lot of talking about land, but as Dr. Montanarella [of the European Union's Joint Research Center] has already argued in the past, land and soil are not the same! Where land is political and economic, soil is natural and scientific.

—A. Perdigão, Portuguese delegate to Global Soil Partnership's Seventh Plenary Assembly

In early June 2019 at the Food and Agriculture Organization's (FAO) headquarters in Rome during an afternoon session of the Global Soil Partnership's (GSP) Seventh Annual Plenary Assembly, a member of the delegation of Portugal intervened with a fiery proclamation, loosely quoted here: *land and soil are not the same*. Despite the lackluster fashion in which it was received by the other attendees at the time, in this chapter I wish to take seriously and interpret this striking statement of geo-philosophy. On its face, we might follow the delegate's own suggestion and conclude that this statement reveals a strategy of depoliticization. Thus, we might interpret the statement as suggesting the following: instead of talking about land, which is too politically sensitive because it draws in questions of, for example, land rights, let's talk about soil and pretend that we can do so under the apolitical cover of scientific objectivity! Though certainly not without its merits, I wish to develop another interpretation: differentiated from those of land, epistemologies of soil open their own modes of politics.

This politics of soil is best understood in terms of cosmopolitics, the ongoing (re)construction of worlds (Hui 2017; Latour 2004, 2009; Stengers 2010). This concept was developed by Stengers and Latour in response to debates in and around science and technology studies regarding the question of how science and technology could be understood as being engaged in *politics by other means* (e.g., de Vries 2007). Questioning the politics of science, Stengers and Latour proposed, cannot be reduced to considering the personal or institutional political values that scientists may mobilize in their work but rather invites reflection on the inherent constructedness of scientific knowledge. Some sociologists of science had problematized this *constructedness* in a critical social constructivist register, as if pointing out the constructedness of scientific knowledge would be enough to unmask scientific claims as all-too-human fabrications (e.g., Knorr-Cetina 1985). By contrast, the philosophy of cosmopolitics proposes that scientific knowledge is constructed akin to the way a bridge is constructed: in a more-or-less robust fashion, arising out of a practical negotiation between materials, knowledges, and values that involves both human questions of power and authority, as well as nonhuman *agencies*. Ultimately at stake in the concept of cosmopolitics is not just a political philosophy of scientific practices alone but a political philosophy of reality-constructing practices as such, including those of, for example, legal, technological, artistic, religious, and more "conventional" political characters (Conway 2020; Latour 2013; Stengers 2005). A cosmopolitical analysis therefore invites questioning how a reality is constructed, how it might be constructed otherwise, and what the consequences of constructing it in this way or that are for the further organization of the cosmos.

Soils and lands, accordingly, are not to be taken for granted as stable entities but interrogated as beings under constant reconstruction and implicated in the reconstruction of other beings, as situated entities whose being is affected by and affecting the relations and contexts in which they feature (Krzywoszynska and Marchesi 2020; Salazar et al. 2020). As such, the soil cultivated by a farmer is admittedly similar but certainly not the same as the soil eaten by a geophage or the soil governed by a state bureaucracy. To interrogate the modes of politics of soil as differentiated from land is to interrogate the way in which this explicit or implicit juxtaposition is made possible through and makes possible particular forms of cosmopolitics. This interrogation I pursue in a sideways manner through an analysis of the European Union's tentative engagement with soil governance since the 1990s and especially since the early 2000s. Facing what it called a series of soil threats culminating in *soil degradation*, the European Commission has launched a series of initiatives around policy, education, science, and monitoring that have reconstituted soil as an object of governance. Despite a lack of success in generating binding soil-protection legislation, these initiatives have been picked up by and given rise to forums like the GSP, an unofficial body of the FAO, in which the European Commission is an important player (De Donà 2021).

This chapter proceeds in analyzing the cosmopolitics of EU soil governance in three registers, drawing on EU policy documents and technical reports, as well as fieldwork in 2019 and 2020 during the meetings of the GSP, the European Soil Partnership (one of the regional bodies of the GSP), and the European Network on Soil Awareness. First, I deconstruct soil as an object and medium of governance on the level of policy discourse through a contextualized reading of main policy documents. Second, I highlight the significance of technoscientific apparatuses in the reconstitution or the *re-sourcing* of soils in a governance context. Third, I engage with the discourses and practices of *soil awareness*, as supported and instigated by EU soil governance. Drawing on this analysis of the mode(s) of cosmopolitics as generative of and generated by soils in an EU governance context, I conclude by returning to the question of differentiating epistemologies of land from soil as raised earlier.

RE-SOURCING SOILS

In 2006, the European Commission launched its Soil Thematic Strategy as part of its sixth Environmental Action Programme, which set out to protect Europe's environmental media, such as air, fresh water, and soil. European soils, the Strategy argues, are increasingly and gravely threatened by a diverse set of anthropogenic degradation processes, such as contamination, erosion, soil sealing, and loss of organic matter and biodiversity. As part of its strategy to protect soils, the Commission has set up a monitoring infrastructure, invested in soil science, promoted soil awareness to various publics, and attempted to launch legislation to protect soils in the European Union (European Commission 2006). In the context of the latter, its most ambitious piece of legislation, the Soil Framework Directive, which was launched shortly after the Strategy, failed to meet the necessary amount of support in the Council of Ministers and was eventually withdrawn in 2013 (Chen 2019). More recently, themes of soil protection have returned to policy prominence through the European Green Deal and its associated policies, including a new Soil Strategy for 2030 and the Soil Deal for Europe mission within the Horizon Europe research and innovation program, which envisages making greater use of soils as a carbon sink and strongly reducing the use of pesticides and fertilizers (Montanarella and Panagos 2021). Notwithstanding these ambitions, these concerns have not found their way into the Common Agricultural Policy plans for the period 2023–2027, partly as the result of the successful lobbying of agribusiness pressure groups like COPA-COGECA in the Parliament and Council of Ministers.

The state-of-the-environment reports by the European Environment Agency, which provides EU policy makers with environmental data every five years, posit that the situation of soils in Europe is, on most accounts and in most geographies, deteriorating as a result of urban development, industrial activity, and "conventional" farming (European Environment Agency 2015, 2019, 114–31; Jones et al. 2012). However, what these reports do not explicate is that the disclosure of soils as degraded presupposes more than the material effects of anthropogenic soil destruction in combination with changing climatic conditions. Rather, the issue of soil degradation also presupposes a changing problematization of soils' values and functions as well as the way these can be destroyed. Concerns with soils and their destruction are certainly as old as the history of agriculture and can be found in the agricultural historical practices and writings of many different societies (e.g., McNeill and Winiwarter 2004). Within the more circumscribed history of the modern European state, a distinct genealogy of soil concerns can be traced that has given rise to different kinds of soil governance projects (Lyons 2020; Pawley 2010; Simmons 2006). Part of what makes this genealogy distinct is the emergence of a particular epistemic authority on soils: soil scientists and their diverging and changing problematizations of soils over time (Brevik, Fenton, and Homburg 2016; Cohen 2009; Marchesi 2020; Sayre 2010). Typically, the cosmopolitics of these soil scientists has revolved around unearthing and operationalizing the nature of the productive power of soils, soils' resourcefulness, while simultaneously encountering soils' fragility, or their resourcelessness.

The concept of soil degradation as mobilized by the European Union presupposes changing definitions of what soils are and what soils do and coemerges with more scientific attention to the role of human activity and soil biodiversity in soil-forming processes and to the role of soils in the Earth's systems (Richter and Yaalon 2012). As Luca Montaranella (2008, 75), a senior soil expert in the Commission's Joint Research Centre (JRC), explains, "[s]oils are no longer considered only as dumping sites, construction surfaces or means for production (agriculture and forestry) but also as a fundamental environmental component." For instance, the 2006 Soil Thematic Strategy acknowledges the importance of soils "as a platform for human activities and landscape and as an archive of heritage" (European Commission 2006), as well as stressing its links to questions of biodiversity; the cycling and storage of such elements as water and carbon; and the more traditional importance for the production of food, biomass, and raw materials.

Without really moving away from a resource-oriented epistemology of soils altogether, the notion of soils' degrading multifunctionality implies a changing understanding of what the resourcefulness of soils, increasingly couched in the language of ecosystem services, entails (Baveye, Baveye, and Gowdy 2016; Krzywoszynska 2020).

In the context of redefining the functionality of soil, the influence of Earth-system science is particularly striking. Problematizing soils through their interaction with other planetary systems, such as the atmosphere, draws attention to the practical conditions under which soils emit or sequester greenhouse gases. Whereas heavy tillage and drainage of soils leads to increased CO_2 emissions, such nonmainstream agricultural practices as no-till farming help soil biota sequester atmospheric carbon. Moreover, in urban spaces, soils are increasingly being returned to public life as a measure of climate adaptation to help improve (rain)water and heat regulation. Both through formal legislation and other measures and programs, especially in the context of the European Green Deal, EU soil policy efforts try to govern and promote such agencies of soils by governing how, for example, farmers till (or, rather, do not till) their soils and promote greater attention to the importance of soils in climate-adaptive cityscapes. In part, then, the concept of soil degradation implicates the re-sourcing of soils through the perspective of what postcolonial historian Chakrabarty (2018, 2019) calls the "planetary," the perspective on life, space, and history that emerges from Earth-system science. By re-sourcing soils through their interactions with parts of the atmosphere and biosphere, this planetary perspective introduces a logic whereby new configurations of environmental policy, agricultural practices, urban planning, and soils can emerge.

This understanding of soil as a multifunctional service provider that operates in EU soil-policy discourses is associated with other, partly preexisting notions on the ways in which soils are entities in need of protection and governance. This includes a particular problematization of soils' nonhuman temporality, which underlies the particular way soils are understood as essentially nonrenewable resources from the perspective of society, despite not being so from a perspective of geological time (see Engel-Di Mauro 2014, 87–90; Shiva 2015). Additionally, emphasis is put on soils' variability in use and composition, which requires the constitution of sufficiently detailed monitoring networks, attention to local socioeconomic and environmental circumstances, and multiscalar soil-protection efforts. In turn, these notions enable particular modes of governance, as seen from the recurring assertion that soils' multitude of functions or ecosystem services pertain to the public nature of soils, which enables European policy makers to govern soils despite their status as private property. The latter crucially echoes the distinction between soil and land proposed by the Portuguese delegation to the 2019 GSP meeting as cited previously: differentiating soils' geo-bio-agency, or their public character, from their private-property status opens particular forms of governing and politicizing soils.

Largely, the process of assembling the different functions, values, and problems of soils takes place not only through the bureaucratic tools of stakeholder meetings and scientific consultations but also through the technical work of determining criteria and indicators used in monitoring soils. As the considerable formal and informal resistance to binding EU soil-protection measures like the Soil Framework Directive suggest, however, the political significance of this seemingly technocratic epistemology of soils is not lost on EU member states and agribusiness lobbyists. Through this contested process of re-sourcing soils, then, soils simultaneously pass into public visibility and become tentatively redefined as objects of governance (Meulemans 2020; Puig de la Bellacasa 2014).

GEO-INFORMATIONAL APPARATUSES

To a significant extent, the output of the European Union's soil-protection efforts is concerned with managing, setting up, and improving the informational flows that connect soils to Europe. This includes funding research projects of various kinds, ranging from studies of agricultural sociology to fundamental research into the importance of soil microbiodiversity or the role of soils in the Earth system. Scientific output resulting from such projects is translated into models, databases, and new indicators that find their way to policy makers through the JRC of the European Commission, which in many ways functions as an institution of translation between science and policy. Many of these indicators are used to set up and inform soil-monitoring efforts in Europe. Monitoring infrastructures exist to varying degrees in EU member states, and an integral effort of the Soil Thematic Strategy has been to improve and harmonize these existing infrastructures by intensifying monitoring efforts and changing, adding, and refining indicators of soil quality, in particular those related to biodiversity. In addition, European institutions have been involved in setting up their own soil-monitoring efforts through such programs as LUCAS, a triennial survey on land use and land cover executed by Eurostat. This involves sending out surveyors to make in situ observations and collect soil samples, which are combined with satellite data and used to continuously update and refine the European Soil Data Centre and the EU Soil Observatory, both hosted by the JRC (Montanarella and Panagos 2021; Panagos et al. 2012).

Thus, students of soil politics in Europe witness the ongoing development of a geo- or pedo- (from *pedon*, the Greek word for *ground*) informational apparatus that connects satellites, sensors, surveyors, soil labs, maps, academics, and data centers. Programs of monitoring, mapping, and studying soils—the networks for which are largely managed and organized by such institutions as the JRC, the European Soil Bureau, the FAO's GSP Secretariat, and national centers of expertise—represent soils to policy makers but also redefine soils, thereby opening new avenues of politicization and governance as argued previously. In this sense, the emergence of soil degradation as a problem of technoscientific governance is similar to issues of climate change and Earth-system science whose emergence on the public space similarly relies on the vast epistemological machines that make them knowable and governable though not necessarily known or governed (Barry 2001; Edwards 2010).

Historically, the sciences of soils have positioned themselves as possessing privileged epistemic authority to speak on matters related to soils, setting themselves apart from other kinds of "experts of the land," like farmers, but also scientific competitors that have sought to reduce soil to larger domains, like geology (Amundson 2006; Evtuhov 2006; Marchesi 2020; Salazar et al. 2020). Crucially, though this privileged perspective on soils lays the groundwork for not just the study but also the governance of soils, the specific epistemic registers through which they do so are open to change and have historically shifted its center from agro-chemistry in the nineteenth century to agrogeology or pedology in the twentieth century and more recently to Earth-system science. The European Union's pedo-informational apparatuses make Europe's soils knowable in new ways and help construct soil degradation as a problem that could be governed while simultaneously highlighting the qualitative and quantitative lack of both basic and applied soil knowledge, such as a better understanding of the importance of soil biodiversity, better soil indicators, and better monitoring systems. Pedo-informational apparatuses are thereby producing not only a particular series of discourses around soil degradation but also the need for an extension of the very same apparatuses. Yet, as Kon Kam King and Granjou (2020) argue, this shift in scientific soil epistemologies toward Earth-system science is not simply productive of scientific attention to soils but also tends to privilege digital kinds of knowing soils over the more qualitative fieldwork-oriented studies that have characterized pedology or more classical soil science in the twentieth century. Though fieldwork still matters, as evidenced through Eurostat's LUCAS program, the logic and practice of fieldwork studies are increasingly dictated by the requirements of modelers rather than the other way around, leading to an increasing *ungrounding* of soil epistemologies (Kon Kam King and Granjou 2020; for similar views, see Frodeman 2003). As an object of knowledge, in other words, the material medium of soil is becoming increasingly entangled with digital media. An exemplary illustration of how this logic operates on and redefines soils is provided by a European critical-zone research project funded under the heading of the Soil Thematic Strategy, titled SoilTrEC.

From 2009 to 2014, the European Commission provided funding to SoilTrEC, which aimed to improve its understanding of the fundamental role of soils in the Earth system's "critical zone" and "to develop a scientific framework to quantify soil functions and threats and design methods for improving soil functions" (Banwart, Bernasconi et al. 2015, 6). Among others, this project included setting up four field laboratories called critical zone observatories (CZOs) in the European Union, selected to represent different stages in the development of soils and different forms of agricultural use (Menon et al. 2014, 3193–94; Montanarella and Panagos 2015). The critical zone is a spatial concept that emerged out of a desire to understand the specific processes involved in the surface system of the Earth in the early 2000s, in the larger field of Earth-system sciences. The critical zone is taken to be the space inhabited by most life forms on Earth, roughly extending from the lowest aquifers to the top of the canopy. This zone is *critical* because it is comprised of a series of relatively fragile processes that are critical to life on Earth and that can be disrupted when put under stress, for example by human activity. Thus, the critical zone embodies a spatial trope encountered in philosophical discussions of the Anthropocene: the rejection of a theatrical metaphor for thinking about the space of human society and politics. Accordingly, the Anthropocene's geologicization of the human and the humanization of the Earth constitutes a rejection of the metaphor that sees the (natural) world as a passive stage or background on which human action takes place (Hamilton 2016; Latour 2017). In the critical zone, foreground and background are no longer straightforwardly separable (Latour 2014, 5; Latour and Weibel 2020).

This planetary surface space is studied through CZOs, which are linked together in various networks. SoilTrEC's CZOs generate the situatedness of the knowledge produced of the critical zone by circumscribing the field through a range of sensory instruments (Walker 1999; see also Krzywoszynska, Banwart, and Blacker 2020). CZOs provide the rough data through satellites, in situ sensors, and manual measurements, which are subsequently used to build and refine digital models of the critical zone, the ultimate deliverable of projects like SoilTrEC. This interdisciplinary field-study orientation gives critical-zone research its innovative character and undergirds its establishment as a novel field of research that asks and answers very basic questions about the composition, architecture, and dynamics of critical zones (Banwart, Chorover et al. 2013, 20; Giardino and Houser 2015, 8). Though the critical zone superficially operates from the general holistic notion that all processes and entities that compose it are interconnected in a myriad of fashions, the concept itself does not specify what *particular* connections it assembles in concrete settings (White et al. 2015, 15–19). Rather than the familiarity of the landscape of one's home, the critical zone is presented as the life support of our existence, of which humans are inescapably an integral ingredient, and yet simultaneously as an unfamiliar space that requires new modes of interrogation, new sensory instruments, and even new forms of heliocentric maps in order to be navigated (Arènes, Latour, and Gaillardet 2018; Latour and Weibel 2020). More significant than this, SoilTrEC redefines soils and thereby redefines what it means to be situated in earthly space through the frame of reference provided by Earth-system science (Banwart, Bernasconi et al. 2015, 6). Exemplary here is the role of soils in the fluxes of carbon. Soils and soil organisms can, under certain conditions, sequester carbon from the atmosphere or alternatively function as a significant source of greenhouse gases. These conditions are affected also by anthropogenic factors, such as methods of cultivation, including tillage and water-level management. Thus, these planetary functionalities of soils, whose understanding presupposes but also promotes new epistemic communities (such as critical-zone science) to concern themselves with the study of soils, opens the space for new geopolitical initiatives, such as the European Green Deal or the French Initiative 4 per 1000 that seek to enhance soil-carbon sequestration by changing land-management practices (Hamilton 2016; Kon Kam King et al. 2018).

SOIL AWARENESS

So far, this chapter argues that soils have returned to public prominence in the European Union as their values and functions are being cosmopolitically reconstituted as objects of governance on the level of policy discourses in tandem with new scientific problematizations of soils. Demonstrating the need of interrogating how such soil practices emerge and operate in particular contexts of governance, the previous section highlights how scientific ideas pertaining to the revaluation of the biophysical agency of soils are informing projects of governing (with) soils. This section extends this line of argumentation to questions of *soil care* and *soil attentiveness*. Here, I elaborate on European practices on soil awareness that largely emerged out of the Thematic Strategy for Soil Protection launched by the European Commission in 2006, which try to reconnect Europeans to the soils on which they unwittingly depend.

Though the state of soils should concern every facet of European societies, according to the European Commission (2006), Europeans do not seem concerned enough. In the face of this lack of interest, a series of soil-advocacy institutions and events have spawned in the wake of the Commission's Soil Thematic Strategy, often under the initial direction of the Commission or its subsidiary bodies. The two main institutional networks engaged in this task are, most importantly, the European Network on Soil Awareness (ENSA) and, to a lesser extent, the working group responsible for the European Soil Partnership's second pillar. ENSA is a loose network of organizations, policy makers, activists, educators, and scientists that are variously involved in awareness raising on soils and their dire state in Europe. ENSA provides a platform for various national soil-awareness organizations, allowing them to exchange information, ideas, and experiences on soil awareness (Broll 2009). Thus, ENSA has close ties with the European Soil Bureau (ESBN), the network of national soil centers of expertise housed at the JRC of the Commission, and such nongovernmental organizations (NGOs) as the European Land and Soil Alliance (ELSA).

As one of its core tasks, ENSA organizes a biannual conference in which representatives from national and regional NGOs in EU member states, such European Commission bodies as the Directorate-General (DG) for the Environment or the JRC, national ministries, and research institutes gather to exchange ideas and experiences and coordinate efforts on soil awareness. The nature of individual contributions varies, from updates over upcoming soil-related conferences to accounts of summer schools, soil-profiling contests, educational programs at schools, artistic and educational exhibitions at museums, social media campaigns, and policy-making efforts at various levels of governance (European Soil Data Centre n.d.). Some of the more striking products coming out of these awareness-raising efforts are the series of soil atlases launched by the European Commission in an attempt to increase knowledge and appreciation of soils, their importance, and the socioenvironmental problems facing them, for both policy makers and the general public (Jeffrey et al. 2010; Jones, Montanarella, and Jones 2005).

Though soil-awareness discourses draw on and incorporate elements from soil science, as well as discussions on soil policy, and are occasionally produced by soil scientists and policy makers, the texts, lectures, movies, and exhibitions concerned with soil awareness do not allow themselves to be straightforwardly categorized in either genre (Jones 2013). Soils are not problematized as a scientific object to be known nor simply a policy object to be governed but an object that first and foremost demands or requires attention from a public that is distracted, inattentive, or ignorant. Rather than governing soils directly, the practice of soil awareness raising therefore aims to govern the cognitive and affective relations European citizens have with soils. This presents itself in at least two relatively distinct guises, in what could be called a narrative of alienation and a narrative of wonder that are sometimes mobilized in isolation and at other times blended.

Typically, soil degradation is presented first and foremost as a problem of negligence and alienation. Soil is posited as vital to society and human life in a plethora of ways—food, water, healthy living environments, and medicine, to name a few—and yet the majority of society remains unaware of its importance. Thus, for example, the 2005 *Soil Atlas of Europe*, published by the European Commission, states in its introduction,

> When different people refer to "The Soil" they usually have rather different ideas of what this means. . . . However, to the vast majority of the human race living in cities and towns, soil is simply the "dirt" or "dust" to be cleaned from their hands or the vegetables that they buy to eat. Many large supermarket retailers in the western world now do this before putting them on display in order to make such produce "more attractive and presentable." (Jones, Montanarella, and Jones 2005, 10)

Implicit or explicit in such narratives is a story of alienation that involves a combination of urbanization, industrialization, and the intensification of agriculture, whereby individual citizens no longer experience their manifold connections to soils while collectively putting an increasing amount of pressure on and pollutants in soils. Documents and authors attending to this narrative spend a lot of time reminding their readers of the various ways in which they are already relying on soils, thus making visible the value of soil that is already there but goes unnoticed. One of the spatial effects that soil-advocacy practices thus seek to generate is the transformation of the awareness of the space necessary for subsistence, extending it beyond the realm of the familiar surface. In addition, the *Soil Atlas of Europe* takes note of humanity's positive soil-producing role, both historically and in contemporary settings (Jones, Montanarella, and Jones 2005, 17). More than simply taking note of various *Anthrosols* and *Technosols*, soil types formed through human activities, the *Soil Atlas* also provides a rudimentary gardening guide to composting. With the collaborative effort of earthworms, soil bacteria, and enzymes, its readers are invited to exert their pedological agency in their own backyard as they turn fruits, vegetables, old socks, and vacuum cleaner waste into valuable organic matter that feeds plants (Jones, Montanarella, and Jones 2005, 19).

Despite the fact that documents like the various soil atlases published by the Commission tend to present European urbanites as generally ignorant of the soils on which they depend, these documents do not seek to erect a dichotomy between urban and rural on the question of soil. In fact, in many ways, the documents reflect a desire to broaden the discussion on soils beyond the narrow domain of agriculture as part of a general strategy of the Commission's DG Environment working on soils (e.g., Pederson et al. 2016). Yet, despite going into extensive detail on the anthropogenic *threats* to soils and soil biota, such as contamination, erosion, or soil sealing and their effects on soils, the soil atlases lack a concrete political analysis that allocates responsibility for the state of soils (Jeffrey et al. 2010, 62–65; Jones, Montanarella, and Jones

2005, 108–18). Rather, these documents present such claims as "Traditional users of the land had a clear view of the key role of the soil in their lives; many modern users of soil are often strong followers of short-term productive goals, ignoring the effects of their practices on the environment" (Jeffrey et al. 2010; Jones, Montanarella, and Jones 2005, 119).

In addition to this narrative of alienation, soil advocacy often operates on the generation of wonder. Here, soils are not just posited as neglected by some unarticulated process of alienation but are instead posited as inherently obscure. Soils are literally and figuratively unseen and below our feet (e.g., Lefèvre et al. 2017; Rodríguez Eugenio, McLaughlin, and Pennock 2018). Rather than a problem of alienation, this line of reasoning argues that soil awareness needs to deal with the fact that soils are out of sight, out of mind, therefore highlighting the need for brightly colored soil maps or vivid imagery of the rich color schemes of soil horizons and strange soil-dwelling organisms (Bartol and White 2015). More than invisible, soil-awareness material ofttimes presents soils as wonderful and alien worlds that are both little understood and teeming with life. Here, authors and artists eagerly reproduce similar figures: that a third of all living organisms are soil dwelling; that a teaspoon of soil contains billions of bacteria, fungi, and other microorganisms; that only 1 percent of soil organisms are identified; and that soils contain more than 90 percent of our planet's biodiversity (e.g., Jeffrey et al. 2010; Keuning 2015, 15–17; Robbins 2013).

Thus, a common trope within soil-awareness campaigns and material is the invitation to explore the "hidden world under our feet" (Puig de la Bellacasa 2019). In doing so, soil-awareness advocates seek to provide a sense of depth or subterraneity to the surface on which we stand in a way that is lacking from ordinary experience of space. Ofttimes, especially in the context of soil-education campaigns in elementary schools and high schools, such explorations are to be taken in a very literal and material sense, as children are taken outside to take soil samples to test the soil quality at their schools, participate in tea bag experiments to demonstrate microorganic activity in a particular soil, and study soil samples under microscopes to see the life they house (Broll 2009). At other times, printed materials, movies, and soil exhibitions seek to recreate the experience of getting one's hands dirty by other means (Exhibition "The Living Soil" n.d.).

Both narratives, whether based on a logic of alienation or of wonder, do not operate within an epistemological regime that is strictly scientific. Instead, soil awareness raising operates in a regime that can be characterized as religious. Religion, here, should be understood in its precise etymological sense as "attention to relations" (Agamben 2007, 74–75). The opposite of religion, in other words, is not atheism—because denial still implies an attention to the nonexistence of god(s)—but negligence. Soil-awareness practices, in this sense, are somewhat akin to conversion practices, as they seek to bring attention of their audience back to the manifold linkages humans have to soils while instilling a sense of wonder about the miraculous living and hidden world beneath their feet (Krzywoszynska 2019; Puig de la Bellacasa 2019; Tironi et al. 2020). In doing so, soil advocates seek to raise soil protection on the public agenda while propagating an underlying *paradigm shift* on what soils are. Thus, according to a Dutch policy maker attending the annual ENSA meeting in 2019, Europeans should move from a perspective of treating soil as a slave to seeing soil as a mother or, ideally, a 'partner' (Cleen and Molenaar 2019).

The introduction to this volume argues that the objectification, commodification, and re-sourcing of land on the one hand and the cultural and religious *subjectification* of land on the other hand are typically opposed when they are mobilized in social struggles around land. The mobilization of soil-awareness strategies as one of the central pillars of EU soil governance indicates, however, that the objectification and subjectification of soils are not necessarily to be considered as irreconcilable in the context of considering the cosmopolitics of soil resourcefulness and soil governance.

CONCLUSION

The previous sections explore how soils' resourcefulness and resourcelessness are constituted through three interacting epistemological domains of EU soil governance: policy discourses, scientific practices and institutions, and soil awareness raising. Yet where does this leave the interpretation of the thesis of the Portuguese GSP delegate? Are soil and land not the same, and what difference does this make?

In the introduction, I posit that the differentiation of soils and lands can be seen as generating and generated by particular forms of cosmopolitics, the politics inherent in the (re)construction of worlds. Throughout the three epistemological domains of EU soil governance explored in this chapter, different interpretations are offered on what is at stake in these forms of cosmopolitics. On a policy level, the differentiation of soils from lands enables the governance of soils' geo-bio-agency, its public functioning as an ecosystem service provider, despite virtually all soils being privately owned as land. Through formal and informal policies, the European Union seeks to limit building, producing, and farming activities that are destructive of soils while promoting activities that enhance soils' functions. On the level of scientific research, the constitution of soils as a specialized epistemological domain, distinct from other terrestrial epistemological categories like land, has enabled soil scientists to play an important role in the ongoing (re)problematization of soils' resourcefulness and resourcelessness. In turn, this continuous *re-sourcing* of soils has constituted and constitutes soils as objects and mediums of governance in particular ways: for example, by enabling soils to sequester carbon dioxide through the governance of tillage and other agricultural practices. Finally, in soil-awareness practices, soils are posited as objects withdrawn from everyday experience of the urban but perhaps also rural life world. Positing soils as such constitutes them as vital but also miraculous entities that require extra attention and care. Together, these interacting epistemologies of soils circumscribe the problem space of soil governance.

In the particular epistemological setting of EU soil governance, the differentiation of soils from lands is productive of a range of governmental and affective epistemologies. This does not mean that epistemologies of lands and soils are to be understood as separate in general, however. A cosmopolitical perspective on soils and lands understands epistemologies—or, indeed, ontologies—of both to be inherently situated in particular practical contexts. From these situations, particular figurations of lands and soils become implicated in the remaking of others. Thus, the soil (as differentiated from land) mobilized as the matter of concern in an EU governance context comes to affect the physical, as well as possibly the financial and legal, interaction between farmers and their lands; the affective relationship between urbanites and their environment; and the biochemical interaction between soil microorganisms and the atmosphere. Thinking about lands and soils cosmopolitically, therefore, invites us not to take them for granted but rather to explore how they figure as sociomaterial constructions in a range of constellations of order, power, and governance.

REFERENCES

Agamben, Giorgio. 2007. *Profanations*. Translated by Jeff Fort. New York: Zone Books.

Amundson, Ronald. 2006. "Philosophical Developments in Pedology in the United States: Eugene Hilgard and Milton Whitney." In *Footprints in the Soil: People and Ideas in Soil History*, edited by Benno P. Warkentin, 149–66. Amsterdam: Elsevier.

Arènes, Alexandra, Bruno Latour, and Jérôme Gaillardet. 2018. "Giving Depth to the Surface: An Exercise in the Gaia-Graphy of Critical Zones." *Anthropocene Review* 5 (2): 120–35. https://doi.org/10.1177/2053019618782257.

Banwart, Steven, Stefano M. Bernasconi, Winfried Blum, Francois Chabaux, Pavel Kram, Danielle Maia de Souza, Lars Lundin, et al. 2015. *SoilTrEC Final Report*. Sheffield, UK: University of Sheffield. https://cordis.europa.eu/docs/results/244/244118/final1-soiltrec-final-report-23-01-2015.pdf.

Banwart, Steven, Jon Chorover, Jerome Gaillardet, Donald Sparks, Tim White, Suzanne Anderson, Anthony Aufdenkampe, et al. 2013. *Sustaining Earth's Critical*

Zone: Basic Science and Interdisciplinary Solutions for Global Challenges. Sheffield, UK: University of Sheffield. http://www.czen.org/sites/default/files/Sustaining-Earths-Critical-Zone_FINAL-290713.pdf.

Barry, Andrew. 2001. *Political Machines: Governing a Technological Society.* London: Athlone Press.

Bartol, Alana, and Amanda White, dirs. 2015. *The Soil Is Teeming with Life*. 5 min. https://vimeo.com/120535980.

Baveye, Philippe C., Jacques Baveye, and John Gowdy. 2016. "Soil 'Ecosystem' Services and Natural Capital: Critical Appraisal of Research on Uncertain Ground." *Frontiers in Environmental Science* 4 (41): 1–49. https://doi.org/10.3389/fenvs.2016.00041.

Brevik, Eric C., Thomas E. Fenton, and Jeffrey A. Homburg. 2016. "Historical Highlights in American Soil Science—Prehistory to the 1970s." *Catena* 146: 111–27. https://doi.org/10.1016/j.catena.2015.10.003.

Broll, Gabriele. 2009. "Soil Awareness and Education." Presentation at the ENSA First Meeting, Ispra, Italy, May 26. https://esdac.jrc.ec.europa.eu/Awareness/Documents/WG_1Meeting/Broll.pdf.

Chakrabarty, Dipesh. 2018. "Anthropocene Time." *History and Theory* 57 (1): 5–32. https://doi.org/10.1111/hith.12044.

———. 2019. "The Planet: An Emergent Humanist Category." *Critical Inquiry* 46 (1): 1–31. https://doi.org/10.1086/705298.

Chen, Yijia. 2019. "Withdrawal of European Soil Framework Directive: Reasons and Recommendations." *Journal of Sustainable Development* 13 (1): 1–9. https://doi.org/10.5539/jsd.v13n1p1.

Cleen, Margot de, and Co Molenaar. 2019. "Global Challenges, Local Solutions! Awareness is needed." Presented at the European Network on Soil Awareness Annual Meeting 2019, Amsterdam, September 19.

Cohen, Benjamin R. 2009. *Notes from the Ground: Science, Soil, and Society in the American Countryside*. New Haven, CT: Yale University Press.

Conway, Philip R. 2020. "On the Way to Planet Politics: From Disciplinary Demise to Cosmopolitical Coordination." *International Relations* 34 (2): 157–79. https://doi.org/10.1177/0047117819879482.

De Donà, Matteo. 2021. "Matching Institutionalized Expertise with Global Needs: Boundary Organizations and Hybrid Management at the Science-Policy Interfaces of Soil and Land Governance." *Environmental Science and Policy* 123: 82–90. https://doi.org/10.1016/j.envsci.2021.05.015.

de Vries, Gerard. 2007. "What Is Political in Sub-Politics? How Aristotle Might Help STS." *Social Studies of Science* 37 (5): 781–809. https://doi.org/10.1177/0306312706070749.

Edwards, Paul N. 2010. *A Vast Machine: Computer Models, Climate Data, and the Politics of Global Warming*. Cambridge, MA: MIT Press.

Engel-Di Mauro, Salvatore. 2014. *Ecology, Soils, and the Left: An Ecosocial Approach*. New York: Palgrave Macmillan.

European Commission. 2006. *Thematic Strategy for Soil Protection [SEC(2006)620] [SEC(2006)1165]: COM/2006/0231 Final: Communication from the Commission to the Council, the European Parliament, the European Economic and Social Committee and the Committee of the Regions*. Brussels: Commission of the European Communities. http://eur-lex.europa.eu/legal-content/EN/TXT/?uri=CELEX:52006DC0231.

European Environment Agency. 2015. *SOER 2015—The European Environment—State and Outlook 2015: A Comprehensive Assessment of the European Environment's State, Trends and Prospects, in a Global Context*. Copenhagen: European Environment Agency. https://www.eea.europa.eu/soer.

———. 2019. *SOER 2020—The European Environment—State and Outlook 2020: Knowledge for Transition to a Sustainable Europe*. Luxembourg: Publications Office of the European Union. https://www.eea.europa.eu/publications/soer-2020.

European Soil Data Centre. n.d. "European Network on Soil Awareness." Accessed January 1, 2018. https://esdac.jrc.ec.europa.eu/networkcooperations/european-network-soil-awareness.

Evtuhov, Catherine. 2006. "The Roots of Dokuchaev's Scientific Contributions: Cadastral Soil Mapping and Agro-Environmental Issues." In *Footprints in the Soil: People and Ideas in Soil History*, edited by Benno P. Warkentin, 125–48. Amsterdam: Elsevier.

Exhibition "The Living Soil." n.d. *Summer of Soil* (blog). Accessed February 8, 2020. https://summerofsoil.nl/en/exhibition/.

Frodeman, Robert. 2003. *Geo-Logic: Breaking Ground between Philosophy and the Earth Sciences*. Albany: State University of New York Press.

Giardino, John R., and Chris Houser. 2015. "Introduction to the Critical Zone." In *Principles and Dynamics of the Critical Zone*, edited by John R. Giardino and Chris Houser, 1–13. Amsterdam: Elsevier.

Hamilton, Clive. 2016. "The Anthropocene as Rupture." *Anthropocene Review* 3 (2): 93–106. https://doi.org/10.1177/2053019616634741.

Hui, Yuk. 2017. "Cosmotechnics as Cosmopolitics." *E-Flux Journal* 86: 1–11. https://www.e-flux.com/journal/86/161887/cosmotechnics-as-cosmopolitics/.

Jeffrey, Simon, Ciro Gardi, Arwyn Jones, Luca Montanarella, Luca Marmo, Ladislav Miko, Karl Ritz, Guénola Pérès, Jörg Römbke, and Wim H. van der Putten, eds. 2010. *European Atlas of Soil Biodiversity*. Luxembourg: Office for Official Publications of the European Communities. https://esdac.jrc.ec.europa.eu/Library/Maps/Biodiversity_Atlas/Documents/Biodiversity_Atlas.pdf.

Jones, Arwyn. 2013. "Communicating the Value of Soil: A JRC Perspective." Presentation at the European Network on Soil Awareness Annual Meeting 2013, Aberdeen, UK, September 18. https://esdac.jrc.ec.europa.eu/Awareness/Documents/ENSA2013/Jones_Activities_ECJRC.pdf.

Jones, Arwyn, Luca Montanarella, and Robert Jones, eds. 2005. *Soil Atlas of Europe*. Luxembourg: Office for Official Publications of the European Communities. https://esdac.jrc.ec.europa.eu/Projects/Soil_Atlas/Download/Atlas.pdf.

Jones, Arwyn, Panos Panagos, Sara Barcelo, Faycal Bouraoui, Claudio Bosco, Olivier Dewitte, Ciro Gardi, et al. 2012. *The State of Soil in Europe: A Contribution of the JRC to the European Environment Agency's Environment State and Outlook Report—SOER 2010*. Luxembourg: Joint Research Centre of the European

Commission. http://publications.jrc.ec.europa.eu/repository/bitstream/JRC68418/lbna25186enn.pdf.

Keuning, Sytze. 2015. *De Magie van de Bodem*. Deventer, Netherlands: Wolters Kluwer.

Knorr-Cetina, Karin. 1985. "Germ Warfare." *Social Studies of Science* 15 (3): 577–86. https://doi.org/10.1177/030631285015003011.

Kon Kam King, Juliette, and Céline Granjou. 2020. "Mapping Soil, Losing Ground? Politics of Soil Mapping." In *Thinking with Soils: Material Politics and Social Theory*, edited by Juan Francisco Salazar, Céline Granjou, Matthew Kearnes, Anna Krzywoszynska, and Manuel Tironi, 39–54. London: Bloomsbury Academic.

Kon Kam King, Juliette, Céline Granjou, Juliette Fournil, and Lauric Cecillon. 2018. "Soil Sciences and the French 4 per 1000 Initiative: The Promises of Underground Carbon." *Energy Research and Social Science* 45: 144–52.

Krzywoszynska, Anna. 2019. "Caring for Soil Life in the Anthropocene: The Role of Attentiveness in More-than-Human Ethics." *Transactions of the Institute of British Geographers* 44 (4): 661–75. https://doi.org/10.1111/tran.12293.

———. 2020. "Nonhuman Labor and the Making of Resources: Making Soils a Resource through Microbial Labor." *Environmental Humanities* 12 (1): 227–49. https://doi.org/10.1215/22011919-8142319.

Krzywoszynska, Anna, Steve Banwart, and David Blacker. 2020. "To Know, to Dwell, to Care: Towards and Actionable, Place-Based Knowledge of Soils." In *Thinking with Soils: Material Politics and Social Theory*, edited by Juan Francisco Salazar, Céline Granjou, Matthew Kearnes, Anna Krzywoszynska, and Manuel Tironi, 89–106. London: Bloomsbury Academic.

Krzywoszynska, Anna, and Greta Marchesi. 2020. "Toward a Relational Materiality of Soils: Introduction." *Environmental Humanities* 12 (1): 190–204. https://doi.org/10.1215/22011919-8142297.

Latour, Bruno. 2004. "Whose Cosmos, Which Cosmopolitics? Comments on the Peace Terms of Ulrich Beck." *Common Knowledge* 10 (3): 450–62. https://doi.org/10.1215/0961754X-10-3-450.

———. 2009. *Politics of Nature*. Translated by Catherine Porter. Cambridge, MA: Harvard University Press.

———. 2013. *An Inquiry into Modes of Existence*. Translated by Catherine Porter. Cambridge, MA: Harvard University Press.

———. 2014. "Some Advantages of the Notion of 'Critical Zone' for Geopolitics." *Procedia Earth and Planetary Science* 10: 3–6. https://doi.org/10.1016/j.proeps.2014.08.002.

———. 2017. *Facing Gaia: Eight Lectures on the New Climatic Regime*. Hoboken, NJ: Wiley.

Latour, Bruno, and Peter Weibel. 2020. *Critical Zones: The Science and Politics of Landing on Earth*. Cambridge, MA: MIT Press.

Lefèvre, Clara, Fatma Rekik, Viridiana Alcantara, and Liesl Wiese. 2017. *Soil Organic Carbon: The Hidden Potential*. Rome: Food and Agriculture Organization of the United Nations.

Lyons, Kristina Marie. 2020. *Vital Decomposition: Soil Practitioners and Life Politics*. Durham, NC: Duke University Press.

Marchesi, Greta. 2020. "Justus von Liebig Makes the World: Soil Properties and Social Change in the Nineteenth Century." *Environmental Humanities* 12 (1): 205–26. https://doi.org/10.1215/22011919-8142308.

McNeill, J. R., and Verena Winiwarter. 2004. "Breaking the Sod: Humankind, History, and Soil." *Science* 304 (5677): 1627–29.

Menon, Manoj, Svetla Rousseva, Nikolaos P. Nikolaidis, Pauline van Gaans, Panos Panagos, Danielle Maia de Souza, Kristin Vala Ragnarsdottir, et al. 2014. "SoilTrEC: A Global Initiative on Critical Zone Research and Integration." *Environmental Science and Pollution Research* 21 (4): 3191–95. https://doi.org/10.1007/s11356-013-2346-x.

Meulemans, Germain. 2020. "Urban Pedogeneses: The Making of City Soils from Hard Surfacing to the Urban Soil Sciences." *Environmental Humanities* 12 (1): 250–66. https://doi.org/10.1215/22011919-8142330.

Montanarella, Luca. 2008. "Towards Protecting Soil Biodiversity in Europe: The EU Thematic Strategy for Soil Protection." *Biodiversity* 9 (1–2): 75–77. https://doi.org/10.1080/14888386.2008.9712889.

Montanarella, Luca, and Panos Panagos. 2015. "Policy Relevance of Critical Zone Science." *Land Use Policy* 49: 86–91. https://doi.org/10.1016/j.landusepol.2015.07.019.

———. 2021. "The Relevance of Sustainable Soil Management within the European Green Deal." *Land Use Policy* 100: 1–6. https://doi.org/10.1016/j.landusepol.2020.104950.

Panagos, Panos, Marc Van Liedekerke, Arwyn Jones, and Luca Montanarella. 2012. "European Soil Data Centre: Response to European Policy Support and Public Data Requirements." *Land Use Policy* 29 (2): 329–38. https://doi.org/10.1016/j.landusepol.2011.07.003.

Pawley, Emily. 2010. "Accounting with the Fields: Chemistry and Value in Nutriment in American Agricultural Improvement, 1835–1860." *Science as Culture* 19 (4): 461–82. https://doi.org/10.1080/09505431.2010.519868.

Pederson, Robert, Ana Frelih-Larsen, Z. Lukacova, A. Crook, Sandra Naumann, Catherine Bowyer, Clunie Keenleyside, and S. Nanni. 2016. "Soil Stakeholders Conference, 5 December 2016—Conference Report." Annex 2 to the report *Updated Inventory and Assessment of Soil Protection Policy Instruments in EU Member States*. Final report to DG Environment. Berlin: Ecologic Institute. http://ec.europa.eu/environment/soil/pdf/soil%20conference%20december%202016/conference_report.pdf.

Puig de la Bellacasa, María. 2014. "Encountering Bioinfrastructure: Ecological Struggles and the Sciences of Soil." *Social Epistemology* 28 (1): 26–40. https://doi.org/10.1080/02691728.2013.862879.

———. 2019. "Re-animating Soils: Transforming Human-Soil Affections through Science, Culture and Community." *Sociological Review* 67 (2): 391–407. https://doi.org/10.1177/0038026119830601.

Richter, Daniel, and Dan H. Yaalon. 2012. "'The Changing Model of Soil' Revisited." *Soil Science Society of America Journal* 76 (3): 766–78.

Robbins, Jim. 2013. "Opinion—The Hidden World under Our Feet." *New York Times*, May 11, 2013. https://www.nytimes.com/2013/05/12/opinion/sunday/the-hidden-world-of-soil-under-our-feet.html.

Rodríguez Eugenio, Natalia, Michael McLaughlin, and Daniel Pennock. 2018. *Soil Pollution: A Hidden Reality*. Rome: Food and Agriculture Organization of the United Nations.

Salazar, Juan Francisco, Céline Granjou, Matthew Kearnes, Anna Krzywoszynska, and Manuel Tironi, eds. 2020. *Thinking with Soils: Material Politics and Social Theory*. London: Bloomsbury Academic.

Sayre, Laura B. 2010. "The Pre-History of Soil Science: Jethro Tull, the Invention of the Seed Drill, and the Foundations of Modern Agriculture." *Physics and Chemistry of the Earth, Parts A/B/C* 35 (15–18): 851–59. https://doi.org/10.1016/j.pce.2010.07.034.

Shiva, Vandana. 2015. *Soil Not Oil: Environmental Justice in an Age of Climate Crisis*. Berkeley, CA: North Atlantic Books.

Simmons, Dana. 2006. "Waste Not, Want Not: Excrement and Economy in Nineteenth-Century France." *Representations* 96 (1): 73–98. https://doi.org/10.1525/rep.2006.96.1.73.

Stengers, Isabelle. 2005. "Introductory Notes on an Ecology of Practices." *Cultural Studies Review* 11 (1): 183–96. https://doi.org/10.5130/csr.v11i1.3459.

———. 2010. *Cosmopolitics I*. Translated by Robert Bononno. Minneapolis: University of Minnesota Press.

Tironi, Manuel, Matthew Kearnes, Anna Krzywoszynska, Céline Granjou, and Juan Francisco Salazar. 2020. "Soil Theories: Relational, Decolonial, Inhuman." In *Thinking with Soils: Material Politics and Social Theory*, edited by Juan Francisco Salazar, Céline Granjou, Matthew Kearnes, Anna Krzywoszynska, and Manuel Tironi, 15–38. London: Bloomsbury Academic.

Walker, James C. G. 1999. "Earth System Science and the Western Worldview." *Chemical Geology* 161 (1): 365–71. https://doi.org/10.1016/S0009-2541(99)00095-9.

White, Timothy, Susan Brantley, Steve Banwart, Jon Chorover, William Dietrich, Lou Derry, Kathleen Lohse, et al. 2015. "The Role of Critical Zone Observatories in Critical Zone Science." In *Principles and Dynamics of the Critical Zone*, edited by John R. Giardino and Chris Houser, 15–78. Amsterdam: Elsevier.

Chapter 9

From Epistemologies of Land to the Lands of Epistemology

Being and Becoming in the Agrocene

Inanna Hamati-Ataya

In inviting us to reflect on the nature, relations, and implications of contemporary epistemologies of land, Felix Anderl has delineated for us a kind of inquiry that is typically ignored in philosophically driven discussions of epistemology in the social sciences and humanities. Such inquiry rests on two sociologically established principles that shift the meaning of epistemology as it is traditionally understood, namely as *the* theory of *human knowledge* in general, abstract terms, and instead redefine it as a properly social and historical phenomenon and practice (Hamati-Ataya 2014, 2016, 2018).

The first principle of which we are here reminded is that epistemology can only ever be an epistemology *of* something because knowledge itself (the object of epistemology) is always deployed on or generated by engagement with some aspect of reality, whether material or ideational, external or self-referential. An inquiry into the epistemology *of land* thereby contributes to the reconstitution of the wider cultural ontology of a society or community (Descola 2005) by identifying *how* it collectively captures and enunciates the "what" of its perceived and lived world.

The second principle is that, beyond the physiological-cognitive structures and processes that make the capacity to know similarly possible for all of us humans (the only universal foundations of knowledge), first- or second-order discourse on reality is always situated in a particular sociohistorical context and configuration of knowing—in other words, knowledge (and knowledge of knowledge) is always strongly determined by sociohistorical contingency. Accordingly, one can meaningfully and seriously speak of epistemology in the singular only in the sense of a historical category whose content is identified inductively and is permanently corrected by a comparative empirical analysis of its varying sociohistorical forms. Hence the meaningfulness—and the necessity—of inquiring into epistemologies of land in the plural and in relation to specific epistemic communities encountering and relating to land in specific historical configurations of life.

The importance of returning epistemology to all its practitioners is worth highlighting here. Epistemology has traditionally been conceived and pursued as a particular kind of theory of a particular kind of knowledge: specifically, an *analytical* theory of *propositional* knowledge (amenable to being formulated in the form of "true statements" about the world) that is itself deployed as a second-order propositional knowledge regulated by logical and linguistic rules of meaning and validity (Hamati-Ataya 2016, 2018). As such, the constitution and practice of philosophical epistemology has naturally entailed the erasure of all forms and types of knowledge and of all conceptions of knowledge that are constituted, manifested, and deployed in nonpropositional terms.[1]

The rationale of this erasure can be traced back sociologically to the beginnings of philosophy as a professionalized field of action that emerged within a specific configuration of the ancient Athenian polity, in which manual, corporeal, and embodied knowledges were systematically devalued to the benefit of the logos-mediated knowledge of the ruling, labor-free elite (Hamati-Ataya 2022). Slaves, cooks, architects, technicians, farmers, and others possessing a "'know-how' without discourse" (de Certeau [1980] 1990, 103) have ever since remained mostly invisible or unrecognized as epistemic laborers, let alone as reflexive workers conscious of the praxical logic of their craft. The notion that their praxis might entail, contain, or generate a distinctive and even valuable philosophy of knowledge in the noblest sense of the term would also have seemed risible or scandalous to most philosophers of the past. A review of contemporary reference books and university curricula in epistemology and philosophy suggests that such a notion would not generate a much different reaction today.

A sociological appraisal of the endurance of idealism in the history of philosophy (Bourdieu 1984, postscript; Collins 1998) and of the erasure of various nonintellectual praxes from the official construction of science (Bangham, Chacko, and Kaplan 2022) can illuminate the processes whereby epistemologies of land anchored in particular forms of experience or labor and validated by mechanisms different from those adopted within the institutions of modern science, the state, or industry can easily fail to be recognized. In its dual (ontological and normative) meaning, recognition entails accepting the particular as an instance of the general and accepting its equal legitimacy to manifest itself as such.

In showcasing a diversity of epistemologies of land and highlighting their existential and material foundations, this volume invites us to recognize and grapple with the plurality of epistemic perspectives that arise from the diversity of experiences of and engagements with our common spaces of life. In exploring the tensions generated by the disjunctions and clashes between these various epistemologies, the volume further inscribes the epistemology of land squarely in the domain of the contested, hierarchical social order. The message that transpires from the examples showcased here is that it is difficult—and perhaps even unwise—to untangle social claims to land from epistemic claims about land and to treat them—analytically and practically—as different categories of statements about the world or even as different types of engagement with the world.

Much of contemporary academic research is dedicated to addressing this entanglement of knowledge and the social order and of knowledge and social action. Many academics are now also exploring ways of rehabilitating and protecting erased and devaluated knowledges and the communities that produce and flourish through them. Our present, anthropogenically created socioenvironmental predicament has relatedly triggered a discussion of the relative value, for human and nonhuman life and for the well-being of the planet as a whole, of various epistemologies, among which epistemologies of land, nature, and the more-than-human world naturally take center stage.

This is an exercise no longer just in *epistemic arbitration* but in *social arbitration*, albeit anchored in a founded conviction in the role of knowledge in human progress: the conviction that an understanding of how modes and uses of knowledge affect a given condition can rationally be used to improve said condition through a correction of the principles and practices that regulate the generation and deployment of that knowledge. As we appear to be the only species on this planet capable of such reflexivity, as well as the only species capable of harm at a planetary scale, the appeal of engaged and responsible scholarship is understandably difficult to resist and is already redefining the good old model of the scholarly vocation.

The extent to which successful social arbitration might in the process also enable or mediate successful epistemic arbitration—that is, establish the capacity to distinguish "valid" or "superior" knowledge according to the criterion of the sustainability of life processes—is an important but difficult case to make. Indeed, settling it might require reaching a universal consensus on what qualifies as well-being, progress, or harm—that is, achieving axiological or ethical invariability—which the very structure of the social order that produces variability in the domain of knowledge and epistemology makes equally unlikely in the domain of values and norms.

Putting aside, then, the question of how to assess the relative worth or validity of sociohistorically constituted epistemologies of land, we are confronted at the very least with the question of understanding what they mean qua social variations or historical forms: that is, of explaining their emergence, as well as how they relate to one another. The most obvious starting point for such an inquiry is the rootedness of land, both as concept and reality, in the agrarian mode of life. It should indeed be a relatively uncontroversial point to agree on that land is not a natural but a cultural object, with no equivalent in human history before the rise of agriculture and no equivalent among the cultural products of any other terrestrial species known to us, even those that engage, like us, in ecosystem engineering.

Some anthropological definition of *land* is therefore needed if we are to elucidate the complex questions that Anderl put to us in this volume's introduction and untangle our discourse from the discourse (or epistemologies) of social actors who are immediately and existentially invested in claiming land's meaning. Perhaps a first step in this direction is to describe land in terms that connect it to human life processes. Land may be conceived, for example, as the product of the taming of natural ecological spaces and relations through the deployment of a coherent and systematic technological culture of energy production that requires and reproduces a territorial form of social organization. Such a description brings forth the overarching *cultural* meaning of agri*culture*, which the major schools of social thought have unfortunately relegated to a secondary dimension by typically approaching and theorizing agricultural practice first and foremost as a socioeconomic mode of production.

As an alternative to this perspective, in which culture is relegated exclusively to the status and role of superstructure, I argue that, once it became consolidated in species-wide lock-in mechanisms of path dependence and social reproduction, the transition to agriculture created a distinctive historical *modality of being*: that is, a specific configuration of human sociality based on a particular articulation of ecology, technology, and social organization. I propose to call this modality in which we find ourselves the Agrocene: a unique biocultural paradigm of human history whose novelty (*kainos*) originates in the constitution of land (*ager*) as a distinctive *artifact* of human knowledge and labor that has become, *as such*, a distinctive *condition* of human life.

The first point I make here is that it is only by approaching the agrarian mode of life as a distinctive cultural (or civilizational) paradigm in the history of humankind that we can make sense of how various epistemologies of land necessarily arise and how they sustain themselves in various configurations of the agrarian order. "Caring" and "extractivist" epistemologies of land, as Anderl refers to them, can accordingly be conceived as the rationalizations, in the realm of knowledge, of different types of material, mental, and symbolic engagements with land that correspond to different modalities of the (re)production of life *within* the Agrocenic cultural paradigm—what are typically classified as traditional or industrial forms of production that should be understood as forms of reproduction, too. "Caring" and "extractivist" (among other) epistemologies of land can, in other words, be understood as phenotypical variations (cultures) of the agrarian genotype (culture) that is distinctive of the Agrocene.

Acknowledging the distinctiveness and historicity of land, of its various epistemologies, and of the agrarian order itself brings us to a third-order question that requires us to shift to a different scale of analysis and a new level of inquiry. If an examination of epistemologies of land as sociohistorical forms of knowing enables us, comparatively, to elaborate a general epistemology of land that is distinctively characteristic of the Agrocene, of what higher-order general category is the epistemology of land itself a sociohistorical variation? In other words, to what extent are our epistemic consciousness (whatever its orders of discourse) and all the tools it mobilizes to make sense of the lived world themselves the product of our agrarian paradigm of life? Knowing what we know of how knowledge is constituted, is it not likely and even certain that the very underlying structures of our consciousness have been shaped or plainly (re)defined by that extraordinary evolutionary divergence that transformed our entire relation to the world and to each other and set us on a cultural path unscripted by our biological evolution?

Thanks to the deployment of sociological and anthropological thinking onto thought itself, it is now understood that the "faculty of understanding" (as per Kant's original conception) is historically constituted—and hence variable—and that it is constituted through a dynamic immersion in the material world. Major shifts in our material relation to natural and social reality, especially via the deployment of labor, infrastructures, technology, and particular modes of exchange (Bourdieu 1972; Childe 1949; Durkheim and Mauss 1963; Heelan 1983; Rosenberger and Verbeek 2015; Sohn-Rethel 1961, 1978; Thomson 1955), have shaped not only our perception of that reality but also the very structures and frames of knowing that underscore such perception and make reality legible and intelligible to us. The carpentry of the world (Segall, Campbell, and Herskovits 1966)—its spaces and times, its colors and sounds, and the rhythms of its life processes—becomes naturalized in(to) our analytical categories (Ihde 1976; Lefebvre 2002; Rosa 2013), either through our direct immersion in these processes or through the disciplining mediation of the social institutions adapted to and reproductive of them (Bourdieu 2012).

Everything we know about the consolidated transition to agriculture on a planetary scale suggests a seismic transformation in our consciousness—from our engagement with space to our consciousness of time, our social organization, and our belief systems. Capturing this transformation requires a new level of reflexivity that extends beyond the self-consciousness of how we are located in and shaped by this or that particular *social structure*. What I envisage here is consciousness as the product, not of a particular structuration of the *social order*, but of the overarching modality of existence of which that social order is a mere historical configuration.

At this juncture we are confronted with the limits and limitations of our sociological reflexivity (Bourdieu 2004; Bourdieu, Passeron, and Chamboredon 1968) and of the fields of knowledge that carried the sociological revolution in thought (Kilminster 1998) and made such reflexivity possible—namely, the sociology of knowledge, ideology critique, and social epistemology more generally (Bloor 1976; Elias 1971a, 1971b; Fuller 1988; Mannheim 1936a, 1936b; Marx 1978; Marx and Engels1978). What is required is an anthropological theory of knowledge of the old kind (Durkheim 1912; Scheler 1980), which inscribes the formation of the structures of our consciousness in the most fundamental life processes that produce and reproduce us as natural and social beings.

As we deploy this anthropological gaze onto earlier periods of our history and zoom out of the Agrocene, the inadequacy of our epistemic tools in making sense of patterns of culture, behavior, and thought in the world of our preagrarian ancestors brings to light the type of agricultural thinking (Gamble et al. 2005) that characterizes our present epistemic consciousness. To the extent that it is possible to reconstruct such past patterns through an engagement with material culture alone in the absence of any written record of past modes of thinking, we may eventually be able to capture the evolution of our epistemic consciousness and the impact the transition to agriculture had on the fundamental structures of the human mind.

Another comparative pathway is available to us if we extend this exercise in deep history (Shryock and Smail 2011) toward the future by deploying futures thinking (Bell 2003; Schreiber and Berge 2019) as a way of identifying future patterns of continuity and change on the basis of similar patterns observed in the deep past. In line with my preliminary definition of how a modality of being is constituted, I suggest that zooming in on emerging technological trends that seem to manifest a new articulation between ecology, technology, and social organization can provide us with a sense of how or what new forms of human consciousness might arise in the future.

The industrial-extractivist model of agriculture that is now universally recognized as a major contributor to planetary-scale environmental damage (Dunlap and Jakobsen 2019; McNeill and Engelke 2014; Smil 2021) is currently being reformed along three major pathways. The first is a return to traditional ("Indigenous") forms of agriculture that constitutes a reversal of the Green Revolution and a scaling down of standardized "world agriculture" back to its local socioecological contexts (Imoro et al. 2021; Singh and Singh 2017). The second pathway represents a continued commitment to the scientific and technological rationale of the Green Revolution but through the deployment of innovations in artificial intelligence, nanotechnology, and genetic engineering that aims to transform the current system into a "smart," sustainable type of agriculture (Bundschuh and Chen 2017; Nhamo, Chikoye, and Gondwe 2017). Neither of these pathways is fundamentally revolutionary in the sense of shifting the underlying rationale of land-based food production. They are essentially variations within the same Agrocenic paradigm.

The third pathway delineates something potentially new and even substantially transformative for our future existence on this planet. Instead of innovating more sustainable ways of engaging with land as a biocultural condition of existence, this pathway is leading to the development of biotechnologies that can do without land entirely. With biomass and precision fermentation (Gyr 2021), cellular agriculture (Eibl et al. 2021; Rischer, Szilvay, and Oksman-Caldentey2020), and vertical farming (Despommier 2010; Kozai, Niu, and Takagaki 2020), a new model of domestication is emerging—the domestication of cells and microorganisms rather than crops and animals and of environments devoid of "natural" soils and resources—that crosses a new threshold in our engagement with nature. At work here is no longer just a taming of nature or an adaptation to its conditions of life but a full hacking of its life processes.

Most importantly for the problem at hand, these innovations prefigure what can only be described as a postagrarian modality of being, in which subsistence is no longer dependent on land, its biota, and its ecosystems as coherent, ecologically distinctive systems of life and (re)production. Viewed from the anthropological perspective of deep history, this uncoupling of food production from land is quite an extraordinary transformation that announces the possibility of a real step change in our species' developmental history—a new evolutionary divergence in our cultural evolution that would bring about a seismic transformation of our consciousness of the world.

Our methodical anticipation of the postagrarian way of life can help us better understand the meaning and historicity of epistemologies of land but also, through them, the meaning and historicity of epistemology tout court. However transient land may be in the history of our kind, it provides us with an entry point into a dimension of our existence that has for far too long been claimed from lofty vantage points unburdened by the materiality of being. In returning epistemology to its original home, we are merely bringing our agrarian metaphors back to life from the subtlety of our sedimented consciousness—our culture as cultivation, our disciplines as fields. Until these metaphors cease to make sense, epistemologies of land could very well be the most insightful pathways into the lands of epistemology.

ACKNOWLEDGMENT

This contribution has benefited from the support of the European Research Council's Horizon 2020 Programme for Research and Innovation (ERC Consolidator Grant no. 724451, Project ARTEFACT, 2017–2023).

NOTE

1. The same erasure has characterized the philosophical field of aesthetics, as it pursued an analytical theory of beauty to the detriment of artists' own praxis-based theory of art (Lichtenstein 2014).

REFERENCES

Bangham, Jenny, Xan Chacko, and Judith Kaplan, eds. 2022. *Invisible Labour in Modern Science*. Lanham, MD: Rowman and Littlefield.

Bell, Wendell. 2003. *Foundations of Futures Studies: Human Science for a New Era*. Vol. 1, *History, Purposes, and Knowledge*. New Brunswick, NJ: Transaction.

Bloor, David. 1976. *Knowledge and Social Imagery*. Chicago: University of Chicago Press.

Bourdieu, Pierre. 1972. *Esquisse d'une théorie de la pratique: Précédé de trois études d'ethnologie kabyle*. Paris: Seuil.

———. 1984. *Distinction: A Social Critique of the Judgement of Taste*. Translated by Richard Nice. Cambridge, UK: Polity.

———. 2004. *Science of Science and Reflexivity*. Translated by Richard Nice. Cambridge, UK: Polity.

———. 2012. *Sur l'état: Cours au Collège de France, 1989–1992*. Paris: Seuil.

Bourdieu, Pierre, Jean-Claude Passeron, and Jean-Claude Chamboredon. 1968. *Le métier de sociologue: Préalables épistémologiques*. Paris: Mouton Bordas.

Bundschuh, Jochen, and Guangnan Chen, eds. 2017. *Sustainable Energy Solutions in Agriculture*. Boca Raton, FL: CRC Press.

Childe, Vere Gordon. 1949. *Social Worlds of Knowledge*. Oxford, UK: Oxford University Press.

Collins, Randall. 1998. *The Sociology of Philosophies: A Global Theory of Intellectual Change*. Cambridge, MA: Belknap Press.

De Certeau, Michel. (1980) 1990. *L'invention du quotidien*. Vol. 1, *Arts de faire*. Paris: Gallimard.

Descola, Philippe. 2005. *Par-delà nature et culture*. Paris: Gallimard.

Despommier, Dickson. 2010. *The Vertical Farm: Feeding the World in the 21st Century*. London: Picador Books.

Dunlap, Alexander, and Jostein Jakobsen. 2019. *The Violent Technologies of Extraction: Political Ecology, Critical Agrarian Studies and the Capitalist Worldeater*. London: Palgrave Macmillan.

Durkheim, Émile. 1912. *Les formes élémentaires de la vie religieuse: Le système totémique en Australie*. Paris: Presses Universitaires de France.

Durkheim, Émile, and Marcel Mauss. 1963. *Primitive Classification*. Translated by Rodney Needham. London: Routledge.

Eibl, Regine, Yannick Senn, Géraldine Gubser, Valentin Jossen, Christian van den Bos, and Dieter Eibl. 2021. "Cellular Agriculture: Opportunities and Challenges." *Annual Review of Food Science and Technology* 12: 51–73.

Elias, Norbert. 1971a. "Sociology of Knowledge: New Perspectives, Part One." *Sociology* 5 (2): 149–68.

———. 1971b. "Sociology of Knowledge: New Perspectives, Part Two." *Sociology* 5 (3): 355–70.

Fuller, Steve. 1988. *Social Epistemology*. Indianapolis: Indiana University Press.

Gamble, Clive, William Davies, Paul Pettitt, Lee Hazelwood, and Martin Richards. 2005. "The Archaeological and Genetic Foundations of the European Population During the Late Glacial: Implications for 'Agricultural Thinking.'" *Cambridge Archaeological Journal* 15 (2): 193–223.

Gyr, Audrey. 2021. *Fermentation: Meat, Seafood, Eggs, and Dairy*. State of the industry report. New York: Good Food Institute.

Hamati-Ataya, Inanna. 2014. "Outline for a Reflexive Epistemology." *Epistemology and Philosophy of Science* 42 (4): 46–66.

———. 2016. "IR Theory and the Question of Science." In *International Relations Theory Today*, 2nd ed., edited by Ken Booth and Toni Erskine, 69–84. Cambridge, UK: Polity.

———. 2018. "The Sociology of Knowledge as Postphilosophical Epistemology: Out of IR's 'Socially Constructed' Idealism." *International Studies Review* 20 (1): 3–29.

———. 2022. "Epistemic Demarcations as Social Erasures: Taste and the Politics of Distinction from the 'Revolutions of Wisdom' to the 'Green Revolution.'" *BJHS Themes* 7: 13–38.

Heelan, Patrick. 1983. *Space-Perception and the Philosophy of Science*. Berkeley: University of California Press.

Ihde, Don. 1976. *Listening and Voice: Phenomenologies of Sound*. Albany, NY: SUNY Press.

Imoro, Ziblim Abukari, Abubakari Zarouk Imoro, Abudu Ballu Duwiejuah, and Ammal Abukari. 2021. "Harnessing Indigenous Technologies for Sustainable Management of Land, Water, and Food Resources Amidst Climate Change." *Frontiers in Sustainable Food Systems* 5: 691603.

Kilminster, Richard. 1998. *The Sociological Revolution: From the Enlightenment to the Global Age*. London: Routledge.

Kozai, Toyoki, Genhua Niu, and Michiko Takagaki, eds. 2020. *Plant Factory: An Indoor Vertical Farming System for Efficient Quality Food Production*. London: Academic Press.

Lefebvre, Henri. 2002. *Critique of Everyday Life*. Vol. 2, *Foundations for a Sociology of the Everyday*. Translated by John Moore. London: Verso.

Lichtenstein, Jacqueline. 2014. *Les raisons de l'art: Essai sur les théories de la peinture*. Paris: Gallimard.

Mannheim, Karl. 1936a. *Essays on the Sociology of Knowledge*. London: Routledge.

———. 1936b. *Ideology and Utopia: An Introduction to the Sociology of Knowledge*. New York: Harvest.

Marx, Karl———. 1978. "Preface to *A Contribution to the Critique of Political Economy*." In *The Marx-Engels Reader*, 2nd ed., edited by Robert C. Tucker, 3–6. New York: W. W. Norton.

Marx, Karl, and Friedrich Engels. 1978. "The German Ideology: Part I." In *The Marx-Engels Reader*, 2nd ed., edited by Robert C. Tucker, 146–200. New York: W. W. Norton.

McNeill, John R., and Peter Engelke. 2014. *The Great Acceleration: An Environmental History of the Anthropocene since 1945.* Cambridge, MA: Cambridge University Press.

Nhamo, Nhamo, David Chikoye, and Therese Gondwe, eds. 2017. *Smart Technologies for Sustainable Smallholder Agriculture: Upscaling in Developing Countries*. London: Academic Press.

Rischer, Heiko, Géza R. Szilvay, and Kirsi-Marja Oksman-Caldentey. 2020. "Cellular Agriculture—Industrial Biotechnology for Food and Materials." *Current Opinion in Biotechnology* 61: 128–134.

Rosa, Hartmut. 2013. *Social Acceleration: A New Theory of Modernity*. Translated by Jonathan Trejo-Mathys. New York: Columbia University Press.

Rosenberger, Robert, and Peter-Paul Verbeek, eds. 2015. *Postphenomenological Investigations: Essays on Human-Technology Relations*. Lanham, MD: Lexington Books.

Scheler, Max. 1980. *Problems of a Sociology of Knowledge*. Translated by Manfred S. Frings. London: Routledge.

Schreiber, D. A., and Z. L. Berge, eds. 2019. *Futures Thinking and Organizational Policy: Case Studies for Managing Rapid Change in Technology, Globalization and Workforce Diversity*. London: Palgrave Macmillan.

Segall, Marshall H., Donald T. Campbell, and Melville J. Herskovits. 1966. *The Influence of Culture on Visual Perception*. Indianapolis: Bobbs-Merrill.

Shryock, Andrew, and Daniel Lord Smail. 2011. *Deep History. The Architecture of Past and Present*. Berkeley: University of California Press.

Singh, Rinku, and G. S. Singh. 2017. "Traditional Agriculture: A Climate-Smart Approach for Sustainable Food Production." *Energy, Ecology and Environment* 2: 296–316.

Smil, Vaclav. 2021. *Grand Transitions: How the Modern World Was Made*. Oxford, UK: Oxford University Press.

Sohn-Rethel, Alfred. 1961. *La pensée-marchandise*. Paris: Éditions du Croquant.

———. 1978. *Intellectual and Manual Labour: A Critique of Epistemology*. London: Humanities Press.

Thomson, George. 1955. *The First Philosophers: Studies in Ancient Greek Society*. London: Lawrence and Wishart.

Index

About the Contributors

Felix Anderl is professor of conflict studies at the Center for Conflict Studies, Philipps University, Marburg. His research focuses on conflicts over land, food, and rural development. He links social movement studies, international relations, and conflict research, drawing on participant observation in social movements and the institutions they oppose.

Eloisa Berman-Arévalo is assistant professor at the Universidad del Norte in Barranquilla, Colombia, and advisor at the Rural Development Agency in Colombia. Her research lies at the intersection between agrarian studies and Black geographies in Latin America. With an emphasis on the Colombian Caribbean, she explores postconflict agrarian capitalism and its racialized and gendered forms of deterritorialization.

Shailaja Fennell is professor of economic security and resilience, Department of Land Economy, University of Cambridge. Her research has focused on institutional reform and collective action, food production, and rural development; gender norms and gender gaps in development interventions; and provision of public goods and the role of partnerships. She has led international research programs in Asia and Africa; TIGR2ESS, a UKRI-funded research program (2018–2022) to study how to improve crop productivity and water use and identify appropriate crops and farming practices for sustainable rural development in India; MillNeti, a sister research program (2019–2021) focused on advancing biofortified millets to reduce iron deficiency of people living in Ethiopia and the Gambia; an ASEAN-funded project (2019–2021), leading a core team responsible for designing the framework, commissioning experts, and compiling the latest research to deliver the first ASEAN development outlook on policies to ensure inclusion and sustainability in Southeast Asia.

Inanna Hamati-Ataya is principal research associate at the Centre for Research in the Arts, Social Sciences and Humanities, and founding director of the Centre for Global Knowledge Studies (gloknos) at the University of Cambridge, where she researches the deep history of knowledge and globalization since the Paleolithic and the transformations of global agrarian orders.

Katarina Kušić is a Marie-Skłodowska Curie Actions Postdoctoral Fellow at the University of Vienna. Her research interests include land politics, statebuilding and peacebuilding interventions, interpretive and fieldwork-based methods, and post-colonial and decolonial thought. Her current work explores international political ecologies of land and human-nature relations more broadly. Her PhD and the ensuing monograph focused on post-war reconstruction efforts in South East Europe.

Maarten Meijer is a doctoral researcher at the Department of International Relations at the University of Groningen. His research focuses on the political history of the sciences of soils and brings in conversation science and technology studies; environmental political philosophy; and critical approaches to the study of power, order, and governance. In addition to his academic work, Meijer works together with the architectural collective Studio Inscape on ecopolitical design interventions in ongoing societal transitions in the Netherlands.

David Nally is a professor of historical geography and fellow of Jesus College at the University of Cambridge. Nally's research interests include critical agrarian studies, histories of the British Empire, the historical geography of American philanthropy, and famine studies.

Sakshi is a lecturer in law and social justice at Newcastle Law School, Newcastle University, United Kingdom. Sakshi's research areas include comparative environmental law, plural sovereignties, legal geography, Marxist legal theory and political economy, and jurisprudence. Sakshi is working on her new research project, "Plural Sovereignties and Climate Justice in the Anthropocene."

Leo Steeds is a research associate on the Adam Smith 300 project at the University of Glasgow. His research focuses on land and environment in the history of political and economic thought. He draws on a range of areas, including political economy, political theory, geography, and contemporary environmental studies to provide insights into the history of ideas that has informed understandings of human-environment relations through to the present.

Anna Wolkenhauer is a postdoctoral researcher at the Collaborative Research Centre 1342: Global Dynamics of Social Policy at the University of Bremen. She works on social protection and agriculture in southern Africa, focusing on visions for rural areas and the politics of knowledge.

www.ingramcontent.com/pod-product-compliance
Lightning Source LLC
LaVergne TN
LVHW102013210926
848483LV00011B/356
9781538176443